THE MOTHER

WITH LETTERS ON THE MOTHER AND
TRANSLATIONS OF PRAYERS AND MEDITATIONS

Sri Aurobindo

The Mother

**WITH LETTERS ON THE MOTHER AND
TRANSLATIONS OF PRAYERS AND MEDITATIONS**

**Sri Aurobindo Ashram
Pondicherry**

First edition: 1972
Eighth impression: 2002

Price: Rs. 120.00
ISBN 81-7058-010-2

Published by Sri Aurobindo Ashram Publication Department,
Pondicherry - 605 002
Printed at Sri Aurobindo Ashram Press, Pondicherry
PRINTED IN INDIA

Contents

CONTENTS

PART THREE

PART ONE

THE MOTHER

1

There are two powers that alone can effect in their conjunction the great and difficult thing which is the aim of our endeavour, a fixed and unfailing aspiration that calls from below and a supreme Grace from above that answers.

But the supreme Grace will act only in the conditions of the Light and the Truth; it will not act in conditions laid upon it by the Falsehood and the Ignorance. For if it were to yield to the demands of the Falsehood, it would defeat its own purpose.

These are the conditions of the Light and Truth, the sole conditions under which the highest Force will descend; and it is only the very highest supramental Force descending from above and opening from below that can victoriously handle the physical Nature and annihilate its difficulties....

There must be a total and sincere surrender; there must be an exclusive self-opening to the divine Power; there must be a constant and integral choice of the Truth that is descending, a constant and integral rejection of the falsehood of the mental, vital and physical Powers and Appearances that still rule the earth-Nature.

The surrender must be total and seize all the parts of the being. It is not enough that the psychic should respond and the higher mental accept or even the inner vital submit and the inner physical consciousness feel the influence. There must be in no part of the being, even the most external, anything that makes a reserve, anything that hides behind doubts, confusions and subterfuges, anything that revolts or refuses.

If part of the being surrenders, but another part reserves itself, follows its own way or makes its own conditions, then each time that that happens, you are yourself pushing the divine Grace away from you.

If behind your devotion and surrender you make a cover for your desires, egoistic demands and vital insistences, if you put these things in place of the true aspiration or mix them with it and try to impose them on the Divine Shakti, then it is idle to invoke the divine Grace to transform you.

If you open yourself on one side or in one part to the Truth and on another side are constantly opening the gates to hostile forces, it is vain to expect that the divine Grace will abide with you. You must keep the temple clean if you wish to instal there the living Presence.

If each time the Power intervenes and brings in the Truth, you turn your back on it and call in again the falsehood that has been expelled, it is not the divine Grace that you must blame for failing you, but the falsity of your own will and the imperfection of your own surrender.

If you call for the Truth and yet something in you chooses what is false, ignorant and undivine or even simply is unwilling to reject it altogether, then always you will be open to attack and the Grace will recede from you. Detect first what is false or obscure in you and persistently reject it, then alone can you rightly call for the divine Power to transform you.

Do not imagine that truth and falsehood, light and

darkness, surrender and selfishness can be allowed to dwell together in the house consecrated to the Divine. The transformation must be integral, and integral therefore the rejection of all that withstands it.

Reject the false notion that the divine Power will do and is bound to do everything for you at your demand and even though you do not satisfy the conditions laid down by the Supreme. Make your surrender true and complete, then only will all else be done for you.

Reject too the false and indolent expectation that the divine Power will do even the surrender for you. The Supreme demands your surrender to her, but does not impose it: you are free at every moment, till the irrevocable transformation comes, to deny and to reject the Divine or to recall your self-giving, if you are willing to suffer the spiritual consequence. Your surrender must be self-made and free; it must be the surrender of a living being, not of an inert automaton or mechanical tool.

An inert passivity is constantly confused with the real surrender, but out of an inert passivity nothing true and powerful can come. It is the inert passivity of physical Nature that leaves it at the mercy of every obscure or undivine influence. A glad and strong and helpful submission is demanded to the working of the Divine Force, the obedience of the illumined disciple of the Truth, of the inner Warrior who fights against obscurity and falsehood, of the faithful servant of the Divine.

This is the true attitude and only those who can take and keep it, preserve a faith unshaken by disappointments and difficulties and shall pass through the ordeal to the supreme victory and the great transmutation.

2

In all that is done in the universe, the Divine through his Shakti is behind all action but he is veiled by his Yoga Maya and works through the ego of the Jiva in the lower nature.

In Yoga also it is the Divine who is the Sadhaka and the Sadhana; it is his Shakti with her light, power, knowledge, consciousness, Ananda, acting upon the Adhara and, when it is opened to her, pouring into it with these divine forces that makes the Sadhana possible. But so long as the lower nature is active the personal effort of the Sadhaka remains necessary.

The personal effort required is a triple labour of aspiration, rejection and surrender, —

an aspiration vigilant, constant, unceasing — the mind's will, the heart's seeking, the assent of the vital being, the will to open and make plastic the physical consciousness and nature;

rejection of the movements of the lower nature — rejection of the mind's ideas, opinions, preferences, habits, constructions, so that the true knowledge may find free room in a silent mind, — rejection of the vital nature's desires, demands, cravings, sensations, passions, selfishness, pride, arrogance, lust, greed, jealousy, envy, hostility to the Truth, so that the true power and joy may pour from above into a calm, large, strong and consecrated vital being, — rejection of the physical nature's stupidity, doubt, disbelief, obscurity, obstinacy, pettiness, laziness, unwillingness to change, Tamas, so that the true stability of Light, Power, Ananda may establish itself in a body growing always more divine;

surrender of oneself and all one is and has and every plane of the consciousness and every movement to the Divine and the Shakti.

*

In proportion as the surrender and self-consecration progress the Sadhaka becomes conscious of the Divine Shakti doing the Sadhana, pouring into him more and more of herself, founding in him the freedom and perfection of the Divine Nature. The more this conscious process replaces his own effort, the more rapid and true becomes his progress. But it cannot completely replace the necessity of personal effort until the surrender and consecration are pure and complete from top to bottom.

Note that a tamasic surrender refusing to fulfil the conditions and calling on God to do everything and save one all the trouble and struggle is a deception and does not lead to freedom and perfection.

3

To walk through life armoured against all fear, peril and disaster, only two things are needed, two that go always together — the Grace of the Divine Mother and on your side an inner state made up of faith, sincerity and surrender. Let your faith be pure, candid and perfect. An egoistic faith in the mental and vital being tainted by ambition, pride, vanity, mental arrogance, vital self-will, personal demand, desire for the petty satisfactions of the lower nature is a low and smoke-obscured flame that cannot burn upwards to heaven. Regard your life as given you only for the divine work and to help in the divine manifestation. Desire nothing but the purity, force, light, wideness, calm, Ananda of the divine consciousness and its insistence to transform and perfect your mind, life and body. Ask for nothing but the divine, spiritual and supramental Truth, its realisation on earth and in you and in all who are called and chosen and the conditions needed for its creation and its victory over all opposing forces.

Let your sincerity and surrender be genuine and entire. When you give yourself, give completely, without demand, without condition, without reservation so that all in you shall belong to the Divine Mother and nothing be left to the ego or given to any other power.

The more complete your faith, sincerity and surrender, the more will grace and protection be with you. And when the grace and protection of the Divine Mother are with you, what is there that can touch you or whom need you fear? A little of it even will carry you through all difficulties, obstacles and dangers; surrounded by its full presence you can go securely on your way because it is hers, careless of all menace, un-affected by any hostility however powerful, whether from this world or from worlds invisible. Its touch can turn difficulties into opportunities, failure into success and weakness into unfaltering strength. For the grace of the Divine Mother is the sanction of the Supreme and now or tomorrow its effect is sure, a thing decreed, inevitable and irresistible.

4

Money is the visible sign of a universal force, and this force in its manifestation on earth works on the vital and physical planes and is indispensable to the fullness of the outer life. In its origin and its true action it belongs to the Divine. But like other powers of the Divine it is delegated here and in the ignorance of the lower Nature can be usurped for the uses of the ego or held by Asuric influences and perverted to their purpose. This is indeed one of the three forces — power, wealth, sex — that have the strongest attraction for the human ego and the Asura and are most generally misheld and misused by those who retain them. The seekers or keepers of wealth are more often possessed rather than its possessors; few escape entirely a certain distorting influence stamped on it by its long seizure and perversion by the Asura. For this reason most spiritual disciplines insist on a complete self-control, detachment and renunciation of all bondage to wealth and of all personal and egoistic desire for its possession. Some even put a ban on money and riches and proclaim poverty and bareness of life as the only spiritual condition. But this is an error; it leaves the power in the hands of the hostile forces. To reconquer it for the Divine to whom it belongs and use it divinely for the divine life is the supramental way for the Sadhaka.

You must neither turn with an ascetic shrinking from the money power, the means it gives and the objects it brings, nor cherish a rajasic attachment to them or a spirit of enslaving self-indulgence in their gratifications. Regard wealth simply as a power to be won back for the Mother and placed at her service.

All wealth belongs to the Divine and those who hold it are trustees, not possessors. It is with them today, tomorrow it may be elsewhere. All depends on the way they discharge their trust while it is with them, in what spirit, with what consciousness in their use of it, to what purpose.

In your personal use of money look on all you have or get or bring as the Mother's. Make no demand but accept what you receive from her and use it for the purposes for which it is given to you. Be entirely selfless, entirely scrupulous, exact, careful in detail, a good trustee; always consider that it is her possessions and not your own that you are handling. On the other hand, what you receive for her, lay religiously before her; turn nothing to your own or anybody else's purpose.

Do not look up to men because of their riches or allow yourself to be impressed by the show, the power or the influence. When you ask for the Mother, you must feel that it is she who is demanding through you a very little of what belongs to her and the man from whom you ask will be judged by his response.

If you are free from the money-taint but without any ascetic withdrawal, you will have a greater power to command the money for the divine work. Equality of mind, absence of demand and the full dedication of all you possess and receive and all your power of acquisition to the Divine Shakti and her work are the signs of this freedom. Any perturbation of mind with regard to money and its use, any claim, any grudging is a sure index of some imperfection or bondage.

The ideal Sadhaka in this kind is one who if required to live poorly can so live and no sense of want will affect him or interfere with the full inner play of the divine consciousness, and if he is required to live richly, can so live and never for a moment fall into desire or attachment to his wealth or to the things that he uses or servitude to self-indulgence or a weak bondage to the habits that the possession of riches creates. The divine Will is all for him and the divine Ananda.

In the supramental creation the money-force has to be restored to the Divine Power and used for a true and beautiful and harmonious equipment and ordering of a new divinised vital and physical existence in whatever way the Divine Mother herself decides in her creative vision. But first it must be conquered back for her and those will be strongest for the conquest who are in this part of their nature strong and large and free from ego and surrendered without any claim or withholding or hesitation, pure and powerful channels for the Supreme Puissance.

5

If you want to be a true doer of divine works, your first aim must be to be totally free from all desire and self-regarding ego. All your life must be an offering and a sacrifice to the Supreme; your only object in action shall be to serve, to receive, to fulfil, to become a manifesting instrument of the Divine Shakti in her works. You must grow in the divine consciousness till there is no difference between your will and hers, no motive except her impulsion in you, no action that is not her conscious action in you and through you.

Until you are capable of this complete dynamic identification, you have to regard yourself as a soul and body created for her service, one who does all for her sake. Even if the idea of the separate worker is strong in you and you feel that it is you who do the act, yet it must be done for her. All stress of egoistic choice, all hankering after personal profit, all stipulation of self-regarding desire must be extirpated from the nature. There must be no demand for fruit and no seeking for reward; the only fruit for you is the pleasure of the Divine Mother and the fulfilment of her work, your only reward a constant progression in divine consciousness and calm and strength and bliss. The joy of service and the joy of inner growth through works is the sufficient recompense of the selfless worker.

But a time will come when you will feel more and more that you are the instrument and not the worker. For first by the force of your devotion your contact with the Divine Mother will become so intimate that at all times you will have only to concentrate and to put everything into her hands to have her present guidance, her direct command or impulse, the sure indication of the thing to be done and the way to do it and the result. And afterwards you will realise that the divine Shakti not only inspires and guides, but initiates and carries out your works; all your movements are originated by her, all your powers are hers, mind, life and body are conscious and joyful instruments of her action, means for her play, moulds for her manifestation in the physical universe. There can be no more happy condition than this union and dependence; for this step carries you back beyond the border-line from the life of stress and suffering in the ignorance into the truth of your spiritual being, into its deep peace and its intense Ananda.

While this transformation is being done it is more than ever necessary to keep yourself free from all taint of the perversions of the ego. Let no demand or insistence creep in to stain the purity of the self-giving and the sacrifice. There must be no attachment to the work or the result, no laying down of conditions, no claim to possess the Power that should possess you, no pride of the instrument, no vanity or arrogance. Nothing in the mind or in the vital or physical parts should be suffered to distort to its own use or seize for its own personal and separate satisfaction the greatness of the forces that are acting through you. Let your faith, your sincerity, your purity of aspiration be absolute and pervasive of all the planes and layers of the being; then every disturbing element and distorting influence will progressively fall away from your nature.

The last stage of this perfection will come when you are completely identified with the Divine Mother and feel yourself to be no longer another and separate being, instrument, servant or worker but truly a child and eternal portion of her consciousness and force. Always she will be in you and you in her;

it will be your constant, simple and natural experience that all
your thought and seeing and action, your very breathing or
moving come from her and are hers. You will know and see
and feel that you are a person and power formed by her out of
herself, put out from her for the play and yet always safe in her,
being of her being, consciousness of her consciousness, force
of her force, Ananda of her Ananda. When this condition is
entire and her supramental energies can freely move you, then
you will be perfect in divine works; knowledge, will, action will
become sure, simple, luminous, spontaneous, flawless, an out-
flow from the Supreme, a divine movement of the Eternal.

6

The four Powers of the Mother are four of her out-
standing Personalities, portions and embodiments of her
divinity through whom she acts on her creatures, orders
and harmonises her creations in the worlds and directs the
working out of her thousand forces. For the Mother is one
but she comes before us with differing aspects; many are her
powers and personalities, many her emanations and Vibhutis
that do her work in the universe. The One whom we adore
as the Mother is the divine Conscious Force that dominates
all existence, one and yet so many-sided that to follow her
movement is impossible even for the quickest mind and for
the freest and most vast intelligence. The Mother is the
consciousness and force of the Supreme and far above all
she creates. But something of her ways can be seen and felt
through her embodiments and the more seizable because more
defined and limited temperament and action of the goddess

forms in whom she consents to be manifest to her creatures.

There are three ways of being of the Mother of which you can become aware when you enter into touch of oneness with the Conscious Force that upholds us and the universe. Transcendent, the original supreme Shakti, she stands above the worlds and links the creation to the ever unmanifest mystery of the Supreme. Universal, the cosmic Mahashakti, she creates all these beings and contains and enters, supports and conducts all these million processes and forces. Individual, she embodies the power of these two vaster ways of her existence, makes them living and near to us and mediates between the human personality and the divine Nature.

The one original transcendent Shakti, the Mother stands above all the worlds and bears in her eternal consciousness the Supreme Divine. Alone, she harbours the absolute Power and the ineffable Presence; containing or calling the Truths that have to be manifested, she brings them down from the Mystery in which they were hidden into the light of her infinite consciousness and gives them a form of force in her omnipotent power and her boundless life and a body in the universe. The Supreme is manifest in her for ever as the everlasting Sachchidananda, manifested through her in the worlds as the one and dual consciousness of Ishwara-Shakti and the dual principle of Purusha-Prakriti, embodied by her in the Worlds and the Planes and the Gods and their Energies and figured because of her as all that is in the known worlds and in unknown others. All is her play with the Supreme; all is her manifestation of the mysteries of the Eternal, the miracles of the Infinite. All is she, for all are parcel and portion of the divine Conscious-Force. Nothing can be here or elsewhere but what she decides and the Supreme sanctions; nothing can take shape except what she moved by the Supreme perceives and forms after casting it into seed in her creating Ananda.

The Mahashakti, the universal Mother, works out whatever is transmitted by her transcendent consciousness from the Supreme and enters into the worlds that she has made; her presence fills and supports them with the divine spirit and the divine all-sustaining force and delight without which they could not exist. That which we call Nature or Prakriti is only her most outward executive aspect; she marshals and arranges the harmony of her forces and processes, impels the operations of Nature and moves among them secret or manifest in all that can be seen or experienced or put into motion of life. Each of

the worlds is nothing but one play of the Mahashakti of that
system of worlds or universe, who is there as the cosmic Soul
and Personality of the transcendent Mother. Each is something
that she has seen in her vision, gathered into her heart of beauty
and power and created in her Ananda.

But there are many planes of her creation, many steps of
the Divine Shakti. At the summit of this manifestation of which
we are a part there are worlds of infinite existence, consciousness, force and bliss over which the Mother stands as the
unveiled eternal Power. All beings there live and move in an
ineffable completeness and unalterable oneness, because she
carries them safe in her arms for ever. Nearer to us are the
worlds of a perfect supramental creation in which the Mother
is the supramental Mahashakti, a Power of divine omniscient
Will and omnipotent Knowledge always apparent in its unfailing works and spontaneously perfect in every process.
There all movements are the steps of the Truth; there all beings
are souls and powers and bodies of the divine Light; there all
experiences are seas and floods and waves of an intense and
absolute Ananda. But here where we dwell are the worlds of
the Ignorance, worlds of mind and life and body separated in
consciousness from their source, of which this earth is a signi-

ficant centre and its evolution a crucial process. This too with all its obscurity and struggle and imperfection is upheld by the Universal Mother; this too is impelled and guided to its secret aim by the Mahashakti.

The Mother as the Mahashakti of this triple world of the Ignorance stands in an intermediate plane between the supramental Light, the Truth life, the Truth creation which has to be brought down here and this mounting and descending hierarchy of planes of consciousness that like a double ladder lapse into the nescience of Matter and climb back again through the flowering of life and soul and mind into the infinity of the Spirit. Determining all that shall be in this universe and in the terrestrial evolution by what she sees and feels and pours from her, she stands there above the Gods and all her Powers and Personalities are put out in front of her for the action and she sends down emanations of them into these lower worlds to intervene, to govern, to battle and conquer, to lead and turn their cycles, to direct the total and the individual lines of their forces. These Emanations are the many divine forms and personalities in which men have worshipped her under different names throughout the ages. But also she prepares and shapes through these Powers and their emanations the minds and bodies of her Vibhutis, even as she prepares and shapes minds and bodies for the Vibhutis of the Ishwara, that she may manifest in the physical world and in the disguise of the human consciousness some ray of her power and quality and presence. All the scenes of the earthplay have been like a drama arranged and planned and staged by her with the cosmic Gods for her assistants and herself as a veiled actor.

The Mother not only governs all from above but she descends into this lesser triple universe. Impersonally, all things here, even the movements of the Ignorance, are herself in veiled power and her creations in diminished substance, her Nature-body and Nature-force, and they exist because, moved by the mysterious fiat of the Supreme to work out something that was there in the possibilities of the Infinite, she has consented to the great sacrifice and has put on like a mask the soul and forms of the Ignorance. But personally too she has stooped to descend here into the Darkness that she may lead it to the Light, into the Falsehood and Error that she may convert it to the Truth, into this Death that she may turn it to godlike Life, into this world-pain and its obstinate sorrow and suffering that she may end it in the transforming ecstasy of her sublime Ananda. In her deep and great love for her children she has consented to put on herself the cloak of this obscurity, condescended to bear the attacks and torturing influences of the powers of the Darkness and the Falsehood, borne to pass through the portals of the birth that is a death, taken upon herself the pangs and sorrows and sufferings of the creation, since it seemed that thus alone could it be lifted to the Light and Joy and Truth and eternal Life. This is the great sacrifice called sometimes the sacrifice of the Purusha, but much more deeply the holocaust of Prakriti, the sacrifice of the Divine Mother.

Four great Aspects of the Mother, four of her leading Powers and Personalities have stood in front in her guidance of this Universe and in her dealings with the terrestrial play. One is her personality of calm wideness and comprehending wisdom and tranquil benignity and inexhaustible compassion and sovereign and surpassing majesty and all-ruling greatness. Another embodies her power of splendid strength and irresistible passion, her warrior mood, her overwhelming will, her impetuous swiftness and world-shaking force. A third is vivid and sweet and wonderful with her deep secret of beauty and harmony and fine rhythm, her intricate and subtle opulence, her compelling attraction and captivating grace. The fourth is equipped with her close and profound capacity of intimate knowledge and

careful flawless work and quiet and exact perfection in all things.
Wisdom, Strength, Harmony, Perfection are their several
attributes and it is these powers that they bring with them into
the world, manifest in a human disguise in their Vibhutis and
shall found in the divine degree of their ascension in those who
can open their earthly nature to the direct and living influence
of the Mother. To the four we give the four great names, Maheshwari, Mahakali, Mahalakshmi, Mahasaraswati.

Imperial MAHESHWARI is seated in the wideness above
the thinking mind and will and sublimates and greatens them into
wisdom and largeness or floods with a splendour beyond them.
For she is the mighty and wise One who opens us to the supramental infinities and the cosmic vastness, to the grandeur of the
supreme Light, to a treasure-house of miraculous knowledge,
to the measureless movement of the Mother's eternal forces.
Tranquil is she and wonderful, great and calm for ever. Nothing
can move her because all wisdom is in her; nothing is hidden
from her that she chooses to know; she comprehends all things
and all beings and their nature and what moves them and the
law of the world and its times and how all was and is and must
be. A strength is in her that meets everything and masters and

none can prevail in the end against her vast intangible wisdom and high tranquil power. Equal, patient and unalterable in her will she deals with men according to their nature and with things and happenings according to their Force and the truth that is in them. Partiality she has none, but she follows the decrees of the Supreme and some she raises up and some she casts down or puts away from her into the darkness. To the wise she gives a greater and more luminous wisdom; those that have vision she admits to her counsels; on the hostile she imposes the consequence of their hostility; the ignorant and foolish she leads according to their blindness. In each man she answers and handles the different elements of his nature according to their need and their urge and the return they call for, puts on them the required pressure or leaves them to their cherished liberty to prosper in the ways of the Ignorance or to perish. For she is above all, bound by nothing, attached to nothing in the universe. Yet has she more than any other the heart of the universal Mother. For her compassion is endless and inexhaustible; all are to her eyes her children and portions of the One, even the Asura and Rakshasa and Pisacha and those that are revolted and hostile. Even her rejections are only a postponement, even her punishments are a grace. But her compassion does not blind her wisdom or turn her action from the course decreed; for the

Truth of things is her one concern, knowledge her centre of power and to build our soul and our nature into the divine Truth her mission and her labour.

MAHAKALI is of another nature. Not wideness but height, not wisdom but force and strength are her peculiar power. There is in her an overwhelming intensity, a mighty passion of force to achieve, a divine violence rushing to shatter every limit and obstacle. All her divinity leaps out in a splendour of tempestuous action; she is there for swiftness, for the immediately effective process, the rapid and direct stroke, the frontal assault that carries everything before it. Terrible is her face to the Asura, dangerous and ruthless her mood against the haters of the Divine; for she is the Warrior of the Worlds who never shrinks from the battle. Intolerant of imperfection, she deals roughly with all in man that is unwilling and she is severe to all that is obstinately ignorant and obscure; her wrath is immediate and dire against treachery and falsehood and malignity, ill-will is smitten at once by her scourge. Indifference, negligence and sloth in the divine work she cannot bear and she smites awake at once with sharp pain, if need be, the untimely slumberer and the loiterer. The impulses that are swift and straight and frank, the movements that are unreserved and absolute, the aspiration that mounts in flame are the motion of Mahakali. Her spirit is tameless, her vision and will are high and far-reaching like the flight of an eagle, her feet are rapid on the upward way and her hands are outstretched to strike and to succour. For she too is the Mother and her love is as intense as her wrath and she has a deep and passionate kindness. When she is allowed to intervene in her strength, then in one moment are broken like things without consistence the obstacles that immobilise or the enemies that assail the seeker. If her anger is dreadful to the hostile and the vehemence of her pressure painful to the weak and timid, she is loved and worshipped by the great, the strong and the noble; for they feel that her blows beat what is rebellious in their material into strength and perfect truth, hammer straight what is wry and perverse and expel what is impure or defective. But for her what is done in a day might have taken centuries; without her Ananda might be wide and grave or soft and sweet and beautiful but would lose the flaming joy of its most absolute intensities. To knowledge she gives a conquering might, brings to beauty and harmony a high and mounting movement and imparts to the slow and difficult labour after perfection an impetus that multiplies the power and shortens the long way. Nothing can satisfy her that falls short of the supreme ecstasies, the highest heights, the noblest aims, the largest vistas. Therefore with her is the victorious force of the Divine and it is by grace of her fire and passion and speed if the great achievement can be done now rather than hereafter.

Wisdom and Force are not the only manifestations of the supreme Mother; there is a subtler mystery of her nature and without it Wisdom and Force would be incomplete things and without it perfection would not be perfect. Above them is the miracle of eternal beauty, an unseizable secret of divine harmonies, the compelling magic of an irresistible universal charm and attraction that draws and holds things and forces and beings together and obliges them to meet and unite that a hidden Ananda may play from behind the veil and make of them its rhythms and its figures. This is the power of MAHALAKSHMI and there is no aspect of the Divine Shakti more attractive to the heart of embodied beings. Maheshwari can appear too calm and great and distant for the littleness of earthly nature to approach or contain her, Mahakali too swift and formidable for its weakness to bear; but all turn with joy and longing to Mahalakshmi. For she throws the spell of the intoxicating sweetness of the Divine: to be close to her is a profound happiness and to feel her within the heart is to make existence a rapture and a marvel; grace and charm and tenderness flow out from her like light from the sun and wherever she fixes her wonderful gaze or lets fall the loveliness of her smile, the soul is seized and made captive and plunged into the depths of an unfathomable bliss. Magnetic is the touch of her hands and their occult and delicate influence refines mind and life and body and where she presses her feet course miraculous streams of an entrancing Ananda.

And yet it is not easy to meet the demand of this enchanting Power or to keep her presence. Harmony and beauty of the mind and soul, harmony and beauty of the thoughts and feelings, harmony and beauty in every outward act and movement, harmony and beauty of the life and surroundings, this is the demand of Mahalakshmi. Where there is affinity to the rhythms of the secret world-bliss and response to the call of the All-Beautiful and concord and unity and the glad flow of many lives turned towards the Divine, in that atmosphere she consents to abide. But all that is ugly and mean and base, all that is poor and sordid and squalid, all that is brutal and coarse repels her advent. Where love and beauty are not or are reluctant to be born, she does not come; where they are mixed and disfigured with baser things, she turns soon to depart or cares little to pour her riches. If she finds herself in men's hearts surrounded with selfishness and hatred and jealousy and malignance and envy and strife, if treachery and greed and ingratitude are mixed in the sacred chalice, if grossness of passion and unrefined desire degrade devotion, in such hearts the gracious and beautiful Goddess will not linger. A divine disgust seizes upon her and she withdraws, for she is not one who insists or strives; or, veiling her face, she waits for this bitter and poisonous devil's stuff to be rejected and disappear before she will found anew her happy influence. Ascetic bareness and harshness are not pleasing to her nor the suppression of the heart's deeper emotions and the rigid repression of the soul's and the life's parts of beauty. For it is through love and beauty that she lays on men the yoke of the Divine. Life is turned in her supreme creations into a rich work of celestial art and all existence into a poem of sacred delight; the world's riches are brought together and concerted for a supreme order and even the simplest and commonest things are made wonderful by her intuition of unity and the breath of her spirit. Admitted to the heart she lifts wisdom to pinnacles of wonder and reveals to it the mystic secrets of the ecstasy that surpasses all knowledge, meets devotion with the passionate attraction of the Divine, teaches to strength and force the rhythm that keeps the might of their acts harmonious and in measure and casts on perfection the charm that makes it endure for ever.

MAHASARASWATI is the Mother's Power of Work and her spirit of perfection and order. The youngest of the Four, she is the most skilful in executive faculty and the nearest to physical Nature. Maheshwari lays down the large lines of the world-forces, Mahakali drives their energy and impetus, Mahalakshmi discovers their rhythms and measures, but Mahasaraswati presides over their detail of organisation and execution, relation of parts and effective combination of forces and unfailing exactitude of result and fulfilment. The science and craft and technique of things are Mahasaraswati's province. Always she holds in her nature and can give to those whom she has chosen the intimate and precise knowledge, the subtlety and patience, the accuracy of intuitive mind and conscious hand and discerning eye of the perfect worker. This Power is the strong, the tireless, the careful and efficient builder, organiser, administrator, technician, artisan and classifier of the worlds. When she takes up the transformation and new-building of the nature, her action is laborious and minute and often seems to our impatience slow and interminable, but it is persistent, integral and flawless. For the will in her works is scrupulous, unsleeping, indefatigable; leaning over us she notes and touches every little detail, finds out every minute defect, gap, twist or incompleteness, considers and weighs accurately all that has been done and all that remains still to be done hereafter. Nothing is too small or apparently trivial for her attention; nothing however impalpable or disguised or latent can escape her. Moulding and remoulding she labours each part till it has attained its true form, is put in its exact place in the whole and fulfils its precise purpose. In her constant and diligent arrangement and rearrangement of things her eye is on all needs at once and the way to meet them and her intuition knows what is to be chosen and what rejected and successfully determines the right instrument, the right time, the right conditions and the right process. Carelessness and negligence and indolence she abhors; all scamped and hasty and shuffling work, all clumsiness and *à peu près* and misfire, all false adaptation and misuse of instruments and faculties and leaving of things undone or half done is offensive and foreign to her temper. When her work is finished, nothing has been forgotten, no part has been misplaced or omitted or left in a faulty condition; all is solid, accurate, complete, admirable. Nothing short of a perfect perfection satisfies her and she is ready to face an eternity of toil if that is needed for the fullness of her creation. Therefore of all the Mother's powers she is the most long-suffering with man and his thousand imperfections. Kind, smiling, close and helpful, not easily turned away or discouraged, insistent even after repeated failure, her hand sustains our every step on condition that we are single in our will and straightforward and sincere; for a double mind she will not tolerate and her revealing irony is merciless to drama and histrionics and self-deceit and pretence. A mother to our wants, a friend in our difficulties, a persistent and tranquil counsellor and mentor, chasing away with her radiant smile the clouds of gloom and fretfulness and depression, reminding always of the ever-present help, pointing to the eternal sunshine, she is firm, quiet and persevering in the deep and continuous urge that drives us towards the integrality of the higher nature. All the work of the other Powers leans on her for its completeness; for she assures the material foundation, elaborates the stuff of detail and erects and rivets the armour of the structure.

There are other great Personalities of the Divine Mother, but they were more difficult to bring down and have not stood out in front with so much prominence in the evolution of the earth-spirit. There are among them Presences indispensable for the supramental realisation, — most of all one who is her Perso-

nality of that mysterious and powerful ecstasy and Ananda which
flows from a supreme divine Love, the Ananda that alone can
heal the gulf between the highest heights of the supramental
spirit and the lowest abysses of Matter, the Ananda that holds
the key of a wonderful divinest Life and even now supports
from its secrecies the work of all the other Powers of the universe.
But human nature bounded, egoistic and obscure is inapt to receive these great Presences or to support their mighty action.
Only when the Four have founded their harmony and freedom
of movement in the transformed mind and life and body, can
those other rarer Powers manifest in the earth movement and the
supramental action become possible. For when her Personalities are all gathered in her and manifested and their separate
working has been turned into a harmonious unity and they rise
in her to their supramental godheads, then is the Mother revealed
as the supramental Mahashakti and brings pouring down her
luminous transcendences from their ineffable ether. Then can
human nature change into dynamic divine nature because all the
elemental lines of the supramental Truth consciousness and
Truth-force are strung together and the harp of life is fitted for
the rhythms of the Eternal.

If you desire this transformation, put yourself in the

hands of the Mother and her Powers without cavil or resistance and let her do unhindered her work within you. Three things you must have, consciousness, plasticity, unreserved surrender. For you must be conscious in your mind and soul and heart and life and the very cells of your body, aware of the Mother and her Powers and their working; for although she can and does work in you even in your obscurity and your unconscious parts and moments, it is not the same thing as when you are in an awakened and living communion with her. All your nature must be plastic to her touch, — not questioning as the self-sufficient ignorant mind questions and doubts and disputes and is the enemy of its enlightenment and change; not insisting on its own movements as the vital in man insists and persistently opposes its refractory desires and ill-will to every divine influence; not obstructing and entrenched in incapacity, inertia and tamas as man's physical consciousness obstructs and clinging to its pleasure in smallness and darkness cries out against each touch that disturbs its soulless routine or its dull sloth or its torpid slumber. The unreserved surrender of your inner and outer being will bring this plasticity into all the parts of your nature; consciousness will awaken everywhere in you by constant openness to the Wisdom and Light, the Force, the Harmony and Beauty, the Perfection that come flowing down from above. Even the body will awake and unite at last its consciousness subliminal no longer to the supramental superconscious Force, feel all her powers permeating from above and below and around it and thrill to a supreme Love and Ananda.

But be on your guard and do not try to understand and judge the Divine Mother by your little earthly mind that loves to subject even the things that are beyond it to its own norms and standards, its narrow reasonings and erring impressions, its bottomless aggressive ignorance and its petty self-confident knowledge. The human mind shut in the prison of its half-lit obscurity cannot follow the many-sided freedom of the steps of the Divine Shakti. The rapidity and complexity of her vision and action outrun its stumbling comprehension; the measures of her movement are not its measures. Bewildered by the swift alteration of her many different personalities, her making of rhythms and her breaking of rhythms, her accelerations of speed and her retardations, her varied ways of dealing with the problem of one and of another, her taking up and dropping now of this line and now of that one and her gathering of them together, it will not recognise the way of the Supreme Power when it is circling and sweeping upwards through the maze of the Ignorance to a supernal Light. Open rather your soul to her and be content to feel her with the psychic nature and see her with the psychic vision that alone make a straight response to the Truth. Then the Mother herself will enlighten by their psychic elements your mind and heart and life and physical consciousness and reveal to them too her ways and her nature.

Avoid also the error of the ignorant mind's demand on the Divine Power to act always according to our crude surface notions of omniscience and omnipotence. For our mind clamours to be impressed at every turn by miraculous power and easy success and dazzling splendour; otherwise it cannot believe that here is the Divine. The Mother is dealing with the Ignorance in the fields of the Ignorance; she has descended there and is not all above. Partly she veils and partly she unveils her knowledge and her power, often holds them back from her instruments and personalities and follows that she may transform them the way of the seeking mind, the way of the aspiring psychic, the way of the battling vital, the way of the imprisoned and suffering physical nature. There are conditions that have been laid down by a Supreme Will, there are many tangled knots that have to be loosened and cannot be cut abruptly asunder. The Asura and Rakshasa hold this evolving earthly nature and have to be met and conquered on their own terms in

their own long-conquered fief and province; the human in us has
to be led and prepared to transcend its limits and is too weak and
obscure to be lifted up suddenly to a form far beyond it. The
Divine Consciousness and Force are there and do at each moment the thing that is needed in the conditions of the labour,
take always the step that is decreed and shape in the midst of
imperfection the perfection that is to come. But only when the
supermind has descended in you can she deal directly as the
supramental Shakti with supramental natures. If you follow your
mind, it will not recognise the Mother even when she is manifest
before you. Follow your soul and not your mind, your soul that
answers to the Truth, not your mind that leaps at appearances;
trust the Divine Power and she will free the godlike elements in
you and shape all into an expression of Divine Nature.

The supramental change is a thing decreed and inevitable
in the evolution of the earth-consciousness; for its upward ascent
is not ended and mind is not its last summit. But that the change
may arrive, take form and endure, there is needed the call from
below with a will to recognise and not deny the Light when it
comes, and there is needed the sanction of the Supreme from
above. The power that mediates between the sanction and the
call is the presence and power of the Divine Mother. The

Mother's power and not any human endeavour and tapasya can alone rend the lid and tear the covering and shape the vessel and bring down into this world of obscurity and falsehood and death and suffering Truth and Light and Life divine and the immortal's Ananda.

LETTERS ON THE MOTHER

I

THE MOTHER
AND THE PURPOSE OF HER EMBODIMENT

THE MOTHER
AND THE PURPOSE OF HER EMBODIMENT

WHO IS THE MOTHER?

Q: Do you not refer to the Mother (our Mother) in your book, "The Mother"?

A: Yes.

Q: Is she not the "Individual" Divine Mother who has embodied "the power of these two vaster ways of her existence"[1] — Transcendent and Universal?

A: Yes.

Q: Has she not descended here (amongst us) into the Darkness and Falsehood and Error and Death in her deep and great love for us?

A: Yes.

17-8-1938

*

[1] Part One, p. 20.

> *Q: There are many who hold the view that she was human but now embodies the Divine Mother and her "Prayers"[1], they say, explain this view. But, to my mental conception, to my psychic feeling, she is the Divine Mother who has consented to put on her the cloak of obscurity and suffering and ignorance so that she can effectively lead us — human beings — to Knowledge and Bliss and Ananda and to the Supreme Lord.*

A: The Divine puts on an appearance of humanity, assumes the outward human nature in order to tread the path and show it to human beings, but does not cease to be the Divine. It is a manifestation that takes place, a manifestation of a growing divine consciousness, not human turning into divine. The Mother was inwardly above the human even in childhood, so the view held by "many" is erroneous.

> *Q: I also conceive that the Mother's "Prayers" are meant to show us — the aspiring psychic — how to pray to the Divine.*

A: Yes.

17-8-1938

THE MOTHER'S MANIFESTATION AND THE SUPRAMENTAL DESCENT

> *Q: Is there any difference between the Mother's manifestation and the descent of the Supramental?*

A: The Mother comes in order to bring down the Supramental and it is the descent which makes her full manifestation here possible.

23-9-1935

*

[1] *Prayers and Meditations of the Mother,* See Part Three.

Q: The Mother does not work on the Sadhak directly from her own plane above, though she can do so if she wants to — she can even supramentalise the world in a day; but in that case the supramental Nature created here would be the same as it is above, and not the earth in Ignorance evolving into the supramental earth, a manifestation which will not be in appearance quite the same as what the Supermind is.

A: That is a very important truth.

17-6-1935

PURPOSE OF THE MOTHER'S EMBODIMENT

Q: Am I right in thinking that she as an individual embodies all the Divine Powers and brings down the Grace more and more to the physical plane, and her embodiment is a chance for the entire physical consciousness to change and be transformed?

A: Yes. Her embodiment is a chance for the earth-consciousness to receive the Supramental into it and to undergo first the transformation necessary for that to be possible. Afterwards there will be a further transformation by the Supramental, but the whole earth-consciousness will not be supramentalised — there will be first a new race representing the Supermind, as man represents the mind.

13-8-1933

*

There is one divine Force which acts in the universe and in the individual and is also beyond the individual and the universe. The Mother stands for all these, but she is working here in the body to bring down something not yet expressed in this material world so as to transform life here — it is so that you should regard her as the Divine Shakti working here for that purpose.

She is that in the body, but in her whole consciousness she is also identified with all the other aspects of the Divine.

*

There are not many Mothers, there is One in many forms. The transcendental is only one aspect of the Mother. I don't know what is meant by the embodied aspect of the transcendental Mother. There is the embodied aspect of the One Mother — what she manifests through it depends on herself.

7-7-1936

*

Q: Why does the Mother in her universal action act according to the law of things, but in her embodied physical by constant Grace?

A: It is the work of the Cosmic Power to maintain the cosmos and the law of the cosmos. The greater transformation comes from the Transcendent above the universal, and it is that transcendent Grace which the embodiment of the Mother is there to bring into action.

13-8-1933

*

Q: What would you say about the utility of the physical approach to the Mother?

A: There is the utility of the physical approach to the Mother — the approach of the embodied mind and vital to her embodied Power. In her universal action the Mother acts according to the law of things — in her embodied physical action is the opportunity of a constant Grace — it is for that that the embodiment takes place.

12-8-1933

DIFFERENT APPEARANCES OF THE MOTHER

The Mother has many different personalities and her appearance varies according as one or another predominates. The something common, of course, exists. There is first, the one whom all these personalities manifest but that cannot be expressed in name or word — there is also the supramental personality which from behind the veil presides over the aim of the present manifestation.

9-11-1933

*

The Mother has not only one appearance, but many at different times.

Behind the physical body there are many forms and powers and personalities of the Mother.

14-5-1933

*

Q: Two days back I saw in a vision that the fire of aspiration was rising from my heart and going upward with the constant remembrance of the Mother. Then I saw that the Mother, as we see her in her physical body, was descending in the fire and filling all my parts with peace and strength. What does this vision indicate? Why did I see the Mother exactly as we see her in her physical body and not in her divine form?

A: It indicates an aspiration and an action for realisation in the external nature and not only in the inner being. When it is an inner action or an action of another plane one can see the Mother in any of her forms, but for realisation in the physical her appropriate form is that which she wears here.

15-7-1933

✵

Q: Why does the Mother appear different at different times, as at Pranam or Prosperity or while giving the interview? Sometimes even anatomical differences are visible. What is the reason of these differences in her appearance? Does it depend on the extent to which she turns outwards?

A: It is rather, I think, dependent on the personality that manifests in front — as she has many personalities and the body is plastic enough to express something of each when it comes forward.

4-12-1933

*

Q: Often when I see the Mother I feel as if she is the image of divine Ananda and her form looks like that of a young girl. Is there any truth in my feeling?

A: Ananda is not the only thing — there is Knowledge and Power and Love and many other powers of the Divine. As a special experience only it may stand.

30-4-1933

*

Yes. Many see like that, as if the Mother were taller than her ordinary physical appearance.

29-9-1933

REVELATION OF THE MOTHER'S COMING

Q: When Ramakrishna was doing Sadhana, Mother was on earth physically for the first eight years of her childhood, from 1878 to 1886. Did he know that Mother had come down? He must have had some vision at least of her coming, but we do not read anywhere definitely about it.

*And when Ramakrishna must have been intensely calling
Mother, she must have felt something at that age.*

A: In Mother's childhood's visions she saw myself whom she
knew as "Krishna" — she did not see Ramakrishna.

It was not necessary that he should have a vision of her
coming down as he was not thinking of the future nor consciously preparing for it. I don't think he had the idea of any
incarnation of the Mother.

11-7-1935

*

I don't say on what plane X is, but his method is that of Adwaita
Knowledge and Moksha — so there is no necessity for him to
recognise the arrival of the Divine. Y's Guru was a *bhakta* of
the Divine Mother, believed in the dynamic side of existence, so
it was quite natural for him to have the revelation of the coming
of the Mother.

23-1-1936

*

X is very much of a Vedantist. He does not believe in what we
believe or in the descent etc. At the same time he himself had
experiences in which the Mother interfered in a visible free
material form and prevented him from doing what he intended
to do.

7-7-1936

SEEING THE DIVINE IN THE MOTHER

*Q: This morning I perceived a great beauty in the Mother.
It was as if her whole body was glowing with a super-
natural light. In fact I felt as if a Supreme Goddess
had come down from the heavens above. Kindly explain
that.*

A: It was only that you felt the Divinity with her which is always there.

20-7-1933

*

As for seeing the Divine in the Mother at first sight, he is not the only one to do that. Plenty of people have done that...e.g. X's cousin, a Musulman girl, who as soon as she met her declared, "This is not a woman, she is a goddess", and has been having significant dreams of her ever since, and whenever she is in trouble, thinks of her and gets helped out of the trouble. It is not so difficult to see the Divine in the Mother as you make it out to be.

23-7-1935

*

Q: I don't know what the Musulman lady exactly saw. From what you say it seems to be a flash of intuition.

A: Not at all, it was a direct sense of the Godhead in her — for I suppose you mean by intuition a sort of idea that comes suddenly? That is what people usually understand by intuition. It was not that in her case nor in X's.

29-7-1935

*

Q: But is it not extremely difficult to see the fully flaming resplendent Divine Mother?

A: I don't believe X or anybody would have that at first view. That can only come if one has already developed the faculty of vision in the occult planes. What is of more importance is the clear perception or intimate inner feeling or direct sense, "This is She." I think you are inclined to be too romantic and poetic and too little spiritually realistic in these things.

With many people the faculty of this kind of occult vision is the first to develop when they begin Sadhana. With others it is there naturally or comes on occasions without any practice of Yoga. But with people who live mainly in the intellect (a few excepted) this faculty is not usually there by nature and most have much difficulty in developing it. It was so even with me.

It would be something of a miracle to see things without the faculty of seeing. We don't deal much in miracles of that kind.

29-7-1935

RECOGNITION OF THE MOTHER'S DIVINITY

There are people who start at once, others take time.

X recognised the Mother as divine at first sight and has been happy ever afterwards; others who rank among Mother's devotees took years to discover or admit it, but they arrived all the same. There are people who had nothing but difficulties and revolts for the first five, six, seven or more years of the Sadhana, yet the psychic ended by awaking. The time taken is a secondary matter: the one thing needful is — soon or late, easily or with difficulty, to get there.

*

Q: Many times I find that old Sanskaras come up and disturb my faith in the Mother and her divinity. How is it possible to prevent it?

A: It is only if you see the divinity of the Mother that there can be a settled conviction — that is a question of the inner consciousness and vision.

5-6-1937

*

Q: How to convince the mind that Mother is divine and that her workings are not human?

A: It is by opening up the psychic and letting it rule the mind and vital that this can be done — because the psychic knows and can see what the mind cannot.

*

Q: *It seems that part of my external being which was not accepting the Mother is now recognising her divinity. But why do I forget it when I physically come before her?*

A: It is the physical mind in its most external action that sees physical things as only physical.

15-8-1937

*

This struggle in you [between *bhakti* for Sri Krishna and the sense of the divinity of the Mother] is quite unnecessary; for the two things are one and go perfectly together. It is he who has brought you to the Mother and it is by adoration of her that you will realise him. He is here in the Ashram and it is his work that is being done here.

1933

*

Q: *Even a good devotee and a brilliant student like X finds it difficult to accept the Mother. I cannot understand why he cannot see the simple truth about her.*

A: If he finds it difficult to accept Mother, how is he a good devotee? A devotee to whom? A brilliant student is another matter; one can be a brilliant student and yet quite incompetent in spiritual matters. If one is a devotee of Vishnu or some other Godhead, then it is different — one may see only one's object of worship and so not be able to accept anything else.

14-11-1934

*

Q: Some people seem to be quite misled in understanding the Mother's status with regard to the higher planes. When they are in these planes or receive something from them, they begin to think that they have reached a great height, and that the higher planes have nothing to do with the Mother. Especially about the Supermind they have such queer notions — that it is something greater than the Mother.

A: If they have a greater experience or consciousness than the Mother, they should not stay here but go and save the world with it.

*

Q: Is the attitude that I am the Brahman not necessary in the Integral Yoga?

A: It is not enough to transform the whole nature. Otherwise there would be no need of the Mother's being here. It could be done by simply thinking of oneself as the Brahman. There would be no need of the Mother's presence or the Mother's force.

27-12-1935

THE MOTHER'S OFFER OF TRUTH

The Mother cannot decide for you whether you should follow the Path of Nirvikalpa Samadhi or accept this Yoga, she can only offer to you the Truth and if you accept it, guide you towards it.

8-9-1933

THE MOTHER AND THE YOGA OF KNOWLEDGE

Why should Mother dislike the Yoga of Knowledge? The realisation of Self and of the Cosmic being (without which the realisation of Self is incomplete) are essential steps in our Yoga; it is the end of other Yogas, but it is, as it were, the beginning of ours, that is to say, the point where its own characteristic realisation can commence.

26-3-1936

*

Certainly, Samadhi is not barred from this Yoga. The fact that the Mother was always entering into it is proof enough of that.

10-6-1936

II

ASPECTS AND POWERS OF THE MOTHER

ASPECTS AND POWERS OF THE MOTHER

EXPLANATION OF SOME TERMS IN "THE MOTHER"

1. FALSEHOOD AND IGNORANCE

Ignorance means Avidya, the separative consciousness and the egoistic mind and life that flow from it and all that is natural to the separative consciousness and the egoistic mind and life. This Ignorance is the result of a movement by which the cosmic Intelligence separated itself from the light of the Supermind (the divine Gnosis) and lost the Truth, — truth of being, truth of divine consciousness, truth of force and action, truth of Ananda. As a result, instead of a world of integral truth and divine harmony created in the light of the divine Gnosis, we have a world founded on the part truths of an inferior cosmic Intelligence in which all is half-truth, half-error. It is this that some of the ancient thinkers like Shankara, not perceiving the greater Truth-Force behind, stigmatised as Maya and thought to be the highest creative power of the Divine. All in the consciousness of this creation is either limited or else perverted by separation from the integral Light; even the Truth it perceives is only a half-knowledge. Therefore it is called the Ignorance.

Falsehood, on the other hand, is not this Avidya, but an extreme result of it. It is created by an Asuric power which intervenes in this creation and is not only separated from the Truth and therefore limited in knowledge and open to error, but in revolt against the Truth or in the habit of seizing the Truth only to pervert it. This Power, the dark Asuric Shakti or Rakshasic Maya, puts forward its own perverted consciousness as true knowledge and its wilful distortions or reversals of the Truth as the verity of things. It is the powers and personalities of this perverted and perverting consciousness that we call hostile beings, hostile forces. Whenever these perversions created by them out of the stuff of the Ignorance are put forward as the Truth of things, that is the Falsehood, in the Yogic sense, *mithyā, moha.*

2. POWERS AND APPEARANCES

These are the forces and beings that are interested in maintaining the falsehoods they have created in the world of the Ignorance and in putting them forward as the Truth which men must follow. In India they are termed Asuras, Rakshasas, Pishachas (beings respectively of the mentalised vital, middle vital and lower vital planes) who are in opposition to the Gods, the Powers of Light. These too are Powers, for they too have their cosmic field in which they exercise their function and authority and some of them were once divine Powers (the former gods, *pūrve devāḥ*, as they are called somewhere in the Mahabharata) who have fallen towards the darkness by revolt against the divine Will behind the cosmos. The word "appearances" refers to the forms they take in order to rule the world, forms often false and always incarnating falsehood, sometimes pseudo-divine.

3. POWERS AND PERSONALITIES

The use of the word Power has already been explained — it can be applied to whatever or whoever exercises a conscious power in the cosmic field and has authority over the world-movement or some movement in it. But the Four[1] of whom you speak are also Shaktis, manifestations of different powers of the Supreme Consciousness and Force, the Divine Mother, by which she rules or acts in the universe. And they are at the same time divine personalities; for each is a being who manifests different qualities and personal consciousness-forms of the Godhead. All the greater Gods are in this way personalities of the Divine — one Consciousness playing in many personalities, *ekam sat bahudhā*. Even in the human being there are many personalities and not only one, as used formerly to be imagined; for all consciousness can be at once one and multiple. "Powers and Personalities" simply describe different aspects of the same being; a Power is not necessarily impersonal and certainly it is not *avyaktam*, as you suggest, — on the contrary, it is a manifestation acting in the worlds of the divine Manifestation.

---

[1] Maheshwari, Mahakali, Mahalakshmi, Mahasaraswati.

4. EMANATIONS

Emanations correspond to your description of the Matrikas of whom you speak in your letters. An emanation of the Mother is something of her consciousness and power put forth from her which, so long as it is in play, is held in close connection with her and, when its play is no longer required, is withdrawn back into its source, but can always be put out and brought into play once more. But also the detaining thread of connection can be severed or loosened and that which came forth as an emanation can proceed on its way as an independent divine being with its own play in the world. All the Gods can put forth such emanations from their being, identical with them in essence of consciousness and power though not commensurate. In a certain sense the universe itself can be said to be an emanation from the Supreme. In the consciousness of the Sadhak an emanation of the Mother will ordinarily wear the appearance, form and characteristics with which he is familiar.

In a sense the four Powers of the Mother may be called, because of their origin, her Emanations, just as the Gods may be called Emanations of the Divine, but they have a more permanent and fixed character; they are at once independent beings allowed their play by the Adya Shakti and yet portions of the Mother, the Mahashakti, and she can always either manifest through them as separate beings or draw them together as her own various Personalities and hold them in herself, sometimes kept back, sometimes at play, according to her will. In the supramental plane they are always in her and do not act independently but as intimate portions of the supramental Mahashakti and in close union and harmony with each other.

5. GODS

These four Powers are the Mother's cosmic Godheads, permanent in the world-play; they stand among the greater cosmic Godheads to whom allusion is made when it is said that the Mother as the Mahashakti of this triple world "stands there (in the Overmind plane) above the Gods."[1] The Gods, as has already been said, are in origin and essence permanent Emanations of the Divine put forth from the Supreme by the Transcendent Mother, the Adya Shakti; in their cosmic action they are Powers and Personalities of the Divine, each with his independent cosmic standing, function and work in the universe. They are not impersonal entities but cosmic Personalities, although they can and do ordinarily veil themselves behind the movement of impersonal forces. But while in the Overmind and the triple world they appear as independent beings, they return in the Supermind into the One and stand there united in a single harmonious action as multiple personalities of the One Person, the Divine Purushottama.

6. Presence

It is intended by the word Presence to indicate the sense and perception of the Divine as a Being, felt as present in one's existence and consciousness or in relation with it, without the necessity of any further qualification or description. Thus, of the "ineffable Presence" it can only be said that it is there and nothing more can or need be said about it, although at the same time one knows that all is there, personality and impersonality, Power and Light and Ananda and everything else, and that all these flow from that indescribable Presence. The word may be used sometimes in a less absolute sense, but that is always the fundamental significance, — the essential perception of the essential Presence supporting everything else.

7. The Transcendent Mother

This is what is termed the Adya Shakti; she is the Supreme Consciousness and Power above the universe and it is by her that all the Gods are manifested, and even the supramental Ishwara comes into manifestation through her — the supramental Purushottama of whom the Gods are Powers and Personalities.

[1] Part One, P. 23.

ADYA SHAKTI

Adya Shakti is the original Shakti, therefore, the highest form of the Mother. Only she manifests in a different way according to the plane on which one sees her.

22-7-1933

THE DIVINE MOTHER

The Divine Mother is the Consciousness and Force of the Divine — which is the Mother of all things.

THE MOTHER AND THE ISHWARA

The Mother is the consciousness and force of the Divine — or, it may be said, she is the Divine in its consciousness-force. The Ishwara as Lord of the cosmos does come out of the Mother who takes her place beside him as the cosmic Shakti — the cosmic Ishwara is one aspect of the Divine.

THE DIVINE MOTHER IN THE GITA, THE TANTRA AND THE INTEGRAL YOGA

The Gita does not speak expressly of the Divine Mother; it speaks always of surrender to the Purushottama — it mentions her only as the Para Prakriti who becomes the Jiva, that is, who manifests the Divine in the multiplicity and through whom all these worlds are created by the Supreme and he himself descends as the Avatar. The Gita follows the Vedantic tradition which leans entirely on the Ishwara aspect of the Divine and speaks little of the Divine Mother because its object is to draw back from world-nature and arrive at the supreme realisation beyond it; the Tantric tradition leans on the Shakti or Ishwari aspect and makes all depend on the Divine Mother because its object is to possess and dominate the world-nature and arrive at the supreme realisation through it. This Yoga insists on both the aspects; the surrender to the Divine Mother is essential for without it there is no fulfilment of the object of the Yoga.

In regard to the Purushottama the Divine Mother is the supreme divine Consciousness and Power above the worlds, Adya Shakti; she carries the Supreme in herself and manifests the Divine in the worlds through the Akshara and Kshara. In regard to the Akshara she is the same Para Shakti holding the Purusha immobile in herself and also herself immobile in him at the back of all creation. In regard to the Kshara she is the mobile cosmic Energy manifesting all beings and forces.

*

The experience of the Mother being the Supreme is the Tantric experience — it is one side of the Truth.

*

> *Q: The Tantrics used to invoke Shakti in their Sadhana. Was it the same Force and Consciousness which is in the Mother here?*

A: It depends on what they invoked — it was usually some aspect of the Mother that they called.

THE WORLD-MOTHER

The Ishwari Shakti, divine Conscious-Force and World-Mother, becomes a mediatrix between the eternal One and the manifested Many. On one side, by the play of the energies which she brings from the One, she manifests the multiple Divine in the universe, involving and evolving its endless appearances out of her revealing substance; on the other, by the reascending current of the same energies she leads back all towards That from which they have issued so that the soul in its evolutionary manifestation may more and more return towards the Divinity there or here put on its divine character. There is not in her, although she devises a cosmic mechanism, the character of an inconscient mechanical Executrix which we find in the first physiognomy of Prakriti, the Nature-Force; neither is there that sense of an Unreality, creatrix of illusions, or semi-illusions, which is attached to our first view of Maya. It is at once clear to the experiencing soul that here is a conscious Power of one substance and nature with the Supreme from whom she came. If she seems to have plunged us into the Ignorance and Inconscience in pursuance of a plan we cannot yet interpret, if her forces present themselves as all these ambiguous forces of the universe, yet it becomes visible before long that she is working for the development of the Divine Consciousness in us and that she stands above drawing us to her own higher entity, revealing to us more and more the very essence of the Divine Knowledge, Will and Ananda. Even in the movements of the Ignorance the soul of the seeker becomes aware of her conscious guidance supporting his steps and leading them slowly or swiftly, straight or by many detours out of the darkness into the light of a greater consciousness, out of mortality into immortality, out of evil and suffering towards a highest good and felicity of which as yet his human mind can form only a faint image. Thus her power is at once liberative and dynamic, creative, effective, — creative not only of things as they are, but of things that are to be; for, eliminating the twisted and tangled movements of his lower consciousness made of the stuff of the Ignorance, it rebuilds and new-makes his soul and nature into the substance and forces of a higher divine Nature.[1]

THE MOTHER AND THE LOWER PRAKRITI

It is a mistake to identify the Mother with the lower Prakriti and its mechanism of forces. Prakriti here is a mechanism only which has been put forth for the working of the evolutionary Ignorance. As the ignorant mental, vital or physical being is not itself the Divine, although it comes from the Divine — so the mechanism of Prakriti is not the Divine Mother. No doubt something of her

[1] *The Synthesis of Yoga* (Centenary Edition, 1972), pp. 116-17.

is there in and behind this mechanism maintaining it for the evolutionary purpose; but what she is in herself is not a Shakti
of Avidya, but the Divine Consciousness, Power, Light, Para
Prakriti to whom we turn for release and the divine fulfilment.

THE COSMIC FORCE OF IGNORANCE AND THE DIVINE MOTHER

There is this much truth that the Cosmic Force works out everything and the Cosmic Spirit (Virat Purusha) supports her action.
The Cosmic Force is a Power that works under the conditions of
the Ignorance — it appears as the lower nature and the lower
nature makes you do wrong things. The Divine allows the play
of these forces so long as you do not yourself want anything
better. But if you are a Sadhak, then you do not accept the play
of the lower nature, you turn to the Divine Mother instead, and
ask her to work through you instead of the lower nature. It is
only when you have turned entirely in every part of your being to
the Divine Mother and to her alone that the Divine will do all
actions through you.

SAGUNA AND NIRGUNA ISHWARA AND THE MOTHER

Nirguna, Saguna are only aspects taken by the Divine in the
manifestation. It is the Mother who manifests (creation is only
manifestation) the Saguna or the Nirguna Ishwara.

                                                    28-6-1933

THE SILENT ATMAN, THE DYNAMIC SELF AND THE MOTHER

The experiences were all right — but they give only one side of
the Divine Truth, that which one attains through the higher
mind — the other side is what one attains through the heart.
Above the higher mind these two truths become one. If one realises the silent Atman above, there is no danger, but there is also
no transformation, only Moksha, Nirvana. If one realises the

cosmic self, dynamic and active, then one realises all as the Self, all as myself, that self as the Divine, etc. This is all true; but the danger is of the ego catching hold of the "my" in that conception of "all is myself". For this "myself" is not my personal self but everybody's self as well as mine. The way to get rid of any such danger is to remember that this Divine is also the Mother, that the personal "I" is a child of the Mother with whom I am one, yet different, her child, servant, instrument. I have said that you should not stop realising the Self as the cosmic consciousness, but should at the same time remember that all this is the Mother.

13-10-1933

*

It is possible to go towards the knowledge by beginning with the experience of dissolution in the One, but on condition that you do not stop there, taking it as the highest Truth, but proceed to realise the same One as the Supreme Mother, the Consciousness-Force of the Eternal. If, on the other hand, you approach through the Supreme Mother, she will give you the liberation in the silent One also as well as the realisation of the dynamic One, and from that it is easier to arrive at the Truth in which both are one and inseparable. At the same time, the gulf created by the mind between the Supreme and his manifestation is bridged, and there is no longer a fissure in the truth which makes all incomprehensible.

*

It is the Divine who is the Master — the Self is inactive, it is always a silent witness supporting all things — that is the static aspect. There is also the dynamic aspect through which the Divine works — behind that is the Mother. You must not lose sight of that, that it is through the Mother that all things are attained.

1-9-1933

*

You are seeking for Self-realisation — but what is that Self if not the Mother's self? There is no other.

29-9-1934

*

The Self has two aspects, passive and active. In the first it is pure silence, wideness, calm, the inactive Brahman, in the second it is the Cosmic Spirit, universal not individual. One can feel in it union or oneness with the Mother. Intimacy is a feeling of the individual, therefore of the psychic being.

12-10-1934

THE MOTHER'S UNIVERSAL AND PERSONAL PRESENCE

What people mean by the formless *svarūpa* of the Mother, — they mean usually her universal aspect. It is when she is experienced as a universal Existence and Power spread through the universe in which and by which all live. When one feels that Presence one begins to feel a universal peace, light, power, bliss without limits — that is her *svarūpa*. One meets this more often by rising in consciousness above the head where one is liberated from this limited body consciousness and feels oneself also as something wide, calm, one self with all beings — free from passion and disturbance in an eternal peace. But it can be felt through the heart also — then the heart too feels itself wide as the world, pure and blissful, filled with the Mother's presence.

There is also the Mother's personal and individual presence in the heart which brings immediately love and Bhakti and the sense of a close intimacy and personal oneness.

9-6-1935

FAITH IN THE DIVINE SHAKTI AND THE ISHWARA

The faith in the divine Shakti must be always at the back of our strength and when she becomes manifest, it must be or grow implicit and complete. There is nothing that is impossible to her who is the conscious Power and universal Goddess all-creative from eternity and armed with the Spirit's omnipotence. All knowledge, all strengths, all triumph and victory, all skill and works are in her hands and they are full of the treasures of the Spirit and of all perfections and Siddhis. She is Maheshwari, goddess of the supreme knowledge, and brings to us her vision for all kinds and widenesses of truth, her rectitude of the spiritual will, the calm and passion of her supramental largeness, her felicity of illumination: she is Mahakali, goddess of the supreme strength, and with her are all mights and spiritual force and severest austerity of Tapas and swiftness to the battle and the victory and the laughter, the *aṭṭahāsya*, that makes light of defeat and death and the powers of the ignorance: she is Mahalakshmi, the goddess of the supreme love and delight, and her gifts are the spirit's grace and the charm and beauty of the Ananda and protection and every divine and human blessing: she is Mahasaraswati, the goddess of divine skill and of the works of the Spirit, and hers is the Yoga that is skill in works, *yogaḥ karmasu kauśalam*, and the utilities of divine knowledge and the self-application of the spirit to life and the happiness of its harmonies. And in all her powers and forms she carries with her the supreme sense of the masteries of the eternal Ishwari, a rapid and divine capacity for all kinds of action that may be demanded from the instrument, oneness, a participating sympathy, a free identity, with all energies in all beings and therefore a spontaneous and fruitful harmony with all the divine will in the universe. The intimate feeling of her presence and her powers and the satisfied assent of all our being to her workings in and around it is the last perfection of faith in the Shakti.

And behind her is the Ishwara and faith in him is the most central thing in the *śraddhā* of the integral Yoga. This faith we must have and develop to perfection that all things are the workings under the universal conditions of a supreme self-knowledge and wisdom, that nothing done in us or around us is in vain or without its appointed place and just significance, that all things are possible when the Ishwara as our supreme Self and Spirit takes up the action and that all that has been done before and all

that he will do hereafter was and will be part of his infallible and
foreseeing guidance and intended towards the fruition of our
Yoga and our perfection and our life work. This faith will be
more and more justified as the higher knowledge opens, we
shall begin to see the great and small significances that escaped
our limited mentality and faith will pass into knowledge. Then
we shall see beyond the possibility of doubt that all happens
within the working of the one Will and that that will was also
wisdom because it develops always the true workings in life of the
self and nature. The highest state of the assent, the *śraddhā* of
the being will be when we feel the presence of the Ishwara and
feel all our existence and consciousness and thought and will
and action in his hand and consent in all things and with every
part of our self and nature to the direct and immanent and occu-
pying will of the Spirit. And that highest perfection of the
śraddhā will also be the opportunity and perfect foundation of
a divine strength: it will base, when complete, the development
and manifestation and the works of the luminous supramental
Shakti.[1]

*

*Q: In "The Mother" you have said that the Mother as
the Cosmic Mahashakti determines "all that shall be in
this universe and in the terrestrial evolution by what she
sees and feels and pours from her, she stands there above
the Gods and all her Powers and Personalities are put
out in front of her for the action and she sends down
emanations of them into these lower worlds to intervene,
to govern, to battle and conquer, to lead and turn their
cycles, to direct the total and the individual lines of their
forces".[2] Does this imply that the World War or the
Bolshevic Revolution or the Satyagraha movement, etc.
were in some manner arranged and determined by the
Mother?*

A: They are incidents in the cosmic plan and so arranged by the

---

[1] *The Synthesis of Yoga* (Centenary Edition, 1972), pp. 752-53.
[2] Part One, p. 23.

Cosmic Mahashakti and worked out by men under the impulse of the forces of Nature.

1-6-1933

THE MOTHER'S SUPRAMENTAL POWER OF LOVE AND ANANDA

Q: In the "Chandi"[1] the names of the four Cosmic Powers of the Mother — Maheshwari, Mahakali, Mahalakshmi, Mahasaraswati — are mentioned along with others, but the name "Radha" is not mentioned. This is a clear proof of the fact that when the "Chandi" was composed the Radha-Power was not manifested to the vision of the saints and that the "Chandi" mentions only the Cosmic Powers of the Mother and not her supramental Powers. In the book "The Mother", after describing the four Powers of the Mother, you have said: "There are other great Personalities of the Divine Mother, but they were more difficult to bring down and have not stood out in front with so much prominence in the evolution of the earth-spirit. There are among them Presences indispensable for the supramental realisation, — most of all one who is her Personality of that mysterious and powerful ecstasy and Ananda which flows from a supreme divine Love, the Ananda that alone can heal the gulf between the highest heights of the supramental spirit and the lowest abysses of Matter, the Ananda that holds the key of a wonderful divinest Life and even now supports from its secrecies the work of all the Powers of the universe."[2] Is not the Personality referred to in this passage the Radha-Power which is spoken of as Premamayi Radha, Mahaprana Shakti and Hladini Shakti?

A: Yes; but the images of the Radha-Krishna *lilā* are taken from the vital world and therefore it is only an inner manifesta-

---

[1] A Tantric scripture forming a part of Markandeya Purana.
[2] Part One, pp. 35-36.

tion of the Radha-Shakti that is there depicted. That is why she is called Mahaprana Shakti and Hladini Shakti. What is referred to [in the passage quoted] is not this inner form but the full Power of Love and Ananda above.

7-2-1934

THE MOTHER'S POWERS ON ALL PLANES

> Q: *Does Maheshwari belong to the Intuitive and the Overmind levels?*

A: These powers can manifest on all levels from the Overmind to the Physical.

25-8-1933

MANY FORMS OF THE MOTHER'S POWERS

As to the gods, man can build forms which they will accept but these forms too are inspired into man's mind from the planes to which the god belongs. All creation has the two sides, the formed and the formless, — the gods too are formless and yet have forms, but a godhead can take many forms, here Maheshwari, there Pallas Athene. Maheshwari herself has many forms in her lesser manifestation, Durga, Uma, Parvati, Chandi, etc. The gods are not limited to human forms — man also has not always seen them in human forms only.

KRISHNA-MAHAKALI

The Mother in her cosmic power is all things and all divine Personalities, for nothing can be in manifestation except by her and as part of her being. But what was meant in the *Visions and Voices*[1] was that the Ishwara and the Divine Shakti were one Person or Being in two aspects and it puts forward this vision of

[1] A book by a Sadhak.

them as Krishna-Mahakali as a great power for the manifestation.

20-10-1936

DURGA

Durga combines the characteristics of Maheshwari and Mahakali to a certain extent, — there is not much connection with Mahalakshmi. The combination of Krishna and Mahakali is one that has a great power in this Yoga and if the names rise together in your consciousness, it is a good sign.

21-3-1938

*

Durga is the Mother's power of Protection.

15-4-1933

*

The lion with Durga on it is the symbol of the Divine Consciousness acting through a divinised physical-vital and vital-emotional force.

*

The lion is the attribute of the Goddess Durga, the conquering and protecting aspect of the Universal Mother.

The Death's Head is the symbol of the Asura (the adversary of the gods) vanquished and killed by the Divine Power.

MAHAKALI AND KALI

Mahakali and Kali are not the same. Kali is a lesser form. Mahakali in the higher planes appears usually with the golden colour.

*

This Kali, Shyama, etc. — are ordinary forms seen through the vital; the real Mahakali form whose origin is in the Overmind is not black or dark or terrible but golden of colour and full of beauty, even when formidable to the Asuras.

10-2-1934

*

Q: While praying today I saw the image of Mother Kali. She was black and naked and was standing with her foot on the back of Shiva — as she is traditionally described. Why is Kali seen in such a form and on what plane is she seen like this?

A: It is in the vital. It is Kali as a destroying Force — a symbol of the Nature Force in the ignorance surrounded by difficulties, wresting and breaking everything in a blind struggle to get through till she finds herself standing with her foot on the Divine itself — then she comes to herself and the struggle and destruction are over. That is the significance of the symbol.

9-2-1934

ACTION OF THE MOTHER'S MAHAKALI POWER

Q: In "The Mother" it is said about the Mahakali power of the Mother that "her hands are outstretched to strike and to succour".[1] What is meant by "strike" here?

A: It expresses her general action in the world. She strikes at the Asuras, she strikes also at everything that has to be got rid of or destroyed, at the obstacles to the Sadhana, etc. I may say that the Mother never uses the Mahakali power in your case nor the Mahakali pressure.

5-6-1936

*

Q: About the Mother's Mahakali aspect it is said in "The Mother": "When she is allowed to intervene in

[1] Part One, p. 29.

> *her strength, then in one moment are broken like things*
> *without consistence the obstacles that immobilise or*
> *the enemies that assail the seeker.*"[1] *How is this inter-*
> *vention of the Mahakali force felt?*

A: It is felt as if something swift, sudden, decisive and imperative. When it intervenes, it has a kind of divine or supramental
sanction behind it and is like a fiat against which there is no
appeal. What is done cannot be reversed or undone. The adverse
forces may try, may even touch or invade, but they retire baffled
and it is seen as soon as they withdraw that the past ground has
remained intact — it is felt even in the attack. Also the difficulties
that were strong before it touched by this fiat lose their power,
their verisimilitude destroyed or are weak shadows that come
only to flicker and fade away. I say "allowed", because this
supreme action of Mahakali is comparatively rare, the action
of the other Powers or a partial action of Mahakali is more
common.

24-8-1933

MITRA[2]

Yes, Mitra is rather a combination of two powers [Mahalakshmi
and Mahasaraswati].

THE TOUCH OF MAHASARASWATI

> *Q: What is the wisdom that brought deeper gyri in the*
> *human brain, the perfect septa in the ventricles of the*
> *heart and such other details of structure? Is it the work*
> *of Mahasaraswati?*

A: Yes — all perfection in intricacy of detail shows the touch
of Mahasaraswati.

19-9-1933

---

[1] Part One, p. 29.   [2] A Vedic god.

THE PRESENT WORKING OF SADHANA

*Q: Is it true that it is mostly the Mahasaraswati aspect
of the Mother that works in our Sadhana here?*

A: At present since the Sadhana came down to the physical
consciousness — or rather it is a combination of Maheshwari-
Mahasaraswati forces.

25-8-1933

THE VIBHUTIS OF THE MOTHER

*Q: What is the difference in the form of expression or
realisation between the Vibhutis of the Ishwara and the
Vibhutis of the Mother?*

A: The Mother's Vibhutis would usually be feminine personalities most of whom would be dominated by one of the four
personalities of the Mother. The others you mention (Christ,
Buddha, Chaitanya, Napoleon, Caesar, etc.) would be personalities and powers of the Ishwara, but in them also, as in all, the
Mother's force would act. All creation and transformation is
the work of the Mother.

29-10-1935

*

*Q: Since all creation is her work, can it be taken that
it is the personalities of the Mother who, behind the veil,
prepare the conditions for the descent of the Avatar or
Vibhutis?*

A: If you mean the divine Personalities of the Mother — the
answer is yes. It may even be said that each Vibhuti draws his
energies from the Four, from one of them predominantly in most
cases, as Napoleon from Mahakali, Rama from Mahalakshmi,
Augustus Caesar from Mahasaraswati.

31-10-1935

CHIT SHAKTI, JIVATMA, SOUL AND EGO

Chit Shakti or Bhagavat Chetana is the Mother — the Jivatma is a portion of it, the psychic or soul a spark of it. Ego is a perverse reflection of the psychic or the Jivatma. If that is what you mean, it is correct.

THE SOUL AND THE DIVINE MOTHER

It is true of every soul on earth that it is a portion of the Divine Mother passing through the experiences of the Ignorance in order to arrive at the truth of its being and be the instrument of a Divine Manifestation and work here.

THE SUPREME MOTHER — A MANTRA[1]

ॐ आनन्दमयि चैतन्यमयि सत्यमयि परमे

OM anandamayi chaitanyamayi satyamayi parame

Sri Aurobindo

----

[1] The last two words in the English transliteration of this Mantra have been added by the Mother as they were not written by Sri Aurobindo in the original.

III

LIGHTS AND VISIONS OF THE MOTHER

LIGHTS AND VISIONS OF THE MOTHER

THE MOTHER AND THE LIGHTS

All the lights are put out by the Mother from herself.

DIFFERENT FORMS OF LIGHT

Light is a general term. Light is not knowledge but the illumination that comes from above and liberates the being from obscurity and darkness.

But this Light also assumes different forms such as the white light of the Mother, the pale blue light of Sri Aurobindo, the golden light of the Truth, the psychic light (pink and rose), etc.

13-10-1934

THE MOTHER'S WHITE LIGHT

The lights are the Mother's Powers — many in number. The white light is her own characteristic power, that of the Divine Consciousness in its essence.

15-7-1934

*

The white light is the Mother's light and it is always around her.

22-8-1933

*

The pale blue light is my light — white light is the Mother's (sometimes gold also). People generally see either the white or both the white and the pale blue around her.

4-9-1933

*

The white light is the Mother's light. Wherever it descends or enters, it brings peace, purity, silence and the openness to the higher forces. If it comes below the navel, that means that it is working in the lower vital.

31-7-1934

*

The important experience is that of the white ray in the heart — for that is a ray of Mother's light, the white light, and the illumining of the heart by the light is a thing of great power in this Sadhana. The intuitions she [a Sadhika] speaks of are a sign of the inner consciousness growing in her — the consciousness which is necessary for Yoga.

28-7-1937

*

It [the Mother's light] is always there in the inner Purusha.

*

That means the light of the divine consciousness (the Mother's Consciousness, white light) in the vital. Blue is the higher mind, gold the divine Truth. So it is the vital with the light of the higher mind and the divine Truth in it emanating the Mother's light.

*

What you saw in vision was a supraphysical body of the Mother made probably of her white light which is the light of the Divine Consciousness and Force that stands behind the Universe.

30-1-1935

*

Q: Today while meditating in the Pranam Hall I saw in vision a range of mountains from which white light was coming out. What does this signify? To which plane does this vision belong?

A: Mental. The mountain is the symbol of the ascent from the lower to the higher. The white light is the Mother's light, the light of the Divine Consciousness descending from the heights.

7-8-1933

*

It [the white water-lily] is the Mother's flower, the flower of divine consciousness.

15-4-1933

*

Q: Today as soon as the Mother took her seat in the Pranam Hall I saw that white light was playing both on her left and right sides. Was there any particular reason why I saw like this?

A: No. One can always see white light around the Mother, for it is her light, always there.

8-8-1933

*

Q: Last evening when the Mother was walking on the terrace I saw a light on Her body. What was it?

A: Many see light around the Mother. The light is there always.

26-7-1933

THE MOTHER'S AURA

What people see around the Mother is first her aura, as it is called nowadays and, secondly, the forces of Light that pour out from her when she concentrates, as she always does on the roof for instance. (Everybody has an aura — but in most it is weak and not very luminous; in the Mother's aura there is the full play of lights and powers.) People do not see it usually because it is a subtle physical and not a gross material phenomenon. They can see only in two conditions, first if they develop sufficient subtle sight, secondly if the aura itself begins to become so strong that it affects the sheath of gross Matter which conceals it. The Mother has certainly no idea of making people see it — it is of themselves that one after another, some 20 or 30 in the Ashram, I believe, have come to see. It is certainly one of the signs that the Higher Force (call it supramental or not) is beginning to influence Matter.

15-11-1933

*

If seeing the Mother's light is a mistake or a mental or vital formation, then the realisation of the Divine and all spiritual experience can be questioned as a mental or vital formation or a mistake and all Yoga becomes impossible.

6-9-1933

THE MOTHER'S DIAMOND LIGHT

(a) It [the diamond light] means the essential Force of the Mother.

(b) The diamond light proceeds from the heart of the Divine Consciousness and it brings the opening of the Divine Consciousness wherever it goes.

(c) The Mother's descent with the diamond light is the sanction of the Supreme Power to the movement in you.

(d) The Mother's diamond light is a light of absolute purity and power.

(e) The diamond light is the central consciousness and force of the Divine.

*

The diamond is the symbol of the Mother's light and energy — the diamond light is that of her consciousness at its most intense.

13-11-1936

THE GOLDEN LIGHT OF THE MOTHER'S MAHAKALI FORM

The Mother's light is white — especially diamond white. The Mahakali form is usually golden, of a very bright and strong golden hue.

12-10-1935

*

The golden light is the light of the Divine Truth on the higher planes above the ordinary mind — a light supramental in origin. It is also the light of Mahakali above the mind. The golden light is also often seen emanating from the Mother like the white light.

17-9-1933

*

Q: I have heard that the colour of Kali is black and she has four hands. But I saw her in my vision with only two hands and her colour was bright white. Why did I see her like this?

A: The black Kali form is a manifestation on the vital plane of Mahakali — but Mahakali herself in the Overmind is golden. What you saw was the Mother herself in her body of light with the Mahakali power in her, but not the actual form of Mahakali.

26-9-1933

*

It depends on the shade of the yellow. If it is golden white it comes from above the mind and the combination suggests the Maheshwari-Mahakali power. Higher Mind colour is pale blue.

21-3-1938

*

The line of golden light is a line of the light of the higher Divine Truth encircling the *ākāśa* of the heart and the diamond mass is the Mother's light pouring into that *ākāśa*. It is therefore a sign of these powers working on the psychic-emotional centre.

17-12-1936

SOME VISIONS AND EXPERIENCES OF THE MOTHER

> *Q: Yesterday when the Mother came down in the evening to give Darshan, I saw her face shining with crimson light like the sun in the early morning. What is the meaning of crimson light?*

A: Crimson light indicates the manifestation of love in the material atmosphere.

5-6-1933

*

> *Q: Today while meditating in the Pranam Hall before the Mother came down, I saw in a vision that from a high place the Mother was descending wearing a rosy-coloured sari and having a "Divine Love" flower in her hair. What is the significance of this?*

A: It is a symbol of the descent of Divine Love.

5-6-1933

*

> *Q: Two days back I saw in a dream that I was lying in a bed in a room and the Mother entered with a rosy-coloured horse. Seeing the horse I told the Mother that he would bite me but the Mother replied that he would not do so. What is the meaning of this dream?*

A: Rose is the colour of psychic love — the horse is dynamic power. So the rosy-coloured horse means that the Mother was bringing with her the dynamic power of psychic love.

3-8-1933

*

> *Q: Today while meditating in the Pranam Hall I saw that from a sky filled with blue light a beautifully-paved*

*path was coming down on earth and the Mother was
slowly descending on this path. The Mother's entire
body was of white and golden light which was spreading
out on all sides. When the Mother reached the end of
the path and came down on earth her body got mixed
with the earth. Then I suddenly woke up from meditation. Was this a vision? What does it signify?*

A: Yes, it is a vision from the plane of mind (not ordinary, but
higher mind). It indicates the descent of the Mother with the
light of purity and Truth (white and golden) into Matter.

5-8-1933

*

*Q: Two days back I saw in a dream that the Mother
was standing on a high place and before her there was a
pillar with the Tulsi plant on it. What does it signify?*

A: That she has brought down and planted Bhakti, I suppose.

5-6-1933

*

Serpents are energies — those of the vital are usually evil forces
and it is these that are usually seen by people. But favourable or
divine forces are also imaged in that form, e.g., the Kundalini
Shakti is imaged in the form of a serpent. Serpents turning over
or round the Mother's head would rather recall the Shivamurti
and would mean numberless energies all finally gathered up into
one infinite energy of which they are the aspects.

28-10-1936

*

*Q: I had a dream in which I saw that the Mother was
near me. Once when she smiled, I felt as if I saw all the
worlds in her mouth, as Jasoda saw them in Krishna's*

mouth. Immediately after seeing this, I felt myself lifted up above the world and looking at it as a free witness. Was this a real dream-experience and did I really see the Mother, or was it some other influence?

A: I don't think it was another influence. It reads like a very genuine experience.

19-6-1935

*

Q: While looking at the Mother when she came on the terrace, I suddenly saw in her lap a baby whom I took to be Jesus Christ as it resembled his figure. The vision lasted for about a minute and I saw it with open eyes. Could it be true?

A: It may be so — as Jesus was the child of the Divine Mother.

25-11-1933

*

You seem to have ascended into a plane of the Higher spiritualised Mind with a descent into it of Maheshwari bringing the power of the Divine Truth. The result in the physical consciousness was a perception of the One Consciousness and Life in all things and an illumination of the cells of the body with golden light of the higher Truth.

October, 1933

*

Q: Last night I saw in a dream that from the Mother's body light was coming into my body and transforming it. Both these bodies were longer than the physical bodies and were of a shadowy colour like that of stones. What does this signify?

A: Good, it is the opening of the physical consciousness to the

Mother. It was probably the subconscient physical that you saw — that would explain the shadowy character — the stone indicates the material Nature.

30-9-1933

*

Q: Recently I notice that before the Mother comes down from the terrace in the evening she stands there for a long time. I feel that at that time she gives us something specially, so I concentrate to receive and feel what she gives. But this evening suddenly I saw (when I was concentrating by looking at her) that her physical body disappeared, — there was no sign of her body, as if she were not there. Then after a few seconds her figure reappeared. I felt at that moment that she mixed with the ether and became one with all things. Why did I see like this?

A: The Mother makes an invocation or aspiration and stands till the movement is over. Yesterday she passed for some time beyond the sense of the body and it is perhaps this that made you see in that way.

29-8-1932

*

Q: Today while meditating in the Pranam Hall I saw in a vision that the Mother was absorbed in deep concentration. Why did I see her like that?

A: The Mother is always in a concentrated consciousness in her inner being — so it is quite natural that you should see like that.

5-6-1933

*

Q: It was in sleep or meditation, I don't remember. I

was approaching the Mother with a dish of various flowers. Before making my Pranams I offered her three flowers of "Divine Love". Has this any correspondence with my Sadhana?

A: It is not quite clear what this number 3 means in this connection. Possibly it is the aspiration for the Divine's Love in the three parts of the being.

12-7-1936

*

Q: I saw the Mother in the colour of the flower "detachment". Does it have any meaning?

A: It must mean that that was the force which she was offering to you or else which you needed from her.

10-1-1934

*

Q: The Mother sitting on the peak of an icy mountain; a narrow path leads there and I am gradually advancing towards that.

A: This is simply a symbol of the purity and silence of the higher consciousness which has to be reached by the path of Sadhana. The mountain symbolises the difficulty because one has not to slip to one side or the other, but go straight.

*

Q: Let me tell you what happened during my noon nap. I was on the lap of the Mother. She had put her transforming palm on my head. With her thumb she was pressing or rather opening the Brahmic centre of my head. I began to feel as if something were received from there. Then all on a sudden there was a shifting of the con-

sciousness into some other world. A supraphysical light was experienced in the cells of the body which was already flooded with the light. The physical itself was taken up. Will you please explain this phenomenon?

A: There is nothing to explain. It was what you describe: At once the raising of the consciousness to a higher plane and the descent of that into the physical.

5-9-1934

*

Q: Over my head I see a plane of infinite and eternal Peace. The Mother is the Queen of this plane. From there I feel a ceaseless glow coming down towards me. It first touches my higher being and passes through it without any resistance. But on its way downwards its flow narrows to a small current which passes through the Brahmic hole. How do you find this description?

A: That is quite correct. In many however it descends in a mass through the whole head and not in a current through the Brahmic hole.

13-2-1936

*

Q: The Mother sitting on her seat. A cobra with many hoods behind her covering the head. It has a shining golden colour; in the centre of each hood a shining red round spot.

A: The cobra is an emblem of Nature-Energy; golden=the higher Truth-Nature; many hoods=many powers. Red is probably a sign of Mahakali power. The cobra covering the head with its hoods is a symbol of sovereignty.

23-1-1937

*

Q: I see a rough rock. The sunlight falls upon it and the figure changes: in the centre a hollow circle is made and rocks arrange themselves round the circle. In the centre of the circle appears a stone image of Shiva about two feet high; afterwards from this image of Shiva emerges the Mother. She is in meditation. The sunlight falls just behind the Mother's body. What does it signify?

A: Rocks=the physical (most material) being.

An opening in the material making room for the formation of the spiritual consciousness there.

Stone image of the Shiva=the realisation of the silent Self or Brahman there (peace, silence, wideness of the Infinite, purity of the witness Purusha).

Out of this silence emerges the Divine Shakti concentrated for the transformation of the material.

Sunlight=Light of Truth.

12-10-1936

*

Q: The other day you asked me to be conscious in trance; I tried it hard and this is the result: I saw a Holy Woman entering a place where a few of the Sadhaks were assembled for her Darshan. She went into a closed room where we were to go one by one. I noticed that everyone was allowed one or two minutes as is done on our Darshan days. My turn was last.

In the centre of the room the Holy Woman was seated wearing simple clothes. Without looking at her face I put my head on her lap. She placed her hands on my head and caressed me softly, meanwhile murmuring to herself something like "Let him have..."; the last word of the sentence I had caught quite distinctly then, but cannot recollect now. It was the name of some spiritual power. No sooner had she said this, I felt a sudden rush of that power entering through my head.

After a few seconds she uttered the name of another

*power. This power knocked me with a tremendous force
— it was shattering in its intensity.*

*After a while I raised my head and looked at the
Holy Woman for the first time. Her face appeared like
the Mother's. Then I told her, "May I ask you a question?" She did not seem to like this, but as she had not
refused, I repeated the question. This time she said, "I
don't like questions." (I wanted to inquire about her
two gifts of different powers conferred on me.) Then I
don't remember what I said. After a long time we both
came back to consciousness, for we had both entered into
a trance together. We knew it only when we asked the
door-keeper how much time we had spent together.
Afterwards I told her, "You must have entered into a
trance and I simply followed you."*

This whole phenomenon is beyond my understanding.

1. Who was the Holy Woman?

2. Why did she grant me the gift of her powers?

3. A trance within a trance! This is something new!

A: Obviously the Holy Woman was the Mother herself in a
supraphysical form. It was natural that she should not like questions — the Mother does not like mental questions very much
at any time and least of all when she is giving meditation as she
was doing in this experience. It is rather funny to ask "why"
(your eternal why) higher powers should be given. People do not
question the gifts of the Shakti or demand reasons for her giving
them, they are only too glad to get them. Trance within trance
of course, since your Sadhana was going on in the trance, according to the ways of trance. It is also in this way that it can go on
in conscious sleep.

*

*Q: Whilst I was having a nap in the afternoon, I had
a vision of a very beautiful woman sitting under the
sun. The rays of the sun were either surrounding her or
were emanating from her body — I can't precisely say*

*which. The appearance and dress seemed to be more
European than oriental.*

A: It is not a woman. A woman does not radiate and is not
surrounded by rays either. Probably a Sun Goddess or a Shakti
of the inner Light, one of the Mother's Powers.

20-12-1935

*

*Q: X told us today that the Mother was trying to
bring down the personality of Durga on the Puja day.*

A: There was no trying — it came down.

*Q: When I came for Pranam, the Mother's appearance
made me feel that she was Durga herself. I don't know
whether such a feeling arose out of the association with
the Puja on that day, or quite independently of it.*

A: All that is the silliness of the physical mind which thinks
itself very clever in explaining away the inner feeling or perception.

*Q: These feelings are so vague and momentary, and
not accompanied by a concrete vision.*

A: What else do you expect the first touches to be!

*Q: To give you one instance: I heard as if the Goddess
Bhagawati were telling me, "I am coming" and many
other things which I don't remember now.*

A: These things are at least a proof that the inner mind and
vital are trying to open to supraphysical things. But if you
belittle it at once the moment it starts how can it ever develop!

Q: I have started concentrating in the heart now. Last Sunday while I was meditating I had the vision of your face floating before me for about an hour or so, accompanied by a deep joy. I was fully conscious, but the body became utterly numb. Has anything in me opened up? Is all this the fulfilment of the promise given by Bhagawati?

A: It looks like it. At any rate there is evidently an opening in the heart-centre or you would not have had the change or the vision with the stilling of the physical consciousness in the body.

VISION OF THE MOTHER AND REALISATION

Q: Could a vision of the Mother or seeing her in dream or in waking be called a realisation?

A: That would be an experience rather than a realisation. A realisation would be of the Mother's presence within, her force doing the work — or of the Peace or Silence everywhere, of universal Love, universal Beauty or Ananda etc., etc. Visions come under the head of experiences, unless they fix themselves and are accompanied by a realisation of which they are as it were the support — e.g. the vision of the Mother always in the heart or above the head etc.

12-3-1934

FACULTY OF VISION AND SPIRITUAL PROGRESS

Q: Some people see light etc. around the Mother but I do not. What is the obstruction in me?

A: It is not an obstruction — it is simply a question of the growth of the inner senses. It has no indispensable connection with spiritual progress. There are some very far on the path who have very little of this kind of vision if any — on the other hand sometimes it develops enormously in mere beginners who have as yet had only very elementary spiritual experiences.

1-12-1933

*

Q: X told me, "I was in constant touch with the Divine Mother long before I entered Pondicherry. I saw her not only in meditation or vision but before my wide-awake eyes, in a concrete form. I often used to converse with her, specially during my difficult periods when she would come and tell me what to do. Only, I did not know till I visited this place that the Divine Mother was no other than the Ashram Mother and had cast herself into a physical mould." Well, I am too prag-magtic to believe all such things, specially her claim of seeing Mother with the naked eyes, which would mean an advanced Sadhana.

A: But there is nothing improbable in it. It means simply that she externalised her inner vision and experience so as to see through the physical eyes also, but it was the inner vision that saw and the inner hearing that heard, not the physical sight or hearing. That is common enough. It does not indicate an "advanced" Sadhana, whatever that phrase may mean, but only a special faculty.

2-7-1936

*

These things [seeing and conversing with the Devata of one's worship] are extremely common among those who practise Yoga everywhere. In the Ashram the Sadhaks are too intelligent, sceptical and matter of fact to have much of that kind of experience. Even those who might develop it are deprived by the outward-mindedness and physical-mindedness that dominates the atmosphere.

2-7-1936

*

It is quite usual at a certain stage of the Sadhana for people who have the faculty to see or hear the Devata of their worship and to receive constant directions from him or her with regard either to action or to Sadhana. Defects and difficulties may remain, but that does not prevent the direct guidance from being a fact. The necessity of the Guru in such cases is to see that it is the right experience, the right voice or vision — for it is possible for a false guidance to come as it did with X and Y.

8-7-1936

SEEING THE MOTHER IN DREAM

Q: I saw Mother's form in a dream last night. Was it real or was imagination only at work?

A: What do you mean by real? It was the form of Mother in a dream experience. Imagination applies only to the waking mind.

3-7-1933

*

Q: But cannot false forces take the form of the Mother?

A: If false forces take the form of the Mother, it will be with some bad object. If there is no attack or wrong suggestion, you need not suppose that it is false forces that have done it.

Of course it is always possible that something in your own consciousness has constructed a dream about the Mother or put her figure there when she herself was not there. That happens when it is only a dream, a number of ideas and memories etc. of the mind put together and not experience on another plane.

5-7-1933

*

Necessarily, Mother can manifest in many other forms besides her physical one, and though I am rather less multitudinous, I can also. But that does not mean that you can take any gentleman for me or any she for her. Your dream-self has to develop a certain discrimination. That discrimination cannot go by signs and forms, for the vital beggars can imitate almost anything — it must be intuitive.

23-5-1935

HEARING THE MOTHER'S VOICE

> *Q: In your book, "Bases of Yoga" one reads, "It is with the Mother who is always with you and in you that you converse." Could you kindly explain to me how one converses with the Mother?*

A: One hears the voice or the thought speaking inwardly and one answers inwardly. Only it is not always safe for the Sadhak if there is any insincerity of ego, desire, vanity, ambition in him — for then he may construct a voice or thought in his mind and ascribe it to the Mother and it will say to him pleasing and flattering things which mislead him. Or he may mistake some other Voice for the Mother's.

2-7-1936

*

> *Q: Can one rely solely upon the voice from within and be thus guided by the Mother?*

A: If it is the Mother's voice; but you have to be sure of that.

7-7-1933

*

> *Q: Is it not a fact that to hear the Mother's voice inwardly and to recognise it as hers is easy?*

A: No, to hear and recognise the Mother's voice within is not easy.

8-7-1933

*

Q: When is one said to be ready to hear the Mother's voice from within?

A: When one has equality, discrimination and sufficient Yogic experience — otherwise any voice may be mistaken for the Mother's.

7-7-1933

*

Q: At Pranam while putting my head in the Mother's lap I heard some voice. It was felt to be the Mother's. Did she really say something to me inwardly or was it a mere illusion of mine?

A: It may have been that the Mother conveyed something to you. At this moment she does not remember.

27-4-1933

IV

THE MOTHER'S PRESENCE

THE MOTHER'S PRESENCE

THE CONSTANT PRESENCE

Live always as if you were under the very eye of the Supreme and of the Divine Mother. Do nothing, try to think and feel nothing that would be unworthy of the Divine Presence.

THE MOTHER'S PERSONAL AND UNIVERSAL PRESENCE

Q: You have written: "Always behave as if the Mother was looking at you; because she is, indeed, always present." You explained to me that this does not mean that she was physically present everywhere because that was impossible. But when I asked the Mother about this, she said that she was personally present at all places. How to reconcile these contradictory statements?

A: If by physically you mean corporeally, in her visible tangible material body, it is obvious that it cannot be. When you asked Mother that question she did not understand you to mean that — she said she could be present everywhere, and she meant, of course, in her consciousness. It is the consciousness and not the body that is the being, the person, the body is only a support and instrument for the action of the consciousness. Mother can be personally present in her consciousness. The universal presence, of course, is always there and the universal and personal are two aspects of the same being.

25-8-1936

*

Q: You have said: "Always behave as if the Mother was looking at you; because she is, indeed, always present." Does this mean that the Mother knows all

our insignificant thoughts at all times, or only when she
concentrates?

A: It is said that the Mother is always present and looking at
you. This does not mean that in her physical mind she is thinking of you always and seeing your thoughts. There is no need of
that, since she is everywhere and acts everywhere out of her
universal knowledge.

12-8-1933

*

Q: In what sense is the Mother everywhere? Does she
know all happenings in the physical plane?

A: Including what Lloyd George had for breakfast today or
what Roosevelt said to his wife about the servants? Why should
the Mother "know" in the human way all happenings in the physical plane? Her business in her embodiment is to know the
workings of the universal forces and use them for her works; for
the rest she knows what she needs to know, sometimes with her
inner self, sometimes with her physical mind. All knowledge is
available in her universal self, but she brings forward only what
is needed to be brought forward so that the working is done.

13-8-1933

*

Q: Someone said that the Mother sees all our physical
movements. How does this happen? Are all our physical
movements reflected on her mind and soon by her as
images or do they occur in her consciousness at the same
time as we do them? But would that not be very puzzling
and cumbersome to her? Moreover, would it not be a
very material kind of telepathy?

A: It would not be worthwhile. Mother can see what people
are doing by images received by her in the subtle state which

corresponds to sleep or concentration or by images or intimations received in the ordinary state; but much even of what comes to her automatically like that is unnecessary, and to be always receiving everything would be intolerably troublesome as it would keep the consciousness occupied with a million trivialities; so that does not happen. What is more important is to know their inner condition and it is this chiefly which comes to her.

29-6-1937

*

Q: (*Re a certain incident that had recently occurred*:) *I was under the impression that Mother could at once know of such things. Some even say that she knows everything — all that is material or spiritual. Others maintain that she knows when the question of consciousness is involved, e.g. sex movements, etc., but not so much about material things.*

A: Good Lord! You don't expect her mind to be a factual encyclopaedia of all that is happening on all the planes and in all the universes? Or even on this earth, e.g. what Lloyd George had for dinner yesterday?

Questions of consciousness, of course, she always knows even with her outermost physical mind. Material facts she can know but is not bound to do it. What would be true to say, is that she can know if she concentrates or if her attention is called to it and she decides to know. I often know from her what has happened before it is reported by anyone. But she does not care to do that on a general scale.

16-7-1935

*

Q: This question of Mother's knowledge became even more interesting for me today. She gave me the flower signifying "Discipline". I began to wonder why this particular flower was given; at last I remembered that

> *yesterday I had not observed the right discipline in the matter of taking food with X and Y.*

A: In this respect the Mother is guided by her intuitions which tell her which flower is needed at the moment or helpful. Sometimes it is accompanied by a perception of a particular state of consciousness, sometimes by that of a material fact; but only the bare fact, usually e.g. — it would not specify that it was "that particular thing" that was done or how X or Y came in. Not that that is impossible, but it is unnecessary and does not happen unless needed.

16-7-1935

*

> Q: *The Mother can know our thoughts, but can she know also the exact words in the thoughts?*

A: If the mind of the person is very clear, yes; otherwise it may be only the substance that comes or a part of the thought or some general idea.

19-5-1933

*

What you write about X is true.... She does not realise that Mother knows all these things by other means and any information given to her only adds certain physical precisions to what she knows already.

How can she be open when she has such ideas against the Mother? They must necessarily shut her up to the Mother's influence.

Mother has written to her that Y had said nothing and that she knew things about X independently of any information, from X's inner being itself which comes to her constantly and tells her or shows her what is in the nature.

The Mother besides sees things in vision and receives the thoughts of the Sadhaks at Pranam and other times.... Only the

Mother never acts on these supraphysical intimations unless there is physical confirmation like the letter itself in this case. For nobody would understand her action — the Sadhaks living in the physical mind would state her action unfounded, and those affected would deny loudly — as many have done in the past — their secret thoughts, feelings and actions. I tell you all this in confidence so that you may understand what is the real basis of Mother's letters to X.

10-9-1936

THE MOTHER'S EMANATIONS

> *Q: What is the exact significance of your statement: "Always behave as if the Mother was looking at you; because she is, indeed, always present"?*

A: It is the emanation of the Mother that is with each Sadhak all the time. In former days when she was spending the night in a trance and not working in the Ashram, she brought back with her the knowledge of all that was happening to everybody. Nowadays she has no time for that.

16-7-1935

*

> *Q: All this is very interesting; and I suppose you have an equal number of emanations yourself. Their object must be to give us protection.*

A: I am not aware of any emanations of mine. As for the Mother's, they are not there for protection, but to support the personal relation or contact with the Sadhak, and to act so far as he will allow them to act.

16-7-1935

*

> *Q: Kindly enlighten us a little more regarding the emanations. How do they support the personal relation? I*

> *thought that all personal relations were with the Mother direct, not through a deputy! When X says that he feels the Mother's physical touch, with whom does he have the contact — the Mother or the emanation? Then again, the different forms of the Mother that one sees in dreams — are they also her emanations?*

A: It is terribly difficult to write of these things, for you are all as ignorant as blazes about these things and misunderstand at every step. The Emanation is not a deputy, but the Mother herself. She is not bound to her body, but can put herself out (emanate) in any way she likes. What emanates, suits itself to the nature of the personal relation she has with the Sadhak which is different with each, but that does not prevent it from being herself. Its presence with the Sadhak is not dependent on his consciousness of it. If everything were dependent on the surface consciousness of the Sadhak, there would be no possibility of the divine action anywhere; the human worm would remain the human worm and the human ass the human ass, for ever and ever. For if the Divine could not be there behind the veil, how could either ever become conscious of anything but their wormhood and asshood even throughout the ages?

> *(By the side of the question, "When X says that he feels the Mother's physical touch, with whom does he have the contact...?" Sri Aurobindo wrote,* "With the Mother — the emanation helping — which is its business.")

19-7-1935

*

The Mother when she works in the supraphysical levels goes out in a different emanation to each Sadhak.

11-12-1933

*

Q: In an experience in the dream-state, we see the

*Mother sometimes. Is that form an emanation of her
or is it her body itself?*

A: An emanation. How can her physical body be seen in a
dream experience?

7-7-1933

*

*Q: During the afternoon sleep I seem to come often into
contact with the Mother. Is it the Mother who sends
her emanation?*

A: Yes, or rather something of her is always with you.

14-12-1933

THE MOTHER'S PRESENCE AND THE DIVINE CONSCIOUSNESS

*Q: Is there any difference between the Mother's presence
and the Divine Consciousness?*

A: One can feel the Divine Consciousness impersonally as a
new consciousness only. The Mother's Presence is something
more — one feels herself there present within or above or enveloping one or all these together.

8-7-1935

THE MOTHER'S PRESENCE WITHIN

He must go into himself and find the presence of the Divine
Mother within and the psychic behind the heart and from there
the knowledge will come and all the power to dissolve the inner
obstacles.

*

The constant presence of the Mother comes by practice; the

Divine Grace is essential for success in the Sadhana, but it is the practice that prepares the descent of the Grace.

You have to learn to go inward, ceasing to live in external things only, quiet the mind and aspire to become aware of the Mother's workings in you.

*

> *Q: We believe that the Mother is doing the Sadhana in all of us, particularly through the heart; but how is it we scarcely feel this? There must be some veil in us.*

A: It is a veil which disappears when the Mother's working as well as her presence is consciously felt at all times.

7-1-1935

*

> *Q: How and when can one feel the Mother's concrete presence all the time?*

A. It is a matter, first of the constant activity of the psychic and secondly of the conversion of the physical and its openness to inner supraphysical experience. Apart from the vital and its disturbances the physical is the chief difficulty in establishing a continuity of Yogic consciousness and experience. If the physical is thoroughly transformed — opened and conscious — then stability and continuity become easy.

16-10-1933

†

It is quite right and part of the right consciousness in Sadhana that you should feel drawn in your heart towards the Mother and aspire for the vision and realisation of her presence. But there should not be any kind of restlessness joined to this feeling. The feeling should be quietly intense. It will then be easier for the sense of the presence to come and to grow in you.

THE PRESENCE AND THE IMAGE

Q: Is it true that when the Presence (image) is seen in the heart all the habits and movements of the lower nature disappear?

A: The image and the Presence are not the same. One can feel the Presence without seeing the image. But to produce the results you speak of, the Presence in the heart is not sufficient, there must be Presence in the whole consciousness and the Force of the Mother governing all the action of the nature.

THE PRESENCE IN FRONT

Q: In the evening meditation, there was an intense movement of surrender from the heart. I had the feeling of Mother's presence immediately in front and aspiration rose from below the feet, from the legs, from the Muladhara centre; there was a willing and loving surrender from the heart, from the entire being, as if for fulfilment. I suppose the psychic being came to the front. But why did I feel the Mother's presence in front and not within me?

A: You had the psychic condition then and that means a coming of the influence of the psychic being to the front. It is when there is complete psychic opening that there is the presence within. The presence in front means that it was with you but had still to enter within.

13-7-1937

THE PRESENCE IN THE HEART-BEATS

But I do not see why I call the feeling sentimental or think that your sense of the presence of the Mother in the heart-beats etc. was unreal. It was your psychic being that suggested it to you and the response showed that the consciousness was ready. Mother felt that something was happening in you and felt that it was the beginning of a realisation — she was encouraging it and did not discourage. If it had been a wrong or vital movement she would not have felt like that.

13-8-1934

THE PRESENCE DURING THE DAY

If you feel the Mother's presence for the greater part of the day, it means that it is your psychic being that is active and feels like that; for without the activity of the psychic it would not be possible. Therefore your psychic being is there and not at all far off.

14-3-1935

THE PRESENCE DURING SLEEP

It [the feeling of the Mother's presence during sleep] follows naturally the presence in the waking state, but it takes a little time.

11-1-1935

*

Q: Can one be wide-awake to the Mother's presence in sleep even?

A: That does happen, but usually only when the psychic is in full activity.

THE PRESENCE IN WORK

It is for most people not easy to feel the Mother's presence with the work — they feel as if they are doing the work, the mind getting busy and not having the right passivity or quietude.

FEELING OF PRESENCE AND ONENESS WITH THE MOTHER

There is no such necessary precedence as that first one must feel the Presence and then only can one feel oneself the Mother's; it is more often the increase of the feeling that brings the Presence. For the feeling comes from the psychic consciousness and it is the growth of the psychic consciousness that makes the constant Presence at last possible. The feeling comes from the psychic and is true of the inner being — its not being yet fulfilled in the whole does not make it an imagination; on the contrary, the more it grows the more is the likelihood of the whole being fulfilling this truth; the inner *bhāva* takes more and more possession of the outer consciousness and remoulds it so as to make it a truth there also. This is the constant principle of action in the Yogic transformation — what is true within comes out and takes possession of the mind and heart and will and through them prevails over the ignorance of the outer members and brings the inner truth out there also.

16-9-1936

*

Q: I wrote to the Mother a prayer in French. Her answer to it was: "Ouvre ton cœur et tu me trouveras déjà là." ("Open your heart and you will find me already there.") What exactly does this signify?

A: What the Mother meant was this that when there is a certain opening of the heart, you find that there was always the eternal union there (the same that you experience always in the Self above).

2-7-1935

*

Q: Some Sadhaks say that they are in union with the Mother. I wonder if it is anything more than a feeling of nearness with the Mother which they sometimes have.

A: I suppose they are trying to feel the Mother's presence, so if they get some sort of feeling of nearness, they call it union. But of course that is only a step towards union. Union is much more than that.

5-3-1934

*

Q: You wrote yesterday, "Openness is not reckoned merely by visions." Quite so. But to have a fusion of the rays of sun and moon on each side of the body and to feel the descent and the Mother's presence in, behind and above oneself, is it not an exceptional vision and experience? Can it occur without sufficient opening to the Mother?

A: Why should it be exceptional to see the Sun and Moon on each side or to feel the Mother's presence everywhere around? There are plenty of Sadhaks who have had these or equivalent experiences. What could be exceptional is to feel the Mother's presence like that always. But occasional experiences like these many have had.

15-9-1936

*

Q: During meditation I feel a sort of oneness with the Mother's consciousness; but these days it is not possible to go deep in meditation at all. Is it not possible to have this feeling of oneness without meditating?

A: What is most important is the change of consciousness of which this feeling of oneness is a part. The going deep in meditation is only a means and it is not always necessary if the great experiences come easily without it.

8-4-1934

WRITING TO THE MOTHER AND FEELING HER PRESENCE

The feeling of the Mother's presence or nearness does not

depend on whether you write or do not write. Many who write often do not feel it, some who write seldom feel her always close.

11-6-1936

VEILING OF THE MOTHER'S PRESENCE

The Mother's presence is always there; but if you decide to act on your own — your own idea, your own notion of things, your own will and demand upon things, then it is quite likely that her presence will get veiled; it is not she who withdraws from you, but you who draw back from her. But your mind and vital don't want to admit that, because it is always their preoccupation to justify their own movements. If the psychic were allowed its full predominance, this would not happen; it would have felt the veiling, but it would at once have said, "There must have been some mistake in me, a mist has arisen in me," and it would have looked and found the cause.

25-3-1932

*

The Presence whose fading you regret can only be felt if the inner being continues to be consecrated and the outer nature is put into harmony or at least kept under the touch of the inner spirit.

But if you do things which your inner being does not approve, this condition will be eventually tarnished and, each time, the possibility of your feeling the Presence will diminish. You must have a strong will to purification and an aspiration that does not flag and cease, if the Mother's grace is to be there and effective.

V

OPENING AND SURRENDER TO THE MOTHER

OPENING AND SURRENDER TO THE MOTHER

THE CENTRAL SECRET OF SADHANA

By remaining psychically open to the Mother, all that is necessary for work or Sadhana develops progressively, that is one of the chief secrets, the central secret of the Sadhana.

13-2-1933

*

But it is not by *upadeśa* that this Sadhana is given or carried on. It is only those who are capable by aspiration and meditation on the Mother to open and receive her action and working within that can succeed in this Yoga.

21-6-1937

*

It is a mistake to exercise the mind about these things and try to arrange them with the ordinary mind. It is by confidence in the Mother that the opening needed will come when your consciousness is ready. There is no harm in arranging your present work so that there will be time and energy for some meditation, but it is not by meditation alone that what is needed will come. It is by faith and openness to the Mother.

*

Keep yourself open to the Mother and in perfect union with her. Make yourself entirely plastic to her touch and let her mould you swiftly towards perfection.

9-3-1934

*

You have only to aspire, to keep yourself open to the Mother, to reject all that is contrary to her will and to let her work in you — doing also all your work for her and in the faith that it is through her force that you can do it. If you remain open in this way, the knowledge and realisation will come to you in due course.

*

To practise Yoga implies the will to overcome all attachments and turn to the Divine alone. The principal thing in the Yoga is to trust in the Divine Grace at every step, to direct the thought continually to the Divine and to offer oneself till the being opens and the Mother's force can be felt working in the *ādhāra*.

*

All things are the Divine because the Divine is there, but hidden not manifest; when the mind goes out to things, it is not with the sense of the Divine in them, but for the appearances only which conceal the Divine. It is necessary therefore for you as a Sadhak to turn entirely to the Mother in whom the Divine is manifest and not run after the appearances, the desire of which or the interest in which prevents you from meeting the Divine. Once the being is consecrated, then it can see the Divine everywhere — and then it can include all things in the one consciousness without a separate interest or desire.

RIGHT WAY OF OPENING

Q: What is the meaning of opening?

A: It is the receptivity to the Mother's presence and her forces.

Q: What is the right and perfect way to get this opening?

A: Aspiration, quietude, widening of oneself to receive, rejection of all that tries to shut you to the Divine.

> *Q: How to know that I am opening to the Mother and not to other forces?*

A: You have to be vigilant and see that there is no movement of disturbance, desire, ego.

> *Q: What are the indications of a real opening to the Mother?*

A: That shows itself at once — when you feel the divine peace, equality, wideness, light, Ananda, Knowledge, strength, when you are aware of the Mother's nearness or presence or the working of her Force, etc., etc. If any of these things are felt, it is the opening — the more are felt, the more complete the opening.

April, 1933

*

> *Q: Opening — what does it mean? Is it: "not to keep anything secret from the Mother"?*

A: That is the first step towards opening.

17-6-1933

*

> *Q: How to open to the Divine Mother?*

A: By faith and surrender in a quiet mind.

18-6-1933

OPENNESS TO THE MOTHER

To be open is simply to be so turned to the Mother that her Force can work in you without anything refusing or obstructing her action. If the mind is shut up in its own ideas and refuses to allow her to bring in the Light and the Truth, if the vital clings to its desires and does not admit the true initiative and impulsions that the Mother's power brings, if the physical is shut up in its desires, habits and inertia and does not allow the Light and Force to enter in it and work, then one is not open. It is not possible to be entirely open all at once in all the movements, but there must be a central opening in each part and a dominant aspiration or will in each part (not in the mind alone) to admit only the Mother's "workings", the rest will then be progressively done.

28-10-1934

*

To remain open to the Mother is to remain always quiet and happy and confident — not restless, not grieving or despondent, to let her force work in you, guide you, give you knowledge, give you peace and Ananda. If you cannot keep yourself open, then aspire constantly but quietly that you may be open.

*

Q: Some dissatisfactions come and affect the heart which is opening to the Mother.

A: Get rid of these dissatisfactions, they prevent the permanent psychic opening.

*

Q: Perhaps it is because the psychic is just opening that it comes under the influence of these dissatisfactions?

A: What the psychic always feels is "What the Mother does is for the best", and accepts all with gladness. It is the vital part of the heart that is easily touched by the suggestions.

OPENING OF THE INNER BEING

Q: Does the inner being open to the Mother by itself?

A: The inner being does not open except by Sadhana, or by some psychic touch in the life.

30-11-1933

*

Q: What is this part which feels like opening to the Mother through writing, even when it is the same thing that goes on being repeated?

A: It may be the inner mental, it may be the psychic.

28-11-1933

RECEIVING THE MOTHER'S GRACE

Q: Is the Mother's Grace only general?

A: Both general and special.

8-2-1934

Q: How to receive what she grants in general?

A: You have only to keep yourself open and whatever you need and can receive at the moment will come.

10-2-1934

*

Q: Is it the Purusha who consents to the action of the Mother's Grace in the whole being?

A: Yes.

Q: If the Purusha does not give consent, does it mean that the other beings also cannot come to the front to enable the Sadhak to receive the Mother's Grace?

A: No. The Purusha often holds back and lets the other beings consent or reject in his place.

*Q: When the Mother's Grace comes down to the
Sadhak, is it by the consent of the Purusha?*

A: What do you mean "by the consent"? The Mother's Grace
comes down by the Mother's will. The Purusha can accept or
reject the Grace.

April, 1933

THE CONDITION FOR PROGRESS

*Q: If a Sadhak even after a long time cannot fully open
himself to the Mother owing to obstacles in his nature,
does it mean that he will not be accepted by the Mother?*

A: There is no meaning in such a question. Those who follow
the Yoga here are accepted by the Mother — for "accepted"
means "admitted into the Yoga, accepted as disciples". But
the progress in the Yoga and the *siddhi* in the Yoga depend on
the degree to which there is the opening.

24-6-1933

SINCERITY, OPENNESS AND TRANSFORMATION

*Q: X says that the Mother told him that if the sincerity
is perfect there would be transformation in a day. I do
not understand how that could be possible — a long process of change and conversion compressed in a single day!*

A. By sincerity Mother meant being open to no influence but
the Divine's only. Now, if the whole being is sincere in that
sense even to every cell of the body, what could prevent the most
rapid transformation? People cannot be like that, however much
the enlightened part of them may want to, because of the nature
of the Ignorance out of which the ordinary *prakṛti* has been built
— hence the necessity of a long and laborious working.

26-7-1934

PROGRESSIVE OPENING

Openness is not always complete from the first — a part of the being opens, other parts of the consciousness remain still closed or half open only — one has to aspire till all is open. Even with the best and most powerful Sadhaks the full opening takes time; nor is there anyone who has been able to abandon everything at once without any struggle. There is no reason to feel therefore that if you call you will not be heard — the Mother knows the difficulties of human nature and will help you through. Persevere always, call always and then after each difficulty there will be a progress.

20-4-1935

THE INNER AND THE HIGHER OPENING

It is by the constant remembrance that the being is prepared for the full opening. By the opening of the heart the Mother's presence begins to be felt and, by the opening to her Power above, the Force of the higher consciousness comes down into the body and works there to change the whole nature.

7-8-1934

*

There is no method in this Yoga except to concentrate, preferably in the heart, and call the presence and power of the Mother to take up the being and by the workings of her force transform the consciousness; one can concentrate also in the head or between the eyebrows, but for many this is a too difficult opening. When the mind falls quiet and the concentration becomes strong and the aspiration intense, then there is a beginning of experience. The more the faith, the more rapid the result is likely to be. For the rest one must not depend on one's own efforts only, but succeed in establishing a contact with the Divine and a receptivity to the Mother's Power and Presence.

*

The direct opening of the psychic centre is easy only when the ego-centricity is greatly diminished and also if there is a strong *bhakti* for the Mother. A spiritual humility and sense of submission and dependence is necessary.

16-7-1936

*

Yes, it is by quieting the mind that you will become able to call the Mother and open to her. The soothing effect was a touch from the psychic — one of the touches that prepare the opening of the psychic with its gift of inner peace, love and joy.

17-9-1934

*

The Mother's peace is above you — by aspiration and quiet self-opening it descends. When it takes hold of the vital and the body, then equanimity becomes easy and in the end automatic.

28-8-1933

OPENNESS TO THE MOTHER'S FORCE AND AVOIDANCE

OF OTHER FORCES

Keep yourself open to the Mother's Force, but do not trust all forces. As you go on, if you keep straight, you will come to a time when the psychic becomes more predominantly active and the Light from above prevails more purely and strongly so that the chance of mental constructions and vital formations mixing with the true experience diminishes. As I have told you, these are not and cannot be the supramental Forces. It is a work of preparation which is only making things ready for a future Yoga-Siddhi.

18-9-1932

*

Let the power of the Mother work in you, but be careful to avoid any mixture or substitution, in its place, of either a magnified ego-working or a force of Ignorance presenting itself as Truth. Aspire especially for the elimination of all obscurity and unconsciousness in the nature.

LOYALTY AND FIDELITY TO THE MOTHER

If an adverse Force comes, one has not to accept and welcome its suggestions, but to turn to the Mother and to refuse to turn away from her. Whether one can open or not, one has to be loyal and faithful. Loyalty and fidelity are not qualities for which one has to do Yoga. They are very simple things which any man or woman who aspires to the Truth ought to be able to accomplish.

THE ONLY WAY TO SUCCEED

There is in a very fundamental part of your nature a strong formation of ego-individuality which has mixed in your spiritual aspiration a clinging element of pride and spiritual ambition. This formation has never consented to be broken up in order to give place to something more true and divine. Therefore, when the Mother has put her force upon you, or when you yourself have pulled the force upon you, this in you has always prevented it from doing its work in its own way. It has begun itself building according to the ideas of the mind or some demand of the ego, trying to make its own creation in its "own way", by its own strength, its own Sadhana, its own Tapasya. There has never been here any real surrender, any giving up of yourself freely and simply into the hands of the Divine Mother. And yet that is the only way to succeed in the supramental Yoga. To be a Yogi, a Sannyasi, a Tapaswi is not the object here. The object is transformation, and the transformation can only be done by a force infinitely greater than your own; it can only be done by being truly like a child in the hands of the Divine Mother.

*

Everyone who is turned to the Mother is doing my Yoga. It is a great mistake to suppose that one can "do" the Purna Yoga — i.e. carry out and fulfil all the sides of the Yoga by one's own effort. No human being can do that. What one has to do is to put oneself in the Mother's hands and open oneself to her by service, by Bhakti, by aspiration; then the Mother by her light and force works in him so that the Sadhana is done. It is a mistake also to have the ambition to be a big Purna Yogi or a supramental being and ask oneself how far have I got towards that. The right attitude is to be devoted and given to the Mother and to wish to be whatever she wants you to be. The rest is for the Mother to decide and do in you.

April, 1935

*

If there is a refusal of the psychic new birth, a refusal to become the child new-born from the Mother, owing to attachment to intellectual knowledge or mental ideas or to some vital desire, then there will be a failure in the Sadhana.

*

> *Q: In our Sadhana, at times we experience large descents of Peace, Force, Ananda, etc. which are usurped by our little human ego to make us feel that we shall belong to the Mother's select band of Supermen. Is this not a mistake?*

A: To want to be a Superman is a mistake. It only swells the ego. One can aspire for the Divine to bring about the supramental transformation, but that also should not be done till the being has become psychic and spiritualised by the descent of the Mother's peace, force, light and purity.

22-2-1936

*

*Q: What poise or mode should we keep for the supra-
mental descent?*

A: As for poise or mode — that you need not trouble yourself about. An entire faith, opening, self-giving to the Mother
are the one condition necessary throughout.

23-9-1935

THE VITAL'S RESISTANCE TO SURRENDER

I have said that the human vital does not like to be controlled or
dominated by another and I said that that also was a reason why
Sadhaks find it difficult to surrender to the Mother. For the vital
wants to affirm its own ideas, impulses, desires, preferences and
to do what it likes, it does not want to feel another force than that
of its own nature leading or driving it; but surrender to the
Mother means that it must give up all these personal things and
allow her Force to guide and drive it in the ways of a higher
Truth which are not its own ways: so it resists, does not want to
be dominated by the Truth Light and the Mother's Force, insists on its own independence and refuses to surrender. These
ideas of breakdown and personal frustration are again wrong
suggestions and the dissatisfaction with yourself is as harmful
almost as dissatisfaction with the Mother would be. It prevents
the confidence and courage necessary for following the path of
the Sadhana. You must dismiss these suggestions from you.

8-10-1936

NECESSITY OF SURRENDER TO THE MOTHER

There is not much spiritual meaning in keeping open to the
Mother if you withhold your surrender. Self-giving or surrender
is demanded of those who practise this Yoga, because without
such a progressive surrender of the being it is quite impossible to
get anywhere near the goal. To keep open means to call in her
Force to work in you, and if you do not surrender to it, it

amounts to not allowing the Force to work in you at all or else only on condition that it will work in the way you want and not in its own way which is the way of the Divine Truth. A suggestion of this kind is usually made by some adverse Power or by some egoistic element of mind or vital which wants the Grace or the Force, but only in order to use it for its own purpose, and is not willing to live for the Divine Purpose, — it is willing to take from the Divine all it can get, but not to give itself to the Divine. The soul, the true being, on the contrary, turns towards the Divine and is not only willing but eager and happy to surrender.

In this Yoga one is supposed to go beyond every mental idealistic culture. Ideas and Ideals belong to the mind and are half-truths only; the mind too is, more often than not, satisfied with merely having an ideal, with the pleasure of idealising, while life remains always the same, untransformed or changed only a little and mostly in appearance. The spiritual seeker does not turn aside from the pursuit of realisation to mere idealising; not to idealise, but to realise the Divine Truth is always his aim, either beyond or in life also — and in the latter case it is necessary to transform mind and life which cannot be done without surrender to the action of the Divine Force, the Mother.

To seek after the Impersonal is the way of those who want to withdraw from life, but usually they try by their own effort, and not by an opening of themselves to a superior Power or by the way of surrender; for the Impersonal is not something that guides or helps, but something to be attained and it leaves each man to attain it according to the way and capacity of his nature. On the other hand, by an opening and surrender to the Mother one can realise the Impersonal and every other aspect of Truth also.

The surrender must necessarily be progressive. No one can make the complete surrender from the beginning, so it is quite natural that when one looks into oneself, one should find its absence. That is no reason why the principle of surrender should not be accepted and carried out steadily from stage to stage, from field to field, applying it successively to all the parts of the nature.

*

It is then a *saṅkalpa* of surrender. But the surrender must be to the Mother — not even to the Force, but to the Mother herself.

4-10-1936

*

If the psychic manifests, it will not ask you to surrender to it, but to surrender to the Mother.

*

The best way is to live in the psychic being, for that is always surrendered to the Mother and can lead the others in the right way. For control one has to centralise somewhere — some do it in the mind or above the mind, others do it in the heart and through the heart in the psychic centre.

11-6-1933

REAL AND COMPLETE SUBMISSION

It is necessary if you want to progress in your Sadhana that you should make the submission and surrender of which you speak sincere, real and complete. This cannot be as long as you mix up your desires with your spiritual aspiration. It cannot be as long as you cherish vital attachment to family, child or anything or anybody else. If you are to do this Yoga, you must have only one desire and aspiration, to receive the spiritual Truth and manifest it in all your thoughts, feelings, actions and nature. You must not hunger after any relations with anyone. The relations of the Sadhak with others must be created for him from within, when he has the true consciousness and lives in the Light. They will be determined within him by the power and will of the Divine Mother according to the supramental Truth for the divine life and divine work; they must not be determined by his mind and his vital desires. This is the thing you have to remember. Your psychic being is capable of giving itself to the Mother and living and growing in the Truth; but your lower vital being has been full of attachments and *samskāras* and an impure movement of desire and your external physical mind was not able to shake off its ignorant ideas and habits and open to the Truth. That was the reason why you were unable to progress, because you were keeping up an element and movements which could not be allowed to remain; for they were the exact opposite of what has to be established in a divine life. The Mother can only free you from these things, if you really want it, not only in your psychic being, but in your physical mind and all your vital nature. The sign will be that you no longer cherish or insist on your personal notions, attachments or desires, and that whatever the distance and wherever you may be, you will feel yourself open and the power and presence of the Mother with you and working in you and will be contented, quiet, confident, wanting nothing else, awaiting always the Mother's Will.

*

Put all before the Mother in your heart so that her Light may work on it for the best.

21-4-1935

*

The life of *samsāra* is in its nature a field of unrest — to go through it in the right way one has to offer one's life and actions to the Divine and pray for the peace of the Divine within. When the mind becomes quiet, one can feel the Divine Mother supporting the life and put everything into her hands.

16-4-1933

THE NECESSARY EFFORT

What you say of Sadhana is true. Sadhana is necessary and the Divine Force cannot do things in the void but must lead each one according to his nature to the point at which he can feel the

Mother working within and doing all for him. Till then the Sadhak's aspiration, self-consecration, assent and support to the Mother's workings, his rejection of all that comes in the way is very necessary — indispensable.

25-9-1936

*

The effort demanded of the Sadhak is that of aspiration, rejection and surrender. If these three are done the rest is to come of itself by the Grace of the Mother and the working of her force in you. But of the three the most important is surrender of which the first necessary form is trust and confidence and patience in difficulty. There is no rule that trust and confidence can only remain if aspiration is there. On the contrary, when even aspiration is not there because of the pressure of inertia, trust and confidence and patience can remain. If trust and patience fail when aspiration is quiescent, that would mean that the Sadhak is relying solely on his own effort — it would mean, "Oh, my aspiration has failed, so there is no hope for me. My aspiration fails, so what can Mother do?" On the contrary, the Sadhak should feel, "Never mind, my aspiration will come back again. Meanwhile I know that the Mother is with me even when I do not feel her; she will carry me even through the darkest period." That is the fully right attitude you must have. To those who have it depression can do nothing; even if it comes it has to return baffled. That is not tamasic surrender. Tamasic surrender is when one says, "I won't do anything; let Mother do everything. Aspiration, rejection, surrender even are not necessary. Let her do all that in me." There is a great difference between the two attitudes. One is that of the shirker who won't do anything, the other is that of the Sadhak who does his best, but when he is reduced to quiescence for a time and things are adverse, keeps always his trust in the Mother's force and presence behind all and by that trust baffles the opposition force and calls back the activity of the Sadhana.

26-10-1936

IN THE MOTHER'S LAP

Q: I find it very difficult to do the right kind of concentration. Since I can't concentrate properly, would it not be best for me to imagine myself lying eternally in the Mother's lap?

A: This is the best possible kind of concentration.

12-8-1935

VI

WORKING OF THE MOTHER'S FORCE

WORKING OF THE MOTHER'S FORCE

THE MOTHER'S FORCE

Nothing can be done except through the force of the Mother.

*

All has to be done by the working of the Mother's force aided by your aspiration, devotion and surrender.

30-10-1934

WHAT IS THE MOTHER'S FORCE?

Q: You often speak of the "Mother's Force". What is it?

A: It is the Divine Force which works to remove the ignorance and change the nature into the divine nature.

18-6-1933

THE FORCE OF PRAKRITI AND THE MOTHER'S FORCE

When I speak of the Mother's force I do not speak of the force of Prakriti which carries in it things of the Ignorance but of the higher Force of the Divine that descends from above to transform the nature.

No, there was no intention on the Mother's part. It is yourself who by coming to Mother became aware of your mistake.

DESCENT AND WORKING OF THE MOTHER'S FORCE

There is a force which accompanies the growth of the new

consciousness and at once grows with it and helps it to come about and to perfect itself. This force is the Yoga-Shakti. It is here coiled up and asleep in all the centres of our inner being (Chakras) and is at the base what is called in the Tantras the Kundalini Shakti. But it is also above us, above our head as the Divine Force — not there coiled up, involved, asleep, but awake, scient, potent, extended and wide; it is there waiting for manifestation and to this Force we have to open ourselves — to the power of the Mother. In the mind it manifests itself as a divine mind-force or a universal mind-force and it can do everything that the personal mind cannot do; it is then the Yogic mind-force. When it manifests and acts in the vital or physical in the same way, it is there apparent as a Yogic life-force or a Yogic body-force. It can awake in all these forms, bursting out-ward and upwards, extending itself into wideness from below; or it can descend and become there a definite power for things; it can pour downwards into the body, working, establishing its reign, extending into wideness from above, link the lowest in us with the highest above us, release the individual into a cosmic universality or into absoluteness and transcendence.

*

Certainly, in a sense the descent of the higher powers is the Divine Mother's own descent — for it is she who comes down in them.

*

When the Peace is established, this higher or Divine Force from above can descend and work in us. It descends usually first into the head and liberates the inner mind centres, then into the heart centre and liberates fully the psychic and emotional being, then into the navel and other vital centres and liberates the inner vital, then into the Muladhara and below and liberates the inner physical being. It works at the same time for perfection as well as liberation; it takes up the whole nature part by part and deals with it, rejecting what has to be rejected, sublimating what has to be sublimated, creating what has to be created. It integrates, harmonises, establishes a new rhythm in the nature. It can bring down too a higher and yet higher force and range of the higher nature until, if that be the aim of the Sadhana, it becomes possible to bring down the supramental force and existence. All this is prepared, assisted, farthered by the work of the psychic being in the heart centre; the more it is open, in front, active, the quicker, safer, easier the working of the Force can be. The more love and Bhakti and surrender grow in the heart, the more rapid and perfect becomes the evolution of the Sadhana. For the descent and transformation imply at the same time an increasing contact and union with the Divine.

That is the fundamental rationale of the Sadhana. It will be evident that the two most important things here are the opening of the heart centre and the opening of the mind centres to all that is behind and above them. For the heart opens to the psychic being and the mind centres open to the higher consciousness and the nexus between the psychic being and the higher consciousness is the principal means of the Siddhi. The first opening is effected by a concentration in the heart, a call to the Divine to manifest within us and through the psychic to take up and lead the whole nature. Aspiration, prayer, Bhakti, love, surrender are the main supports of this part of the Sadhana — accompanied by a rejection of all that stands in the way of what we aspire for. The second opening is effected by a concentration of the consciousness in the head (afterwards, above it) and an aspiration and call and a sustained will for the descent of the divine Peace, Power, Light, Knowledge, Ananda into the being — the Peace first or the Peace and Force together. Some indeed receive Light first or Ananda first or some sudden pouring down of Knowledge. With some there is first an opening which reveals to them a vast infinite Silence, Force, Light or Bliss above them and afterwards either they ascend to that or these things begin to descend into the lower nature. With others there is either the descent, first into the head, then down to the heart level, then to the navel and below and through the whole body, or else an inexplicable opening — without any sense of descent — of peace, light, wideness or power, or else a horizontal opening into the cosmic consciousness or in a suddenly widened mind an outburst of knowledge. Whatever comes has to be welcomed — for there is no absolute rule for all — but if the peace has not come first, care must be taken not to swell oneself in exultation or lose the balance. The capital movement however is when the Divine Force or Shakti, the Power of the Mother comes down and takes hold, for then the organisation of the consciousness begins and the larger foundation of the Yoga.

*

What you feel streaming down must be the Mother's overhead Force. It flows usually from above the head and works at first in the mind-centres (head and neck) and afterwards goes down into the chest and heart and then through the movement of the whole body.

It is the effect of this working which you must be feeling in the head up to the shoulders. The Force that comes down from above is the one that works to transform the consciousness into that of a higher spiritual being. Before that the Mother's Force works in the psychic, mental, vital and the physical plane itself to support, purify and psychically change the consciousness.

*

The stream which you feel coming down on the head and pouring into you is indeed a current of the Mother's Force; it is so that it is often felt; it flows into the body in currents and works there to liberate and change the consciousness. As the consciousness changes and develops, you will begin yourself to understand the meaning and working of these things.

21-8-1936

*

The feeling of the vibration of the Mother's Force around the head is more than a mental idea or even a mental realisation, it is an experience. This vibration is indeed the action of the Mother's

Force which is first felt above the head or around it, then afterwards within the head. The pressure means that it is working to open the mind and its centres so that it may enter. The mind-centres are in the head, one at the top and above it, another between the eyes, a third in the throat. That is why you feel the vibration around the head and sometimes up to the neck, but not below. It is so usually, for it is only after enveloping and entering the mind that it goes below to the emotional and vital parts (heart, navel, etc.) — though sometimes it is more enveloping before it enters the body.

24-3-1937

*

This is the meaning of your experiences:

1. The power of the Divine Mother from above is descending upon you and the pressure you feel on your head and the workings of which you are aware are hers.

Put yourself completely into her hands, have entire confidence, observe carefully and accurately all that happens and write that here. There is no need of special instructions since what is needed is being done for you.

2. The first pressure was on your mind. The centres of the mind are: (a) the head and above it, (b) the centre of the forehead between the eyes, (c) the throat and the vital-mental (emotional) and sensational mind-centres from the breast downward. It is this latter which is the first *prāṇa* of which you became aware. The action of the Power was to widen these two parts of you and raise them up towards the lowest centre of the higher consciousness above your head, so that hereafter they might both be consciously governed from there and that these might both move in a wide universal consciousness not limited by the body.

3. The other *prāṇa*, the restless one of which you became aware is the vital being, the being of desire and life-movement. The work of the Power has been directed towards quieting the restless movements and making it wide in consciousness as with the mind. The large body you felt was the vital body, not the physical, *sthūla śarīra*.

4. The basis of your Sadhana must be silence and quiet.
You must remain and grow always more and more deeply
quiet and still both in yourself and in your attitude to the world
around you. If you can do this, the Sadhana is likely to go on
progressing and enlarging itself with a minimum of trouble and
disturbance.

Go on quietly trusting to the Power that is at work in
you.

*

This weight or pressure on the head is always the sign that the
Mother's Force is in contact with you and pressing from above
to envelop your being and enter the *ādhāra* and pervade it; —
usually passing by degrees through the centres on its way downward. Sometimes it comes first as Peace, sometimes as Force,
sometimes as the Mother's consciousness and her presence, sometimes as Ananda.

When you lost it before, it must have been due either to
some uprising of vital imperfections in yourself or an attack
from outside. Of course, the pressure need not always be there;
but if things take the ordinary course, it usually recurs or else continues until the *ādhāra* is open and there is no further obstacle
to the descent of the higher consciousness.

18-9-1933

*

It is the descent of the Mother's Force from above through the
spinal cord, it is a well-known movement. There are two or
three kinds of descent. One is this touching the base of the
centres which rest on the spinal cord. Another is through the
head into the body going from level to level till the whole body is
filled and opening all the centres of consciousness. Another is a
descent enveloping the *ādhāra* from outside.

1-2-1934

*

What the Mother did was to light the fire within — if you did not feel it, it must be because the outer covering has not yet allowed it to come through into the outer consciousness. But something in the inner being must have kept it and opened more widely — that is shown by your experience in sleep, for that was evidently an action of the Mother in the inner being. The descent of the current in the spine is always a descent of the Mother's Force working in the centres to open them, and the strong force of the current you felt is an evident proof that the wider opening is there. You have only to persist and the effect both of the fire and the force will come out in the surface consciousness — for always there is a preparatory work behind the veil in the inner being before the veil thins or disappears and all the working can be done with the participation of the outer consciousness.

22-4-1937

*

Something is growing in you, but it is all inside — still if there is the steady persistence it is bound to come out. For instance, this white dazzling light with currents, it is a sure sign of the Force (the Mother's) entering and working in the *ādhāra*, but it came to you in sleep — that is to say, in the inner being, still behind the veil. The moment it came out, the dryness would disappear.

5-2-1937

*

Q: Since the evening the working of the Force has begun. During the evening Darshan of the Mother my consciousness opened itself before her more widely than ever before.

A: Very good. The Force usually works in that way with interruptions and returns growing each time stronger and fuller.

4-8-1934

ONENESS WITH THE MOTHER'S UNIVERSAL CONSCIOUSNESS

The consciousness of the mind, life, body in each person is ordinarily shut up in itself; it is narrow, not wide, sees itself as the centre of everything, judges all things according to its own impressions — it does not know anything as it really is. But when by Yoga one begins to open to the true consciousness then this barrier begins to break down. One feels the mind grow wider, even in the end the physical consciousness grows wider and wider, until you feel all things in yourself, yourself one with all things. You then become one with the Mother's universal Consciousness. That is why you feel the mind becoming wide. But also there is much above the human mind and it is this which you feel like a world above your head. All these are the ordinary experiences of our Yoga. It is only a beginning. But in order that it may go on developing, you must become more and more quiet, more and more able to hold whatever comes without getting too eager and excited. Peace and calmness are the first thing, and with it wideness — in the peace you can bear whatever love or Ananda comes, whatever strength comes or whatever knowledge.

THE UNIVERSAL AND THE TRANSFORMING POWER

> *Q: The more we open individually to the Mother's Light and Force, the more her power is established in the universal — is it not?*

A: It is the transforming power that is established — the universal power is always there.

12 8 1933

THE MOTHER'S FORCE AND THE GUNAS

> *Q: When one feels the Mother's Force acting through him and not his own, is it the Mother's Force alone that works in his actions and the Gunas remain quiescent?*

A: No, the *guṇas* are there and not quiescent — for they are the intermediation. If the force and the inner consciousness are very strong, then there is a tendency for the *rajas* to become like some inferior form of *tapas* and the *tamas* to become more like a kind of inert *śama*. That is how the transformation begins, but usually it is very slow in its process.

29-1-1936

THE MOTHER'S FORCE IN THE MATERIAL

Q: When can it be said that the material is ready for the Divine?

A: If the material consciousness is open, feels the Mother's Force working in it and responds, then it is ready.

11-6-1933

*

It [the Mother's consciousness] can be there in all the atoms of the body since all is secretly conscious.

5-10-1933

*

For the Mother's Force to work fully in the body, the body itself and not only the mind must have faith and open.

9-10-1933

*

Q: Is it that Mother begins to work on the physical nature after the inner parts are made ready?

A: It is the usual course, but some work is always being done in the inner parts at all times, because they are interdependent.

THE MOTHER'S INFLUENCE ON THE SUBCONSCIENT
AND THE ENVIRONMENTAL

Q: Since morning I was having intense aspiration to get lost in the Mother's Consciousness. Then I felt my consciousness frequently rising and stationing itself above. Before Pranam I felt as if even the parts near the navel and below were being drawn upwards. After Pranam I experienced for some time a different kind of atmosphere almost concretely around me. So I imagined that the Mother may have put a strong spiritual influence on my subconscient and environmental consciousness.

A: It is very good, you are right about the subconscient and environmental, — for it is there that the influence must fall so that the consciousness may go upward and spread itself out widely in a free peace, light and joy connecting them down to the subconscient with the higher consciousness. It is then that the loss of the ego in the Mother's Consciousness becomes possible.

25-9-1935

ASSIMILATION OF THE MOTHER'S FORCE

As for Mother's force when one receives it the best way is to be quiet till it is assimilated. Afterwards it is all right, not lost by outward movement or mixing.

*

If the meditation brings poise, peace, a concentrated condition or even a pressure or influence, that can go on in the work, provided one does not throw it away by a relaxed or dispersed state of consciousness. That was why the Mother wanted people not only to be concentrated at Pranam or meditation but to remain silent and absorb or assimilate afterwards and also insisted on avoiding things that relax or disperse or dissipate too much — precisely for this reason that so the effects of what she put in them might continue and the change of attitude will take place. But I am afraid most of the Sadhaks have never understood or practised anything of the kind — they could not appreciate or understand her directions.

*

Allow a quiet and steady will to progress to be settled in you; learn the habit of a silent, persistent and thorough assimilation of what the Mother puts into you. This is the sound way to advance.

March, 1928

PULLING AT THE MOTHER'S FORCES

When one is open and too eager and tries to pull down the force, experience, etc., instead of letting it descend quietly, that is called pulling. Many people pull at the Mother's forces — trying to take more than they can easily assimilate and disturbing the working.

April, 1935

*

Q: *What is meant by pulling? When we want something from the Mother with a vital desire, is it pulling? What is its effect on us?*

A: Yes; that is one kind of pulling — its effect is to blind and confuse the consciousness. But there is also a pulling for right things which is not bad in itself, and most people use — e.g. for Light, Force, Ananda. But it brings more reactions than a quiet opening to the Divine.

1-6-1933

*

No, to make people ill in order to improve or perfect them is not Mother's method. But sometimes things like headache come because the brain either tried too much or does not want to receive or makes difficulties. But the Yogic headaches are of a special kind and after the brain has found out the way to receive or respond they don't come at all.

20-6-1935

*

Q: Is the heat, felt in the body, of the fever or of the Mother's Force which has exerted a tremendous pressure on my Adhara?

A: That has still to be seen. It is most probably the Tapas heat; the question is whether it is turned partially in the body into fever.

7-6-1936

PSYCHIC OPENNESS TO THE MOTHER'S FORCE

What is needed is to profit by the discovery and get rid of the impediment. The Mother did not merely point out the impediment; she showed you very expressly how to get rid of it and at that time you understood her, though now (at the time of writing your letter to me) the light which you saw seems to have been clouded by your indulging your vital more and more in the bitter pastime of sadness. That was quite natural, for that is the result sadness always does bring. It is the reason why I object to the gospel of sorrow and to any Sadhana which makes sorrow one of its main planks (*abhimāna*, revolt, *viraha*). For sorrow is not, as Spinoza pointed out, a passage to a greater perfection, a way to Siddhi; it cannot be, for it confuses and weakens and distracts the mind, depresses the vital force, darkens the spirit. A relapse from joy and vital elasticity and Ananda to sorrow, self-distrust, despondency and weakness is a recoil from a greater to a lesser consciousness, — the habit of these moods show a clinging of something in the vital to the smaller, obscurer, dark and distressed movement out of which it is the very aim of Yoga to rise.

It is, therefore, quite incorrect to say that the Mother took away the wrong key with which you were trying to open the faery palace and left you with none at all. For she not only showed you the true key but gave it to you. It was not a mere vague exhortation to cheerfulness she gave you, but she described exactly the condition felt in the right kind of meditation — a state of inner rest, not of straining, of quiet opening, not of eager or desperate pulling, a harmonious giving of oneself to the Divine Force for its working, and in that quietude a sense of the Force working and a restful confidence allowing it to act without any unquiet interference. And she asked you if you had not experienced that condition and you said you had and knew it very well. Now that condition is the beginning of psychic opening and, if you have had it, you know what the psychic opening is; there is of course much more that afterwards comes to complete it but this is the fundamental condition into which all the rest can most easily come. What you should have done was to keep the key the Mother gave you present in your consciousness and apply it — not to go back and allow sadness and the repining view of the past to grow upon you. In this condition, which we term the right or the psychic attitude, there may and will be call, prayer, aspiration. Intensity, concentration will come of themselves, not by a hard effort or tense strain on the nature. Rejection of wrong movements, frank confession of defects are not only not incompatible, but helpful to it; but this attitude makes the rejection, the confession easy, spontaneous, entirely complete and sincere and effective. That is the experience of all who have consented to take this attitude.

I may say in passing that consciousness and receptivity are not the same thing; one may be receptive, yet externally unaware of how things are being done and of what is being done. The Force works, as I have repeatedly written, behind the veil; the results remain packed behind and come out afterwards, often slowly, little by little, until there is so much pressure that it breaks through somehow and forces itself upon the external nature. There lies the difference between a mental and a vital straining and pulling and a spontaneous psychic openness, and it is not at all the first time that we have spoken of the difference.

The Mother and myself have written and spoken of it times without number and we have deprecated pulling[1] and straining and advocated the attitude of psychic openness. It is not really a question of the right or the wrong key, but of putting the key in the lock in the right or the wrong way; either, because of some difficulty, you try to force the lock turning the key this way and that with violence or confidently and quietly give it the right turn and the door opens.

5-5-1932

HINDRANCE OF THE ACTIVE MIND

Q: My mind was trying to become conscious of the Mother's thoughts and to receive them. Is this activity right?

A: It is not altogether the way — if the mind is active it is more difficult to become aware of what the Mother is bringing. It is not thoughts she brings, but the higher light, force etc.

22-3-1933

*

Q: Today I felt the Mother filling my head with her light. Was I imagining things or did she really do so?

A: She does it every time, only today you not only received but were consciously receptive.

8-5-1933

UNDERSTANDING OF THE ACTION OF THE MOTHER'S FORCE

Q: Is it always necessary for us to understand what the Mother's Force is doing in us for the progress of our Yoga?

[1] There is a steady drawing of the Force possible which is not what I mean by pulling — drawing of the Force is quite common and helpful.

A: Plenty of people progress rapidly without understanding what the Force is doing — they simply observe and describe and say "I leave all to the Mother." Eventually knowledge and understanding come.

17-7-1933

*

Q: With reference to the Mother you once said, "Ask for the consciousness of her force". Does it mean that I should aspire to know about her Force?

A: Yes, not know with the mind only, but to feel it and see it with the inner experience.

18-6-1933

*

Q: Suppose I am in a fix and call down the Mother's Force which is above me. Now, how am I to know whether or not it has descended?

A: By the feeling of it or the result.

26-6-1933

*

Q: Grant that it has descended, and I have started doing my lessons; could I then order it to guard me from outer influences and simultaneously keep me in complete touch with the Mother even when my mind is occupied in some other work?

A: You can't order anything to the Mother's force, the Mother's force is the manifestation of the Mother herself.

26-6-1933

*

Q: I am unable to understand how this force can deal with action.

A: You think the Mother's force has nothing to do with the action or that it is too feeble to act? Or what? What is a force meant for but to act?

26-6-1933

MIXTURE OF THE LOWER NATURE WITH THE
MOTHER'S FORCE

Q: As to the Force, you said, "It creates its own activities in the mind or elsewhere." In that case the mind or any other part on which it acts will express only what the Force has created.

A: That is the ideal condition when the Force is the true Force only — but there is too much mixture in the nature for that to be possible at this stage of Sadhana.

3-8-1934

*

Q: In that case, does it not mean that what my consciousness feels as the Force is not the real Force of the Mother?

A: I have said that it gets mixed with the action of the present mind, vital and body. That is inevitable since it has to work upon them. It is only after the transformation that it can be fully the Mother's Force with no mixture of the separate personality. If the Divine Force in all its perfection without mixture were to act from the beginning, not taking any account of the present nature, then there would be no Sadhana, only a miraculous substitution of the Divine for the Human without any reason or process.

4-8-1934

NECESSITY OF DISCRIMINATION

It is dangerous to think of giving up "all barrier of discrimination and defence against what is trying to descend" upon you. Have you thought what this would mean if what is descending is something not in consonance with the divine Truth, perhaps even adverse? An Adverse Power would ask no better condition for getting control over the seeker. It is only the Mother's force and the divine Truth that one should admit without barriers. And even there one must keep the power of discernment in order to detect anything false that comes masquerading as the Mother's force and the divine Truth, and keep too the power of rejection that will throw away all mixture.

Keep faith in your spiritual destiny, draw back from error and open more the psychic being to the direct guidance of the Mother's light and power. If the central will is sincere, each recognition of a mistake can become a stepping-stone to a truer movement and a higher progress.

*

Q: How to recognise that a particular thought, feeling or impulse to action has come from the Mother herself and not from some universal force? If it is apparently of falsehood it can be recognised as such, but there are many others of a different character and sometimes one goes on thinking that they are prompted by the Mother from within even though they are not.

A: It can only be done by discrimination, care, sincerity, a constant control with regard to the mind's movements and the growth of a certain kind of psychic tact which detects any mental imitation or false suggestion of its being the Mother's.

27-4-1933

SAFEGUARDS AGAINST DANGERS IN DESCENT

In this process of the descent from above and the working it is most important not to rely entirely on oneself, but to rely on the guidance of the Guru and to refer all that happens to his judgment and arbitration and decision. For it often happens that the forces of the lower nature are stimulated and excited by the descent and want to mix with it and turn it to their profit. It often happens too that some Power or Powers undivine in their nature present themselves as the Supreme Lord or as the Divine Mother and claim the being's service and surrender. If these things are accepted, there will be an extremely disastrous consequence. If indeed there is the assent of the Sadhak to the Divine working alone and the submission or surrender to that guidance, then all can go smoothly. This assent and a rejection of all egoistic forces or forces that appeal to the ego are the safeguard throughout the Sadhana. But the ways of nature are full of snares, the disguises of the ego are innumerable, the illusions of the Powers of Darkness, Rakshasi Maya, are extraordinarily skilful; the reason is an insufficient guide and often turns traitor; vital desire is always with us tempting to follow any alluring call. This is the reason why in this Yoga we insist so much on what we call *samarpaṇa* — rather inadequately rendered by the English word surrender. If the heart centre is fully opened and the psychic is always in control, then there is no question; all is safe. But the psychic can at any moment be veiled by a lower upsurge. It is only a few who are exempt from these dangers and it is precisely those to whom surrender is easily possible. The guidance of one who is himself by identity or represents the Divine is in this difficult endeavour imperative and indispensable.

*

Let nothing and nobody come between you and the Mother's force. It is on your admitting and keeping that force and responding to the true inspiration and not on any ideas the mind may form that success will depend. Even ideas or plans which might otherwise be useful, will fail if there is not behind them the true spirit and the true force and influence.

*

If you want to get back your faith and keep it, you must first quiet your mind and make it open and obedient to the Mother's Force. If you have an excited mind at the mercy of every influence and impulse, you will remain a field of conflicting and contrary forces and cannot progress. You will begin to listen to your own ignorance instead of the Mother's knowledge and your faith will naturally disappear and you will get into a wrong condition and a wrong attitude.

March, 1928

HELP OF THE MOTHER'S FORCE FOR CHANGE

It is to be assumed that you are capable of the change since you are here in the presence and under the protection of the Mother. The pressure and help of the Mother's Force is always there. Your rapidity of progress depends upon your keeping yourself open to it and rejecting calmly, quietly and steadily all suggestions and invasions of other forces. Especially, the nervous excitement of the vital has to be rejected; a calm and quiet strength in the nervous being and the body is the only sound basis. It is there for you to receive, if you open to it always.

27-8-1932

*

Do not allow yourself to be troubled or discouraged by any difficulties, but quietly and simply open yourself to the Mother's force and allow it to change you.

*

The Mother's Force is not only above on the summit of the being. It is there with you and near you, ready to act whenever your nature will allow it. It is so with everybody here.

15-11-1936

*

The Mother's Force may do everything, but one has to become more and more conscious of one's own being and nature and what is below in it.

It is not a question of mental judgment, — that is of little use in these matters, but of the consciousness, feeling and seeing.

Supermind is not organised in the lower planes as the others are. It is only a veiled influence. Otherwise the supramental realisation would be easy.

22-5-1934

*

You should not rely on anything else alone, however helpful it may seem, but chiefly, primarily, fundamentally on the Mother's Force. The Sun and the Light may be a help, and will be if it is the true Light and the true Sun, but cannot take the place of the Mother's Force.

*

The steadiness you have gained is not a personal virtue but depends on your keeping the contact with the Mother — for it is her Force that is behind it and behind all the progress you can make. Learn to rely on that Force, to open to it more completely and to seek spiritual progress even not for your own sake but for the sake of the Divine — then you will go more smoothly.

*

They are unable to progress for two reasons: (1) because they yield to despair and gloom and the illusion of impotence; (2) because they try only with their own strength and do not care or know how to call in the working of the Mother's force.

10-6-1936

RESISTANCE TO THE MOTHER'S FORCE

The illnesses you have are the signs of the resistance of your physical consciousness to the action of the Divine Power.

If you cannot advance in your Sadhana, it is because you are divided and do not give yourself without reserve. You speak of surrendering everything to the Mother but you have not done even the one thing which she asked of you and which you have promised more than once. If after having called the action of the Divine Force, you allow other influences to prevail, how can you expect to be free from obstruction and difficulties?

20-11-1928

THE MOTHER'S USE OF PRESSURE

I was speaking of your case only — it was not my intention to say that the Mother never uses pressure. But pressure also can be of various kinds. There is a pressure of the Force when it is entering the mind or vital or body — a pressure to go faster, a pressure to build or form, a pressure to break and many more. In your case if there is any pressure it is that of help or support or removal of an attack, but it does not seem to me that that can properly be called pressure.

THE MOTHER'S WORKING IN THE PREPARATORY
CONSCIOUSNESS

The experiences you have are a good starting-point for realisation. They have to develop into the light of a deeper state in which there will be the descent of a higher consciousness into you. Your present consciousness in which you feel these things is only a preparatory one — in which the Mother works in you through the cosmic power according to your state of consciousness and your Karma, and in that working both success and failure can come — one has to remain equal-minded to both while trying for success. A surer guidance can come even in this preparatory consciousness if you are entirely turned towards her alone in such a way that you can feel her direct guidance and follow it without any other influence or force intervening to act upon you,

but that condition is not easy to get or to keep — it needs a great
one-pointedness and constant single-minded dedication. When
the higher consciousness will descend, then a closer union, a
more intimate consciousness of the Presence and a more illumined intuition will become possible.

17-11-1934

RECEIVING THE MOTHER'S FORCE AT A DISTANCE

As to what your other friend asks, it is quite possible for him to
receive where he is without coming here if he has the adoration of
the Mother in his heart and an intense call.

25-8-1935

*

*Q: You said regarding my friend X that he was receiving
the force of the Mother. I am a little puzzled because
I cannot understand to which Mother you are referring. Is it our Mother or some other, called the Universal
Mother by the people? I am puzzled because he does
not invoke the Mother and still he gets the Mother's
force!*

A: "In contact with" the Divine Force which is the force of the
Mother — that was what I wrote, I believe. Have you not put
him, by the photograph and his letter, in connection with us?
Has he not turned in this direction? Has he not met Y and been
impressed by him — a third channel of contact? That is quite
sufficient to help him to a contact if he has the faith and the
Yogic stress in him.

1936

*

I don't know whether Mother is sending force in the accepted
sense; I haven't asked her. In any case, anyone can receive the

force who has faith and sincerity, whose psychic being has begun to wake and who opens himself, — whether he knows or not that he is receiving. If X even imagines that he is receiving, that may open the way to a real reception, — if he *feels* it, why question his feeling? He is certainly trying hard to change and that is the first necessity; if one tries it can always be done, in more or less time.

28-6-1943

*

It is quite possible for you to do Sadhana at home and in the midst of your work — many do so. What is necessary in the beginning is to remember the Mother as much as possible, to concentrate on her in the heart for a time every day, if possible thinking of her as the Divine Mother, to aspire to feel her there within you, offer her your works and pray that from within she may guide and sustain you. This is a preliminary stage which often takes long, but if one goes through it with sincerity and steadfastness, the mentality begins little by little to change and a new consciousness opens in the Sadhak which begins to be aware more and more of the Mother's presence within, of her working in the nature and in the life or of some other spiritual experience which opens the gate towards realisation.

*

Remember the Mother and, though physically far from her, try to feel her with you and act according to what your inner being tells you would be her Will. Then you will be best able to feel her presence and mine and carry our atmosphere around you as a protection and a zone of quietude and light accompanying you everywhere.

12-12-1936

RECEIVING FORCE FROM THE MOTHER'S PHOTOGRAPHS

Q: When I sit in meditation before the Mother's photo-

graphs or the drawing of her feet, I receive Force. Is
this only a subjective feeling?

A: No, it is not subjective merely. By your meditating near
them you have been able to enter through them into communion
with the Mother and something of Her Power and Her Presence
is there.

14-7-1934

THE MOTHER AND THE ACTION OF THE HEALING FORCE

Q: I had an animated but friendly discussion with X
about the action of the healing force. He was of the
opinion that now that it has been brought down here it
is likely to operate in other parts of the world and that
any Tom, Dick and Harry can wield it even if spiri-
tually undeveloped. Is this true?

A: It may operate but not through every T, D and H, at first at
least.

3-2-1936

*

Q: I contended that the healing force will act only through
the Mother and others will be able to wield it if they are
in some way open to or in conscious rapport with her
and in physical contact with her. Nobody will be able to
use it without fulfilling these conditions. What do you
say?

A: At first it will be no doubt like that, if it is to be the true
Force, but when once it is settled in the earth-consciousness, a
more general use of the supraphysical Force for healing may
become possible.

It is not always necessary either that the rapport you speak
of should be conscious. Coué, for instance, was in rapport with

the Mother without knowing it. She told me of his getting something of the Force and of the beginning of his work long before he was known to anyone (of course, she did not know his name, but described him and his work in such a way that the identification was evident).

3-2-1936

VII

TRUE RELATION WITH THE MOTHER

TRUE RELATION WITH THE MOTHER

SPECIAL RELATIONS WITH THE MOTHER

It is certainly true that the Divine has no preferences or dislikes and is equal to all, but that does not prevent there being a special relationship with each. This relation, however, does not depend on the more or less identification or union. The purer soul has an easier access to the Divine. The more developed nature has more lines on which to meet Him. The identification creates a spiritual oneness. But there are other personal relations which are created by other causes. It is too complex for all relations to be determined by one cause.

Yes, Yogis whose progress does not depend on the personal intervention of the Mother, need have no personal relation with her — only the spiritual contact in distance. Some may have a special relation, but that is due to special aspects of their Sadhana. On the other hand, one may have a personal relation with the Mother even though no progress has been made in the Sadhana. There are all kinds of possibilities in this matter.

There is such a relation with all of those who have come here with a psychic sufficiently developed to admit of the relation. In other cases it is more a possibility than a thing realised.

There are, roughly speaking, three parts of the being in manifestation which come into play here: (1) the psychic being in evolution which brings with it its past experience of past lives and something of the old personalities, so much as it can make helpful for the present life; (2) the present formation due to this birth and made up of many complex factors; (3) the future being, which in our case means the great lines of higher consciousness above the present manifestation by joining which the transformation becomes more possible and the work attempted can be done.

It is the psychic being which brings in the contact through past lives or personalities, i.e. through something essential and still operative in them which it has kept.

But, in addition, some psychic beings have come here who are ready to join with great lines of consciousness above, represented often by beings of the higher planes and are therefore specially fitted to join with the Mother intimately in the great work that has to be done. These have all special relation with the Mother which adds to the past one.

As for the present formation, it may obviously have elements which, not being joined or met with the Mother, may feel themselves strange to her. It is such an element which may feel standing in the way; but it is an exterior formation and does not belong to the past or to the future evolution, at any rate in its present figure. It must either disappear or change.

10-6-1935

*

To launch into too many mental subtleties in this connection is not very helpful; it is a subject which is beyond mental analysis and the constructions of the mind about it are apt to be either very partially true or else erroneous.

There is a universal Divine Love which is equal for all. There is also a psychic connection which is individual; it is essentially the same for all, but it admits of a special relation with each which is not the same for all but different in each case. This special relation stands apart in each case and has its own nature, it is, as is said, *sui generis*, of its own kind and cannot be compared, balanced or measured with other relations, for each of these again is *sui generis*. The question of less or more is therefore perfectly irrelevan. here.

It is quite wrong to say that the Mother loves most those who are nearest to her in the physical. I have often said this but people do not wish to believe it, because they imagine that the Mother is a slave of the vital feelings like ordinary people and governed by vital likes and dislikes. "Those she likes she keeps near her, those she likes less she keeps less near, those she dislikes or does not care for she keeps at a distance," that is their childish reasoning. Many of those who feel the Mother's presence and love always with them hardly see her except once in six months or once in a year; — apart from the Pranam and meditation. On the other hand one near her physically or seeing her often may not feel such a thing at all; he may complain of the absence of the Mother's help and love altogether or as compared to what she gives to others. If the childishly simple rule of three given above were true, such outbursts would not be possible.

Whether one feels the Mother's love or not depends on whether one is open to it or not. It does not depend on physical nearness. Openness means the removal of all that makes one unconscious of the inner relation — nothing can make one more unconscious than the idea that it must be measured only by some outward manifestation instead of being felt within the being; it makes one blind or insensitive to the outer manifestations that are there. Whether one is physically far or near makes no difference. One can feel it, being physically far or seeing her little. One can fail to feel it when it is there even if one is physically near or often in her physical presence.

11-6-1935

*

If the Sadhak becomes unfaithful to the Mother, it means that he did not want the Sadhana or the Mother but the satisfaction of his desires and his ego. That is not Yoga.

The Mother meets nobody for "hours" — if anybody stayed for hours she would get very tired.

Mother did not meet X more than others because she loved him more than others but because she was trying to get something done through him for the work, which, if done, would have been a great victory for all. But precisely because he took it in the wrong way, grasping at it as a personal physical relation and satisfaction of his egoistic desire, he failed and had to go away. Your "part" makes the same stupid ignorant claim of the sensuous ego and if the Mother were so foolish as to satisfy it, it would turn up like X.

Mother has taken the body because a work of a physical nature (including a change in the physical world) had to be done, she has not come to establish a "physical relation" with people.

Some have come with her to share in the work, others she had called, others have come seeking for the light. With each she has a personal relation or a possibility of the personal relation, but each is of its own kind and no one can say that she must do equally the same thing with each person. No one can claim as a right that she must be physically near to him because she is physically near to others. Some have chosen personal relation with her yet she sees little of them — some have a less close personal relation yet for one reason or another may see her much oftener or longer. To apply silly mathematical rules of the physical mind here is absurd. Your physical mind cannot understand what the Mother does, its values and standards and ideas are not hers. It is still worse to make your personal vital demand or desire the measure of what she ought to do. That way spiritual ruin lies. She acts in each case for different reasons suitable to that case.

TRUE CHILDREN OF THE MOTHER

Those are the Mother's children closest to her who are open to her, close to her in their inner being, one with her will — not those who come bodily nearest to her.

*

If one has the close inner relation, one feels the Mother always near and within and round and there is no insistence on the closer physical relation for its own sake. Those who have not this, should aspire for this and not hanker after the other. If they get the outer closeness, they will find that it means nothing without the inner oneness and closeness. One may be physically near the Mother and yet as far from her as the Sahara desert.

11-6-1934

INNER UNION AND EXTERNAL CONTACT
WITH THE MOTHER

The spiritual union must begin from within and spread out from there; it cannot be based on anything exterior — for, if so based, the union cannot be spiritual or real. That is the great mistake which so many make here: they put the whole emphasis on the external vital or physical relation with the Mother, insist on a vital interchange or else physical contact and when they do not get it to their satisfaction, enter into all kinds of disturbances, revolt, doubt, depression. This is a wrong viewpoint altogether and has caused much obstruction and trouble. The mind, vital, physical can participate and are intended to participate in the union, but for that they must be submitted to the psychic, themselves psychicised; the union must be an essentially psychic and spiritual union spreading out to the mind, vital and physical. Even the physical must be able to feel invisibly the Mother's closeness, her concrete presence — then alone can the union be truly based and completed and then alone can any physical closeness or contact find its true value and fulfil its spiritual purpose. Till then any physical contact is of value only so far as it helps the inner Sadhana, but how much can be given and what will help or hinder, the Mother only can judge, the Sadhak cannot be the judge — he will be led away by the desires and lower vital ego, as so many have been in fact. When the vital demand is there with its claims and revolts and takes the desire for the exterior contact or closeness as a cause or occasion for these things, then it becomes a serious hindrance to the development of the inner union, it does not help at all. The Sadhaks always imagine in their ignorance that when the Mother sees more of one person than of another, it is because of personal preference and that she is giving more love and help to that person. That is altogether a mistake. Physical closeness and contact can be a severe ordeal for the Sadhak; it may raise the vital demands, claims, jealousies, etc. to a high pitch; it may, on the other hand, leave him satisfied with an outer relation without making any serious effort for the inner union; or it becomes for him something mechanical, because ordinary and familiar, and for any inner purpose quite ineffective — these things are not only possible but have happened in many cases. The Mother knows that and her arrangements in this matter are therefore dictated by quite other reasons than those which are attributed to her.

The only safe thing is to concentrate on the inner union foremost and altogether, to make that the one thing to be achieved and to leave aside all claims and demands for anything external, remaining satisfied with what the Mother gives and relying wholly on her wisdom and solicitude. It ought to be quite evident that a desire which raises revolt, doubt, depression, desperate struggles cannot be a true part of the spiritual movement. If your mind tells you that it is the right thing, then surely you must distrust the mind's suggestions. Concentrate entirely on the one thing needful and put away, if they come, all ideas and forces that want to disturb it or make you deviate. The vital assent to these things has to be overcome, but for that the first thing is to refuse all mental assent, for the mental support gives them a greater force than they would otherwise have. Fix the right attitude in the mind and the deeper emotional being — cling to that when contrary forces arise and by your firmness in that psychic attitude repel them.

14-3-1937

THE OUTER AND THE INNER MOTHER

It is true that the Mother is one in many forms, but the distinction between the outer and the inner Mother must not be made too trenchant; for she is not only one, but the physical Mother contains all the others in herself and in her is established the communication between the inner and the outer existence. But to know the outer Mother truly one must know what is within her and not look at the outer appearances only. That is only possible if one meets her with the inner being and grows into her consciousness — those who seek an outer relation only cannot do that.

10-8-1936

*

I do not know how you are going to *live into* the manifested form. To live in the Mother's consciousness even to the physical with the manifested form as the centre of this unity is possible. Perhaps you mean that? But how are you going to do that if the other parts are left to remain as they are? They will go on pulling you out of the true consciousness as they do now. And how are they to be changed if the Mother's Force is not there in them to change them?

14-1-1936

TRUE INNER RELATION WITH THE MOTHER

An inner (soul) relation means that one feels the Mother's presence, is turned to her at all times, is aware of her force moving, guiding, helping, is full of love for her and always feels a great nearness whether one is physically near her or not. This relation takes up the mind, vital and inner physical till one feels one's mind close to the Mother's mind, one's vital in harmony with hers, one's very physical consciousness full of her. These are all the elements of the inner union, not only in the spirit and self but in the nature.

I do not recollect what I had written, but this is the close inner relation as opposed to an outer relation which consists only in how one meets her in the external physical plane. It is quite possible and actual to have this close inner relation even if physically one sees her only at Pranam and meditation and once a year perhaps on the birthday.

*

The connection is always there, in the self and in the psychic; but if there are obstacles in the mind, vital and the physical, then the connection cannot manifest or, if at all manifest, it is mixed with elements which make it imperfect and unsuitable. The true connection is the psychic and spiritual relation; the relation in other parts must be kept up on the basis of this psychic and spiritual connection and then it can be permanent.

*

The relation with the Divine, the relation with the Mother must be one of love, faith, trust, confidence, surrender; any other relation of the vital ordinary kind brings reactions contrary to the Sadhana, — desire, egoistic *abhimāna*, demand, revolt and all the disturbance of ignorant rajasic human nature from which it is the object of the Sadhana to escape.

26-4-1933

THE CONSTANT PSYCHIC NEARNESS

Q: I am feeling very close to the Mother as if there is no difference. But how can this be possible, as there is such a great gulf between her and me — she being on the Supramental and I on the mental plane?

A: But the Mother is there not only on the Supramental but on all the planes. And especially she is close to everyone in the psychic part (the inner heart), so when that opens, the feeling of nearness naturally comes.

11-12-1933

*

All that is needed is for your psychic being to come forward and to open you to the direct and real and constant inner contact of myself and the Mother. Hitherto your soul has expressed itself through the mind and its ideals and admirations or through the vital and its higher joys and aspirations; but that is not sufficient to conquer the physical difficulty and enlighten and transform Matter. It is your soul in itself, your psychic being that must come in front, awaken entirely and make the fundamental change. The psychic being will not need the support of intellectual ideas or outer signs and helps. It is that alone that can give you the direct feeling of the Divine, the constant nearness, the inner support and aid. You will not then feel the Mother remote or have any further doubt about the realisation; for the mind thinks and the vital craves, but the soul feels and knows the Divine.

*

What you write here is an exact description of the psychic being and its relation to the Mother. That is the true relation. If you want to succeed in this Yoga, you must take your stand on the psychic relation and reject the egoistic vital movement. The psychic being coming to the front and staying there is the decisive movement in the Yoga. It is that which happened when you saw the Mother last, the psychic came in front. But you must keep it in front. You will not be able to do that if you listen to the vital ego and its outcries. It is by faith and surrender and the joy of pure self-giving — the psychic attitude — that one grows into the Truth and becomes united with the Divine.

26-2-1933

*

Q: When I could not properly concentrate, I called down Purity from above. At once the whole being was filled with Peace and Purity and, without any difficulty, I felt the Mother's Presence in the heart. An intense aspiration rose from the heart, from below, in fact, from all parts of the being. The heart was filled with adoration for the Mother; there was devotion, a genuine surrender, a great relief in union with the Mother. There was an intense aspiration for Purity. Was it a psychic opening?

A: Yes, certainly, it was a psychic opening and at the point emphasised which is very important, the opening to the higher Purity. That is one of the most important things for the psychic opening and the inner relation with the Mother.

14-7-1937

*

That which calls is your own psychic being whose place is deep behind the heart-centre. Many people feel at times the call for the Mother going on from there. It comes more easily in sleep or in a half-waking condition because then the surface mind is not active so that what is going on within in the inner being can manifest itself.

29-10-1934

THE TRUE BASIS OF SADHANA

Yes, that is the true basis. In the perfect equality wholly united with the Mother — so the higher consciousness can be lived and brought even into the outermost parts of the nature.

22-5-1934

*

The more the union with the Mother increases, the better for the Sadhana.

2-10-1933

*

Yes, it is a very encouraging progress. If you keep the wideness and calm as you were keeping it and also the love for the Mother in the heart, then all is safe — for it means the double foundation of the Yoga — the descent of the higher consciousness with its peace and freedom and serenity from above and the openness of the psychic which keeps all the effort or all the spontaneous movement turned towards the true goal.

10-10-1934

THE MOTHER'S LOVE

You are the Mother's child and the Mother's love to her children is without limit and she bears patiently with the defects of their nature. Try to be the true child of the Mother: it is there within you, but your outward mind is occupied by little futile things and too often in a violent fuss over them. You must not only see the Mother in dream but learn to see and feel her with you and within you at all times. Then you will find it easier to control yourself and change, — for she being there would be able to do it for you.

*

As for the feelings about the Mother and that her love is only

given for a return in work or to those who can do Sadhana well,
that is the usual senseless idea of the vital-physical mind and has
no value.

17-1-1937

*

If meditation brings a headache, you should not meditate. It
is a mistake to think that meditation is indispensable to the
Sadhana. There are so many who do not do it, but they are near
to the Mother and progress as well as those who have long meditations.

The one thing necessary is to be turned to the Mother and
that is all that is needed. Do not fear or be sad, but let the
Mother do quietly her work in you and through you and all will
be well.

16-3-1935

*

Certainly, it is not necessary for you to become "good" in order
that the Mother may give you her love. Her love is always there
and the imperfections of human nature do not count against that
love. The only thing is that you must become aware of it always
there. For that it is necessary for the psychic to come in front
— for the psychic knows, while the mind, vital and physical look
only at surface appearances and misinterpret them.

24-6-1936

*

X is probably making two mistakes — first, expecting outward
expressions of love from the Mother; second, looking for
progress instead of concentrating on openness and surrender
without demand of a return. These are two mistakes which
Sadhaks are constantly making. If one opens, if one surrenders,
then as soon as the nature is ready, progress will come of itself;
but the personal concentration for progress brings difficulties

and resistance and disappointment because the mind is not looking at things from the right angle. The Mother has a special
kindness for X and every day at Pranam she is trying to put a
sustaining force upon him. He must learn to be very quiet in
mind and vital and consecrate himself so that he may become
conscious as well as receive. The Divine Love, unlike the human,
is deep and vast and silent; one must become quiet and wide to
be aware of it and reply to it. He must make it his whole object
to be surrendered so that he may become a vessel and instrument
— leaving it to the Divine Wisdom and Love to fill him with what
is needed. Let him also fix this in the mind not to insist that in a
given time he must progress, develop, get realisations — whatever time it takes, he must be prepared to wait and persevere and
make his whole life an aspiration and an opening for the one
thing only, the Divine. To give oneself is the secret of Sadhana,
not to demand and acquire a thing. The more one gives oneself,
the more the power to receive will grow. But for that all impatience and revolt must go; all suggestions of not getting, not being
helped, not being loved, going away, of abandoning life or the
spiritual endeavour must be rejected.

1-9-1936

*

Obviously, if people expect the ordinary kind of love from the
Mother they must be disappointed — the love based on the vital
and its moods. But that is just the kind of love that has to be
overpassed in Yoga or transformed into something else.

14-3-1936

*

All that is quite correct. Even the human or the psychic love
[of the Mother] many are unable to feel or understand because it
is not quite in the ordinary human way.

5-5-1935

*

But why do you want to meet her as a "human" Mother? If you can see the Divine Mother in a human body that should be enough and a more fruitful attitude. Those who approach her as a human Mother often get into trouble by their conception making all sorts of mistakes in their approach to her.

2-5-1934

*

Q: The Sadhak feels alone and suffers when he does not have the Mother's presence. Does the embodied Mother feel the absence of her child as the human mother does? Or is she more miserable than the human for the reason that she cannot express her feeling as openly as the human mother?

A: If that were the case the Mother would have to be in a profound state of millionfold misery all the time — for why should she be miserable only for the Sadhaks? Why not for each soul that is wandering in the Ignorance? The child need not be miserable but simply come back when the Mother calls.

24-9-1934

*

This thought of yours that Mother cares for all as her children and does not care for you is evidently a quite groundless idea and does not rest on any solid basis. She is as affectionate in her love and care for you and in her way...towards you as to any others and more than to most. There is nothing solid or specific that we can see on which the idea can rest. Certainly, it corresponds to no reality in the Mother's feelings.

But I have noted that this kind of idea *always* comes up in the minds of Sadhaks and Sadhikas (especially the latter) when they become despondent or listen to the suggestions from outside them. Always they say the same thing as you, "You love and care for all; only for me you do not love and care. I am evidently unfit for the Yoga or you would not keep me far from you like

that. I shall never arrive at anything. What is the use of remaining here only to trouble you. What have I to live for?"
But when the psychic being is well awake, then these thoughts,
this despondency, these wrong notions are bound to go away.
What you feel therefore is just this despondency and the wrong
suggestions it brings; it does not correspond to any reality in the
Mother's feelings or behaviour towards you. It will go with the
rest as the inner being, the soul in you comes more and more
forward — for the soul in you knows that it loves the Mother
and the Mother loves you; it cannot be blinded by the suggestions that deceive the mind and the vital nature.

Do not therefore remain in these thoughts that have no
foundation but are only a mood of despondency or a suggestion
from outside. Let the psychic being in you grow and the
Mother's force work. The relation of the child and the Mother is
there in your soul; it will make itself felt in your mind and the
vital and physical consciousness till it becomes the foundation of
the whole consciousness on which all the Sadhana can be firm
and secure.

26-7-1935

*

All the Mother's love and help will remain with you unchanged
as before. The whole difficulty comes from a vital movement
which wants to possess in the wrong way, by comparison with
others, instead of living fully in close relation of your heart and
soul with the Mother's. It is the same in your relation with X.
But this is a defect common in human nature and many here
have it. It is not a thing that cannot be removed from the nature.
Indeed since your heart and soul want to be free from it, it cannot but go. Do not be discouraged therefore when it returns
owing to old habit. With the Mother's love and help what your
heart and soul desire will surely come and the wrong obscuring
element disappear.

25-9-1935

*

*Q: Am I right in my feeling that my psychic being is
always active in the front for some years now?*

A: If your psychic is in front and active, i.e. busy changing and
controlling the mind, vital and physical, how is it that there is an
upsetting of your nature by the Mother's dealings with you? If
the psychic is in front and active, it would immediately tell any
part of the nature that wanted to get upset "Whatever the Mother
does or decides must be accepted with surrender and gladness.
The mind must not believe that it knows better than the Mother
what ought to be done, the vital must not want the Mother to act
according to its wants and preferences. For such ideas and desires belong to the old nature and have no place in the psychic
and spiritual. They are the errors of the ego." And if it had the
control of the nature, the upsetting would at once cease or fade
away. Indeed if it had full control, such upsettings would be impossible. It must be assumed therefore that the psychic may
have been exerting some influence on the being but that its
control is far from complete or that the vital has risen up and
covered the psychic and suspended its influence. But if the psychic is fully in front, not veiled or not merely emerging, then it
would be impossible to cover it up altogether — there could
only be at most an upsetting on the surface while within all
remained quiet, conscious and devoted.

2-7-1936

TRUE LOVE FOR THE MOTHER

The love which is turned towards the Divine ought not to be the
usual vital feeling which men call by that name; for that is not
love, but only a vital desire, an instinct of appropriation, the
impulse to possess and monopolise. Not only is this not the divine
Love, but it ought not to be allowed to mix in the least degree in
the Yoga. The true love for the Divine is self-giving, free of demand, full of submission and surrender; it makes no claim, imposes no condition, strikes no bargain, indulges in no violences of
jealousy or pride or anger — for these things are not in its com-

position. In return the Divine Mother also gives herself, but freely — and this represents itself in an inner giving — her presence in your mind, your vital, your physical consciousness, her power re-creating you in the divine nature, taking up all the movements of your being and directing them towards perfection and fulfilment, her love enveloping you and carrying you in its arms Godwards. It is this that you must aspire to feel and possess in all your parts down to the very material, and here there is no limitation either of time or of completeness. If one truly aspires and gets it, there ought to be no room for any other claim or any other disappointed desire. And if one truly aspires, one does unfailingly get it, more and more as the purification proceeds and the nature undergoes its needed change.

Keep your love pure of all selfish claim and desire; you will find that you are getting all the love that you can bear and absorb in answer.

Realise also that the Realisation must come first, the work to be done, not the satisfaction of claim and desire. It is only when the Divine Consciousness in its supramental Light and Power has descended and transformed the physical that other things can be given a prominent place — and then too it will not be the satisfaction of desire, but the fulfilment of the Divine Truth in each and all and in the new life that is to express it. In the divine life all is for the sake of the Divine and not for the sake of the ego.

I should perhaps add one or two things to avoid misapprehensions. First, the love for the Divine of which I speak is not a psychic love only; it is the love of all the being, the vital and vital-physical included, — all are capable of the same self-giving. It is a mistake to believe that if the vital loves, it must be a love that demands and imposes the satisfaction of its desire; it is a mistake to think that it must be either that or else the vital, in order to escape from its "attachment", must draw away altogether from the object of its love. The vital can be as absolute in its unquestioning self-giving as any other part of the nature; nothing can be more generous than its movement when it forgets self for the Beloved. The vital and physical should both give themselves in the true way — the way of true love, not of ego desire.

1-8-1931

REAL LOVE AND EGOISM

Q: We all want the Mother's love but I wonder how many of us really love the Mother. Most of us live in our own likes and dislikes, joys and miseries, satisfactions and disappointments but hardly anyone has real love for the Mother.

A: It does not mean that there is no love, but that the love is mixed up and covered with egoism, demand and vital movements. At least that is the case with many. There are some, of course, who have no love at all or "love" — if it can be called so — only for what they get, one or two who love truly, but in a great many there is a psychic spark hidden in much smoke. The smoke has to be got rid of so that the spark may have a chance of growing into a blaze.

9-11-1934

PSYCHIC, MENTAL AND VITAL DEVOTION

Q: What is the difference between psychic devotion, mental devotion and vital devotion for the Mother?

A: The psychic is made up of love and self-giving without demand, the vital of the will to be possessed by the Mother and serve her, the mental of faith and unquestioning acceptance of all that the Mother is, says and does. These, however, are outside signs — it is in inner character quite recognisable but not to be put into words that they differ.

28-4-1933

*

> *Q: Is there no place for mental and vital devotion in this Yoga?*

A: Who says there is not? So long as it is real devotion, all *bhakti* has a place.

28-4-1933

*

It is the old vital with its ego which comes up again and again. It refuses to follow the higher being and be as the true Bhaktas are who ask nothing and are content with all that the Mother does or does not do, because whatever she does must be good since she is the Mother. You must impose the truth on this vital part.

6-5-1935

*

> *Q: How to get a pure and complete devotion?*

A: Get quiet first — then from the quietude aspire and open yourself quietly and sincerely to the Mother.

15-11-1933

*

> *Q: Grant me one little bit of devotion, Mother, just a little bit of it. Otherwise I do not know what will happen to me, I do not indeed know how I can live here. And I do not want to leave the shelter of Thy Lotus-Feet.*

A: Do not allow mental anxiety to harass you. Wait on the working of the Mother's force which will open the lotus of the heart. In the light from above devotion will blossom in you.

25-10-1936

FAITH AND LOVE

> *Q: Is it not true that those who have faith in the Mother*

have also love for her? Do not faith and love go together?

A: Not always. There are plenty of people who have some faith without love, though they may have a certain kind of mental *bhakti*, and plenty who have some love but no faith. But if it is the true psychic love, then faith goes with it, and if there is the entire faith, then the psychic love becomes soon awake. What you say is right if it is the soul's faith, the soul's love — but in some there is only a vital feeling and that brings, when it is disappointed, revolt and anger and they go away.

8-5-1933

PSYCHIC FEELING FOR THE MOTHER

Q: What kind of feeling is that which gets satisfaction and joy only in seeing the Mother?

A: It is psychic.

Q: What kind of feeling is that which gets satisfaction and joy only in remembering the Mother?

A: Psychic.

Q: What kind of feeling is that which gives a wound in the heart on hearing anything against the Mother?

A: Psychic.

Q: What kind of feeling is that by which one feels close to the Mother's presence in the heart even though she is physically far?

A: Psychic.

Q: How shall I find out that I am in the full state of psychic love?

A: By the absence of ego, by pure devotion, by submission and surrender to the Divine.

9-5-1933

*

Q: When the whole nature is engrossed in feeling, thinking, acting round the word "Mother", would the psychic be realised?

A: That would of itself be the psychic state.

*

Q: Can there be a conscious contact with the Mother through the psychic before the latter comes forward fully?

A: Yes, the psychic is always there.

*

Q: Why do I not feel love and Ananda every time I see the Mother?

A: As for the love and Ananda, it depends on the psychic coming up.

29-7-1934

*

Q: Whenever an inner love springs out for the Mother, tears rush out too.

A: These are psychic tears of devotion etc.

25-8-1934

*

Q: A lady visitor was leaving the Ashram today. No sooner did the Mother finish the Pranam ceremony than this lady began to weep. In fact, she tried hard to check herself as we all were still there, but it seems she could not help it. Was it not due to her psychic coming in front for the time?

A: It is not a question of the psychic coming in front. She has a psychic being which is awake and has long been in connection with the Mother on the inner plane.

28-8-1934

*

Q: A thrill comes from above and passes through my body, making the Adhara stilled for a while. I don't understand it much. What exactly is it?

A: Of course it is the thrill of the Mother's touch coming from above and felt by the psychic and vital together.

28-8-1934

*

Q: We find that in the Mother's presence or by meeting her we come out of depression and experience ecstasy of joy. Does this take place by a psychic meeting or meeting on the inner vital level?

A: It depends on whether it comes by drawing vital force from her or simply by the joy of seeing her or by receiving something from her. In the 2 latter cases it is usually psychic or psychic-vital, in the former it is vital.

*

Q: If a man feels that he is the happiest child of the Mother, is it due to ego-feeling?

A: It depends on the source of the feeling. If it is true happiness, then it is not ego. If it is due to a feeling of superiority, then it is ego.

*

Q: My psychic sometimes feels sad and lonely because it feels it cannot properly love the Mother.

A: It can't be the psychic in that case. The psychic never feels that it cannot love the Divine.

*

Q: Psychic love for the Mother — or else death: this is what one feels at times as a final resolution.

A: That is altogether the wrong attitude. It is once more the vital coming in — it is not a psychic attitude. If in asking for the psychic love, you take an attitude that is vital not psychic, how do you expect the psychic to come?

2-3-1935

*

Q: To concentrate only on being with the Mother's heart and want only to be hers and live for her and care for no other experience: what do you think of this attitude?

A: The attitude is good for awakening the psychic being and the inner being generally. But if the higher experience comes it should not be stopped.

12-3-1935

*

Q: Even higher or deeper experiences do not seem

*valuable at all if one cannot love the Mother with the
true heart.*

A: It is a mistake to think like that. The experiences prepare the
different parts of the being for loving in the right way, so that
it is not the soul alone that loves. So long as they are open to
ignorance and ego they cannot receive and hold the love
rightly.

23-10-1935

PSYCHIC AND VITAL LOVE

Love and devotion depend on the opening of the psychic and for
that the desires must go. The vital love offered by many to the
Mother instead of the psychic love brings more disturbance than
anything else because it is coupled with desire.

8-9-1936

*

There is no harm in the vital love provided it is purified of all
insincerity (as, for example, self-importance etc.) and from all
demand. To feel joy in seeing the Mother is all right, but to
demand it as a right, to be upset or in revolt or *abhimāna* when
it is not given, to be jealous of others who get it — all that is
demand and creates an impurity which spoils both the joy and
the love.

13-9-1934

*

As for the *eagerness* to see the Mother, it depends on the nature
of the feeling. If there is no demand or claim in it, no dissatisfaction when it is not fulfilled, but only the feeling of the will to
see her whenever possible and the joy of seeing her, then it is all
right. Of course no trace of anger or jealousy must be there.
The vital has also to participate in the Sadhana, so the mere fact

that there is a vital element does not make the thing wrong, provided it is a vital element of the right kind.

6-12-1931

*

If you have no *abhimāna* against the Mother, that also is surely very desirable. *Abhimāna*, disturbance, etc. may be signs of life but of a vital, not of the inner life. They must quiet down and give room for the inner life. At first the result may be a neutral quiet, but one has often to pass through that to arrive at a more positive new consciousness.

2-1-1937

*

It will not do to indulge this restless vital movement. It is not by that that you can have the union with the Mother. You should aspire calmly — eat, sleep, do your work. Peace is the one thing you have to ask for now — it is only on the basis of peace and calm that the true progress and realisation can come. There must be no vital excitement in your seeking or your aspiration towards the Mother.

20-10-1933

VITAL BARGAINING AND TRUE SELF-GIVING

What you have felt is a revival or return on you of the lower vital with its demands and desires. Its suggestion is, "I am doing the Yoga, but for a price. I have abandoned the life of vital desire and satisfaction but in order to get intimacy with the Mother — instead of satisfying myself with the world, to satisfy myself and get my desires fulfilled by the Divine. If I do not get the intimacy of the Mother and immediately and as I want it, why should I give up the old things?" And as a natural result the old things start again — "X and Y and Y and X and the wrongs of Z." You must see this machinery of the lower vital and dismiss it.

It is only by the full psychic relation of self-giving that unity and closeness with the Divine can be maintained — the other is part of the vital ego movement and can only bring a fall of the consciousness and disturbance.

20-6-1933

*

You are concerned only with yourself and the Divine. In your relations with the Divine you are concerned not with the Divine's satisfaction of your personal desires, but with being pulled out of these things and raised to your highest spiritual possibilities, so that you may become united with the Mother within and as a result in the outer being also. That cannot be done by satisfying your vital desires — to do so would only increase them and give you into the hands of the ignorance and restless confusion of the ordinary Nature. It can be done only by your inner trust and surrender and by the pressure of the Mother's peace and Force working from within and changing your vital nature. It is when you forget this that you go wrong and suffer; when you remember it you progress and the difficulties become less and less insistent.

13-9-1933

*

If it is the same part of the vital that was on the right side and has now turned against the Mother, the explanation is very obvious. It gave its adhesion formerly because it thought that by its adhesion it could make her satisfy its desires; finding its desires not indulged, it turns against her. That is the usual vital movement in ordinary man and in ordinary life, and it has no true place in Yoga. It was just the introduction of this attitude into Yoga by the Sadhaks and its persistence which has at last made it necessary for the Mother to draw back as she has done. What you have to do is to get these lower parts to understand that they exist not for themselves but for the Divine and to give their adhesion, without claim or *arrière-pensée* or subterfuge. It is the whole issue at the present moment in the Sadhana; for it is only if this is done that the physical consciousness can change and become fit for the descent. Otherwise there will always be these ups and downs in some part of the being — at least, delay, confusion and disorder. This is the only true basis for fixity in the true consciousness and for a smooth course in the Sadhana.

14-12-1931

OBSTACLE OF FEAR IN INTIMACY WITH THE MOTHER

All fear ought to be cast out. This movement of fear belongs to a still unchanged part of the vital which answers to the old ideas, feelings and reactions. Its only effect is to make you misinterpret the Mother's attitude or the intention in her words or looks or expression. If the Mother becomes serious or has an ironic smile, that does not in the least mean that she is angry or has withdrawn her affection; on the contrary, it is with those with whom she is most inwardly intimate that she feels most free to become like that — even to give them severe chidings. They in their turn understand her and do not get upset or afraid, — they only turn to look inside themselves and see what it is on which she is putting her pressure. That pressure they regard as a privilege and a sign of her Grace. Fear stands in the way of this complete intimacy and confidence and creates only misunderstanding; you must cast it out altogether.

22-5-1932

*

There is no need to ask for pardon, for the Mother has not in the least been angry or displeased with you. You may be sure of her love always.

29-9-1933

*

It is always a mistake to attach importance to what others say — it is enough to have true devotion and the right attitude towards the Mother. You need have no apprehension of this kind at all.

28-4-1933

THREE RULES FOR REMAINING OPEN TO THE MOTHER

Nothing is more dangerous than the influences of the physical mind trying to build up conclusions upon outward appearances — they have nine chances out of ten of being false. One must learn to distrust hasty conclusions from surface appearances — is not that the first condition of true knowledge? — and learn to see and know things from within.

You ask how to stop these movements? To begin with, observe three rules:

1. Keep always confidence in the Mother's care and love — trust in them and distrust every suggestion, every appearance that seems to contradict.

2. Reject immediately every feeling, every impulse that makes you draw back from the Mother — from your true relation with her, from inner nearness, from a simple and straightforward confidence in her.

3. Do not lay too much stress on outward signs — your observation of them may easily mislead you. Keep yourself open to her and feel with your heart, — the inner heart, not the surface vital desire, but the heart of the true emotion, — there you are more likely to find her and be always near her in yourself and receive what constantly she is working to give you.

1931

*

If you bring somebody between you and the Mother, it is bound to give trouble.

5-4-1933

DIRECT RELATION WITH THE MOTHER

The direct relation with the Mother is always open to you and it is there whenever you can feel it; for it is a thing of the inner being. Whenever you go deep within yourself you find it; it has to come out and govern the outer nature and life. That is why

I want you to give time for going inside and for inner progress in the Sadhana. The relation with X which the Mother thought of establishing was of two friends and fellow-workers in her work, it was never intended that she should be between you and the Mother. In Y's case there was a help to be given to you so that you might not be carried away by the attacks from which you suffered and might have time and support till you could reach a point at which you could seek the Mother's presence within you and with you. That you can do now and there is no reason why anyone should be asked to intervene in any way — our work is directly in you and upon you and not through anyone.

22-12-1936

*

Do not think whether people agree with you or do not agree with you or whether you are good or bad, but think that "the Mother loves me and I am the Mother's". If you base your life on that thought, everything will soon become easy.

30-4-1935

*

It is because of the thoughts about others and your "badness" that you feel far from the Mother. All the time she is very near to you and you to her. If you take the position I told you and make it the basis of your life, "the Mother loves me and I am hers", the curtain would soon disappear, for it is made of these thoughts and nothing else.

1-5-1935

*

It was your mistake to listen to what people say about you and X and Y and attach any value to their foolish chatter.... It is what the Mother says that is true and matters and not what people say; if you listen to what people say, you will lose touch with the Mother's consciousness. It is because of that that these thoughts

have come back on you about your badness and the rest of it....
For many days you had peace and joy and freedom from the restless mind and you had the psychic opening. Now you must go
back to that and do as you were doing before. Turn to the
Mother only and let her consciousness and her will work in you.
Then you will recover what you had got, silence the mind and
be free.

29-4-1933

VIII

SADHANA THROUGH WORK FOR THE MOTHER

SADHANA THROUGH WORK FOR THE MOTHER

WORK FOR THE MOTHER AND SADHANA

Work for the Mother done with the right concentration on her is as much a Sadhana as meditation and inner experiences.

*

Those who do work for the Mother in all sincerity are prepared by the work itself for the right consciousness even if they do not sit down for meditation or follow any particular practice of Yoga. It is not necessary to tell you how to meditate; whatever is needful will come of itself, if in your work and at all times you are sincere and keep yourself open to the Mother.

NECESSITY OF WORK IN INTEGRAL YOGA

To go entirely inside in order to have experiences and to neglect the work, the external consciousness, is to be unbalanced, one-sided in the Sadhana — for our Yoga is integral; so also to throw oneself outward and live in the external being alone is to be unbalanced, one-sided in the Sadhana. One must have the same consciousness in inner experience and outward action and make both full of the Mother.

*

It is not well to spend the whole time or the greater part of the time in meditation unless one is very strong in mind — for one gets into the habit of living in an inner world entirely and losing touch with external realities — this brings in a one-sided inharmonious movement and may lead to disturbance of balance. To do both meditation and work and dedicate both to the Mother is the best thing.

6-8-1933

*

It is not our experience that by meditation alone it is possible to change the nature, nor has retirement from outward activity and work much profited those who have tried it; in many cases it has been harmful. A certain amount of concentration, an inner aspiration in the heart and an opening of the consciousness to the Mother's presence there and to the descent from above are needed. But without action, without work the nature does not really change; it is there and by contact with men that there is the test of the change in the nature. As for the work one does, there is no higher or lower work; all work is the same provided it is offered to the Mother and done for her and in her power.

6-10-1934

*

This happens when the work is always associated with the Mother's thought, done as an offering to her, with the call to do it through you. All ideas of ego, all association of egoistic feelings with the work must disappear. One begins to feel the Mother's force doing the work; the psychic grows through a certain inner attitude behind the work and the *ādhāra* becomes open both to the psychic intuitions and influences from within and to the descent from above. Then the result of meditation can come through the work itself.

*

> Q: X says that he cannot feel your presence during work as he can during meditation. He does not understand how work can help him.

A: He has to learn to consecrate his work and feel the Mother's power working through it. A purely sedentary subjective realisation is only a half realisation.

23-1-1934

*

The Mother does not think that it is good to give up all work and only read and meditate. Work is part of the Yoga and it gives the best opportunity for calling down the Presence, the Light and the Power into the vital and its activities; it increases also the field and the opportunity of surrender.

It is not enough to remember that the work is the Mother's — and the results also. You must learn to feel the Mother's forces behind you and to open to the inspiration and the guidance. Always to remember by an effort of the mind is too difficult; but if you get into the consciousness in which you feel always the Mother's force in you or supporting you, that is the true thing.

The Mother does not usually give specific advice such as you ask for in regard to the Insurance Company. You must learn to get the true inspiration in the mind's silence.

18-8-1932

*

Q: Will those who live in peace and Samata but do no work for the Mother or do little work get transformation?

A: No, they do not get transformed at all.

7-5-1933

TWO STAGES OF UNION WITH THE MOTHER'S FORCE

The feeling that all one does is from the Divine, that all action is the Mother's is a necessary step in experience, but one cannot remain in it — one has to go farther. Those can remain in it who do not want to change the nature, but only to have the experience of the Truth behind it. Your action is according to universal Nature and in that again it is according to your individual nature, and all Nature is a force put out by the Divine Mother for the action of the universe. But as things are it is an action of the Ignorance and the ego; while what we want is an action of the divine Truth unveiled and undeformed by the Ignorance and the ego.

So when you feel that your actions are all done by the force
(Shakti) of the Mother, that is the true experience. But the will
of the Mother is that all you do should be done not by her force
in Nature as now, but her own direct force in the Truth of her
nature, the higher divine Nature. So also it was correct, what
you thought afterwards, that unless there is this change, the
experience that all you do is done by her will cannot be altogether
true. So it will not be permanent till then. For if it were permanent now, it might keep you in the lower action as it does many
and prevent or retard the change. What you need as a permanent
experience now is that of the Mother's Force working in you in
all things to change this ignorant consciousness and nature into
her divine consciousness and nature.

It is the same with the truth about the instrument. It is true
that each thing is an instrument of the cosmic Shakti, therefore
of the Mother. But the aim of the Sadhana is to become a conscious and perfect instrument instead of one that is unconscious
and therefore imperfect. One can be a conscious and perfect
instrument only when one is no longer acting in obedience to the
ignorant push of the lower nature but in surrender to the Mother
and aware of her higher Force acting within oneself. So here too
your intuition was perfectly true.

But all this cannot be done in a day. So you are once more
right in not being anxious or uneasy. One must be vigilant, but
not anxious and uneasy. The Mother's Force will act and bring
the result in its own time, provided one offers all to her and
aspires and is vigilant, calling and remembering her at all times,
rejecting quietly all that stands in the way of the action of her
transforming Force.

Your second view of this was more from the right angle of
vision than the first. To say, "it is not I who have to act, so I
need not mind", is to say too much — one has to act in so far
as one has to aspire, offer oneself, assent to the Mother's working, reject all else, more and more surrender. All else will be
done in time, there is no need for anxiety or depression or
impatience.

13-7-1935

*

At first one must put one's will in union with the Mother's will knowing that it is an instrument only and that it is the Mother's will behind that alone can give the result. Afterwards when one becomes conscious fully of the Mother's force working within, then the personal will is replaced by the divine.

15-7-1935

*

There should be not only a general attitude, but each work should be offered to the Mother so as to keep the attitude a living one all the time. There should be at the time of work no meditation, for that would withdraw the attention from the work, but there should be the constant memory of the One to whom you offer it. This is only a first process; for when you can have constantly the feeling of a calm being within concentrated in the sense of the Divine Presence while the surface mind does the work, or when you can begin to feel always that it is the Mother's force that is doing the work and you are only a channel or an instrument, then in place of memory there will have begun the automatic constant realisation of Yoga, divine union, in works.

*

Everybody is in the Mother, but one must become conscious of that, not of the work only.

1-4-1935

*

Q: Is it true that one should feel that it is the Divine Presence which moves one and does everything for one? Would it be possible to feel it without a union with the Divine Mother?

A: No — that is itself a union with her — to feel the Divine Presence above or in you and moving you.

14-7-1933

*

Q: Today I felt as if someone else than myself was carrying out my actions. Of course I was there, but in the background. Was it not the Mother's Force trying to take me into itself integrally?

A: It is too much to say that. What you say amounts only to some glimpse of the cosmic Force behind all the actions.

2-6-1934

*

Q: How can the will be made one with the Mother's Will?

A: The will can be made one with the Mother's by establishing a constant contact of the consciousness with hers.

24-6-1933

*

Q: What is meant by "establishing a constant contact of the consciousness" with the Mother's which you say is necessary for union with her Will? Does it mean mental contact or psychic?

A: It means the whole — with the psychic as the base.

25-6-1933

*

Q: My psychological analysis indicates that it is not always possible for us, Sadhaks, to let the Mother work in us spontaneously. For often something in us keeps off and closes the doors against her. I think the best course would be to develop our will-power, so that something might be always there to help us reopen the doors. I mean here the will not of the vital or mental kind but the true will-power. Would you kindly enlighten me as to how to develop it?

A: The only way to do it is (1) to become aware of a conscious Force behind that uses the mind etc. (2) to learn by practice to direct that Force towards its object. I don't suppose you will find it easy to do either of these things at once — one must first learn to live more deeply in the inner consciousness than you have done hitherto.

16-7-1934

CONDITIONS FOR FOLLOWING THE MOTHER'S WILL

The conditions for following the Mother's Will are to turn to her for Light and Truth and Strength, and aspire that no other force shall influence or lead you, to make no demands or conditions in the vital, to keep a quiet mind ready to receive the Truth, but not insisting on its own ideas and formations, — finally, to keep the psychic awake and in front, so that you may be in a constant contact and know truly what her will is; for the mind and vital can mistake other impulsions and suggestions for the Divine Will, but the psychic once awakened makes no mistake.

A perfect perfection is only possible after supramentalisation; but a relative good working is possible on the lower planes, if one is in contact with the Divine and careful, vigilant and conscious in mind and vital and body. That is a condition, besides, which is preparatory and almost indispensable for the supreme liberation.

THE BASIS OF DIVINE LIFE

To be entirely sincere means to desire the divine Truth only, to surrender yourself more and more to the Divine Mother, to reject all personal demand and desire other than this one aspiration, to offer every action in life to the Divine and do it as the work given without bringing in the ego. This is the basis of the divine life.

One cannot become altogether this at once, but if one aspires at all times and calls in always the aid of the Divine Shakti with

a true heart and straightforward will, one grows more and more
into this consciousness.

TRUE CONSCIOUSNESS OF KARMAYOGA

He should carry on his work and do all things else in the right
consciousness, offering all he does to the Mother and keeping in
inner touch with her. All work done in that spirit and with that
consciousness becomes Karmayoga and can be regarded as part
of his Sadhana.

*

What you received and kept in the work is indeed the true basic
consciousness of Karmayoga — the calm consciousness from
above supporting and the strength from above doing the work,
with that the Bhakti which feels it to be the Mother's Consciousness present and working. You know now by experience
what is the secret of Karmayoga.

15-9-1936

RIGHT ATTITUDE IN WORK

Not only in your inward concentration, but in your outward
acts and movements you must take the right attitude. If you do
that and put everything under the Mother's guidance, you will
find that difficulties begin to diminish or are much more easily
got over and things become steadily smoother.

In your work and acts you must do the same as in your concentration. Open to the Mother, put them under her guidance,
call in the peace, the supporting Power, the protection and, in
order that they may work, reject all wrong influences that might
come in their way by creating wrong, careless or unconscious
movements.

Follow this principle and your whole being will become one,
under one rule, in the peace and sheltering Power and Light.

*

The Truth for you is to feel the Divine in you, open to the Mother and work for the Divine till you are aware of her in all your activities. There must be the consciousness of the divine presence in your heart and the divine guidance in your acts. This the psychic being can easily, swiftly, deeply feel if it is fully awake; once the psychic has felt it, it can spread to the mental and vital also.

*

Demands should not be made; what you receive freely from the Mother helps you; what you demand or try to impose on her is bound to be empty of her force.

The Mother deals with each person differently according to his true need (not what he himself fancies to be his need) and his progress in the Sadhana and his nature.

For you the most effective way to get the strength you need should be to do the work consciously and scrupulously, allowing nothing to interfere with its exact discharge. If you did that, opening yourself at the same time to the Mother in your work, you would receive more constantly the grace and would come to feel her power doing the work through you; you would thus be able to live constantly with the sense of her presence. If, on the contrary, you allow your fancies or desires to interfere with your work or are careless and negligent, you interrupt the flow of her grace and give room for sorrow and uneasiness and other foreign forces to enter into you. Yoga through work is the easiest and most effective way to enter into the stream of this Sadhana.

8-3-1930

*

Even the most purely physical and mechanical work cannot be properly done if one accepts incapacity, inertia and passivity. The remedy is not to confine yourself to mechanical work, but to reject and throw off incapacity, passivity and inertia and open yourself to the Mother's force. If vanity, ambition and self-conceit stand in your way, cast them from you. You will not get rid of these things by merely waiting for them to disappear. If you merely wait for things to happen, there is no reason why they should happen at all. If it is incapacity and weakness that oppose, still, as one opens oneself truly and more and more to the Mother's force, the strength and capacity necessary for the work will be given and will grow in the *ādhāra*.

*

The advantage of being in the true consciousness is that you have the right awareness and its will being in harmony with the Mother's will, you can call in the Mother's Force to make the change. Those who live in the mind and the vital are not so well able to do this; they are obliged to use mostly their personal effort and as the awareness and will and force of the mind and vital are divided and imperfect, the work done is imperfect and not definitive. It is only in the Supermind that Awareness, Will, Force are always one movement and automatically effective.

*

Q: I am always in touch with the Mother during work. Not only do I remember her but the contact with her remains during work. Her Force constantly flows into the Adhara and the work is done automatically, but swiftly, perfectly, unhesitatingly — without personal anxieties and responsibilities; instead, there is confidence, sureness, strength, calmness. I feel that if I can do work in this attitude, it will be perfect, flawless, the work of the Mother's child, not of an egoistic man. Kindly let me know if I am correct.

A: Yes, it is a very good progress and the first step towards the right use of the Power for action.

*

Q: I have read both in "The Synthesis of Yoga" and

*the Mother's "Conversations" that every act and move-
ment, thought and word should be an offering. Even if
this is a strictly mental effort without the heart's devotion, as it may be at first, it is sure to lead to devotion,
provided the effort is sincere. This discipline is quite possible in acts of a more or less mechanical nature like
walking or eating, but where the work involves mental
concentration, as in reading or writing, it seems well-
nigh impossible. If the consciousness has to be busy
with the remembrance, the attention will get divided and
the work will not be properly done.*

A: It is because people live in the surface mind and are identified with it. When one lives more inwardly, it is only the surface consciousness that is occupied and one stands behind it in
another which is silent and self-offered.

*

*Q: Does this consciousness come only by aspiration or
can one have it by following a mental discipline?*

A: One starts by a mental effort. Afterwards it is an inner consciousness that is formed which need not be always thinking of
the Mother.

*

*Q: There are two ways of making an offering to the
Mother: one is to offer an act at her feet as one might
offer a flower; the other is to withdraw one's personality
altogether and to feel as if she is doing all the actions
which one performs. In the first way there is duality
between the worker and her; but in the second there is a
close intimacy and union. Which of these two ways is
better for the Sadhana?*

A: There is no need to ask which is the better as they are not
mutually exclusive. It is the mind that regards them as opposites.

The psychic being can offer the act while the nature is passive to the Force (the ego being expunged or having withdrawn) and feels the Mother's Force doing the act and her Presence in it.

5-11-1938

*

Q: When one works, one aspires for the Mother's Force to take up one's activity in due course. What should one aspire for when one is not working?

A: For the Mother's power to work and bring down by the proper stages the higher consciousness. Also for the system to be more and more fit — quiet, egoless, surrendered.

NEED OF MASTERY IN WORK

Mother does not disapprove of your writing a book — what she does not like is your being so lost in it that you can do nothing else. You must be master of what you do and not possessed by it. She quite agrees to your finishing and offering the book on your birthday if that can be done. But you must not be carried away — you must keep your full contact with higher things.

1-5-1934

CONDITIONS OF PERFECT SERVICE

Efface the stamp of ego from the heart and let the love of the Mother take its place. Cast from the mind all insistence on your personal ideas and judgments, then you will have the wisdom to understand her. Let there be no obsession of self-will, ego-drive in the action, love of personal authority, attachment to personal preference, then the Mother's force will be able to act clearly in you and you will get the inexhaustible energy for which you ask and your service will be perfect.

27-11-1940

*

Yes, that is the most important thing — to get over ego, anger, personal dislikes, self-regarding sensitiveness, etc. Work is not only for work's sake, but as a field of Sadhana, for getting rid of the lower personality and its reactions and acquiring a full surrender to the Divine. As for the work itself, it must be done according to the organisation arranged or sanctioned by the Mother. You must always remember that it is her work and not personally yours.

23-3-1935

*

I can only repeat what I have already written whenever these circumstances and feelings come to you. To leave your work is not a solution — it is through work that one can detect and progressively get rid of the feelings and movements that are contrary to the Yogic ideal — those of the ego.

Work should be done for the Mother and not for oneself, — that is how one encourages the growth of the psychic being and overcomes the ego. The test is to do the work given by the Mother without *abhimāna* or insistence or personal choice or prestige, — not getting hurt by anything that touches the pride, *amour-propre* or personal preference.

It is a high and great ideal that is put before the Sadhak through work and it is not possible to realise it suddenly, but to grow steadily into it is possible, if one keeps the aim always before one — to be a selfless and perfectly tempered instrument for the work of the Divine Mother.

28-9-1935

THE IMPERSONAL WORKER

To be impersonal generally is not to be ego-centric, not to regard things from the point of view of how they affect oneself, but to see what things are in themselves, to judge impartially, to do what is demanded by the purpose of things or by the will of the Master of things, not by one's own personl point of view or egoistic interest or ego-formed idea or feeling. In work it is to do what is best for the work, without regard to one's own prestige or convenience, not to regard the work as one's own but as the Mother's, to do it according to rule, discipline, impersonal arrangement, even if conditions are not favourable to do the best according to the conditions, etc., etc. The impersonal worker puts his best capacity, zeal, industry into the work, but not his personal ambitions, vanity, passions. He has always something in view that is greater than his little personality and his devotion or obedience to that dictates his conduct.

29-6-1935

*

It would be dangerous to take every "inner prompting" as if it were a prompting or initiation of action from the Mother. What seems an inner prompting may come from anywhere, any force good or bad seeking to fulfil itself.

One may have ego about the work even if the work itself comes from the Mother. The ego of the instrument is one of the things against which there must be special care in the Yoga.

When one is doing the work, usually the urge of the force that works and the preoccupation of doing it and getting it done or the pleasure of doing it are sufficient and the mind does not think of anything else. Afterwards the sense of "I did it" comes up. With some, however, the ego is active during the work itself.

3-11-1935

*

Q: If I work for the Mother alone, the interference of the ego would mean that it comes from outside. For I can't do work only for the Mother along with my ego.

A: Of course it is a way. But one has still to be careful about the ego. Even people who sincerely think that they are doing only the Mother's will are yet actuated by ego without knowing it.

4-4-1936

PROFIT FROM DIFFICULTIES IN WORK

I am glad of your resolution. The greater the difficulties that rise in the work the more one can profit by them in deepening the equality, if one takes it in the right spirit. You must also keep yourself open to receive the help towards that, for the help will always be coming from the Mother for the change of the nature.

29-9-1935

*

Do not allow yourself to be grieved or discouraged. Human beings have unfortunately the habit of being unkind to each other. But if you do your work in all sincerity, the Mother will be satisfied and all the rest will come afterwards.

*

You need not mind X's quick temper. Remind yourself always it is Mother's work you are doing and if you do it as well as you can remembering her, the Mother's Grace will be with you. That is the right spirit for the worker, and if you do it in that spirit, a calm consecration will come.

1-3-1933

ACTION FROM INNER COMMUNION WITH THE MOTHER

You must gather yourself within more firmly. If you disperse yourself constantly, go out of the inner circle, you will constantly move about in the pettinesses of the ordinary outer nature and under the influences to which it is open. Learn to live within, to act always from within, from a constant communion with the Mother. It may be difficult at first to do it always and completely, but it can be done if one sticks to it — and it is at that price, by learning to do that, that one can have the Siddhi in the Yoga.

5-6-1934

*

When things become confused outside, you must fix on your mind at once the rule of not judging by appearances — refer all to the Mother's Light within with the confidence that all will be clear.

The Mother says that if at any time you feel too much strain of work, you must tell her at once so that she may see what to do.

16-9-1933

OPENNESS TO THE MOTHER'S FORCE IN WORK
AND NEED OF REST

In the ordinary condition of the body if you oblige the body to do too much work, it can do with the support of vital force. But as soon as the work is done, the vital force withdraws and then the body feels fatigue. If this is done too much and for too long a time, there may be a breakdown of health and strength under the overstrain. Rest is then needed for recovery.

If, however, the mind and the vital get the habit of opening to the Mother's Force, they are then supported by the Force and may even be fully filled with it — the Force does the work and the body feels no strain or fatigue before or after. But even then, unless the body itself is open and can absorb and keep the Force, sufficient rest in between the work is absolutely necessary. Otherwise, although the body may go on for a very long time, yet in the end there can be a danger of a collapse.

The body can be sustained for a long time when there is the full influence and there is a single-minded faith and call in the mind and the vital; but if the mind or the vital is disturbed by other influences or opens itself to forces which are not the Mother's, then there will be a mixed condition and there will be sometimes strength, sometimes fatigue, exhaustion or illness or a mixture of the two at the same time.

Finally, if not only the mind and the vital, but the body also is open and can absorb the Force, it can do extraordinary things in the way of work without breaking down. Still even then rest is necessary. That is why we insist on those who have the impulse of work keeping a proper balance between rest and labour.

A complete freedom from fatigue is possible, but that comes only when there is a complete transformation of the law of the body by the full descent of a supramental Force into the earth-nature.

*

This is the thing that used to happen daily to the physical workers in the Ashram. Working with immense energy and enthusiasm, with a passion for the work they might after a time feel tired, then they would call the Mother and a sense of rest came into them and with or after it a flood of energy so that twice the amount of work could be done without the least fatigue or reaction. In many there was a spontaneous call of the vital for the Force, so that they felt the flood of energy as soon as they began the work and it continued so long as the work had to be done.

26-3-1936

VITAL ENERGY IN WORK

Don't be afraid of vital energy in work. Vital energy is an invaluable gift of God without which nothing can be done — as the Mother has always insisted from the beginning; it is given that His work may be done. I am very glad that it has come back, the cheerfulness and optimism with it. That is as it should be.

IX

THE MOTHER AND THE WORKING
OF THE ASHRAM

THE MOTHER AND THE WORKING
OF THE ASHRAM

THE MOTHER'S SADHANA IN THE SADHAKS

Naturally, the Mother does the Sadhana in each Sadhak — only it is conditioned by their zeal and their receptivity.

4-1-1935

*

The Mother has her own experience in bringing down the things that have to be brought down — but what the Sadhaks experience she had long ago. The Divine does the Sadhana first for the world and then in others.

12-9-1934

*

I have said that the Divine does the Sadhana first for the world and then gives what is brought down to others. There can be no Sadhana without realisations and experiences. The *Prayers*[1] are a record of Mother's experiences.

4-1-1935

PSYCHIC CONTACT IN THE ASHRAM AND OUTSIDE

It is certainly quite true that the psychic contact can exist at a distance and that the Divine is not limited by place but is everywhere. It is not necessary *for everybody* to be in the Ashram or physically near the Mother in order to lead the spiritual life or to practise the Yoga, especially in its earlier stages. But that is only one side of the truth, there is another. Otherwise the logical conclusion might be that there was no necessity for the Mother to be here at all, or for the existence of the Ashram, or for anyone to come here.

[1] *Prayers and Meditations* of the Mother. See Part Three.

The psychic being is there in all, but in very few is it well developed, well built up in the consciousness or prominent in the front; in most it is veiled, often ineffective or only an influence, not conscious enough or strong enough to support the spiritual life.

It is for this reason that it is necessary for those drawn towards this Truth to come here in order that they may receive the touch which will bring about or prepare the awakening of the psychic being — that is for them the beginning of the effective psychic contact.

It is also for this reason that a stay here is needed for many — if they are ready — in order that under the direct influence and nearness they may have the development or building up of the psychic being in the consciousness or its coming to the front. When the touch has been given or the development effected, so far as the Sadhak is at the moment capable of it, he returns to the outside world and under the protection and guidance even at a distance is able to keep the contact and go on with his spiritual life. But the influences of the outside world are not favourable to the psychic contact and the psychic development and, if the Sadhak is not sufficiently careful or concentrated, the psychic contact may easily be lost after a time or get covered over and the development may become retarded, stationary or even diminished by adverse movements or influences. It is therefore that the necessity exists and is often felt of a return to the place of the central influence in order to fortify or recover the contact or to restore or give a fresh forward impulse to the development. The aspiration for such nearness from time to time is not a vital desire; it becomes a vital desire only when it is egoistically insistent or mixed with a vital motive, but not if it is an aspiration of the psychic being calm, deep and without clamour in it or perturbing insistence.

This for those who are not called upon or are not *yet* called upon to live in this Ashram under the direct pressure of the central Force and Presence. Those who must so live are those called from the very beginning or who have become ready or who are for some reason or another given a chance to form a part of the work or creation which is being prepared by Yoga. For them the stay here in the atmosphere, the nearness are indispensable; to depart would be for them a renunciation of the opportunity given them, a turning of the back upon the spiritual destiny. Their difficulties are often in appearance greater than the struggle of those who remain outside because the demand and the pressure are greater; but so also is their opportunity greater and the power and the influence for development poured upon them and that too which they can spiritually become and will become if they are faithful to the choice and the call.

7-10-1931

*

Q: Is there any special effect of physical nearness to the Mother?

A: It is indispensable for the fullness of the Sadhana on the physical plane. Transformation of the physical and external being is not possible otherwise.

18-8-1933

*

Q: Is it possible to receive the Mother's contact and help almost in the same way at a great distance — say Bombay or Calcutta — as here in the Ashram?

A: One can receive everywhere and if there is a strong spiritual consciousness one can make great progress. But experience does not support the idea that it makes no difference or is almost the same.

18-8-1933

DECISION TO JOIN THE ASHRAM

There should be no desire or anxiety in your mind to get these people or others to come here. These things ought to be decided on one side by their call and fitness and on the other by the will of the Mother.

28-6-1936

CHOICE FROM WITHIN

It is not possible for the Mother to tell you to remain, if you are yourself in your mind and vital eager to go. It is from within yourself that there must come the clear will on one side or the other.

24-2-1932

PERIOD OF PROBATION

Well, it is better not to write anything too positive. Nowadays, especially, the Mother takes people in such circumstances on probation, she does not give them large immediate assurances, but waits to see how they open. If he justifies his aspiration all will be well.

26-2-1943

FULL ACCEPTANCE BY THE MOTHER

Q: When a person begins to do Yoga under the Mother's care, is he not fully taken up by her?

A: Not until he is ready. He has first to accept her and then to give up more and more his ego. There are Sadhaks who at every step revolt, oppose the Mother, contradict her will, criticise her decisions. How can she take them up fully in such conditions?

21-6-1933

*

Q: Is there really any difference between the Guru, the

Divine and the Truth in our Yoga? I have been consider-
ing that the Mother and yourself are not only the Gurus
but also the Divine, and that whatever either of you say
is the law of the Truth. Why then are you using (in reply
to my question on discipline) these three different words?

A: I wrote the general law of spiritual life and obedience. You
have to know that as well as its special application here. Moreover many here are satisfied with saying, "The Mother is divine,"
but they do not follow her commands — others do not really
regard her as Divine — they treat her as if she were an ordinary
Guru.

13-6-1933

*

Q: Yesterday you spoke about the Mother's commands.
What are they? I want to try to follow them.

A: They are supposed to be known. You have to do the right
thing and follow the Yoga sincerely.

14-6-1933

*

Q: We are told the Mother can act best if a Sadhak is
sincere. But what is meant by this?

A: What is meant by sincere Sadhana? In the Mother's definition of sincere, it means "opening only to the Divine Forces"
i.e. rejecting all the others even if they come.

21-4-1936

SPIRITUAL POSSIBILITY DUE TO THE MOTHER'S PRESENCE

Certainly very few seem to realise what a possibility has been
given them here — all has been turned into an opportunity for

the bubbling of the vital or the Tamas of the physical rather than used for the intended psychic and spiritual purpose.

7-3-1936

*

I was not speaking of any particular thing — but the whole spiritual possibility due to the Mother's presence here. Very few realise what that means and even those who have some idea of it take little advantage and allow their lower nature to block the progress.

9-3-1936

*

Because people are living here under the Mother's shelter and saved from the great sufferings and tragedies of human life, they must needs spin despairs and tragedies out of nothing. The vital wants to indulge its sorrow sense and shout and groan and weep and if it can't have a good or big reason for doing it, it will use a bad or small one.

1-3-1936

NECESSITY OF TRANSFORMING THE VITAL

FOR SUCCESS IN YOGA

Q: I had a belief that all those who have been called to do this Yoga will realise the Divine in this very birth sooner or later. But I heard from someone: "The Mother has of course chosen only those who have got capacity to do this Yoga, but they will reach the goal only if the vital gets transformed. If not, they will realise in the next birth." Is it so?

A: Mother has never spoken anything to be done in the next birth. Naturally the vital has to be transformed if one is to succeed.

15-1-1934

REASONS FOR SADHAKS GOING AWAY FROM THE MOTHER

> *Q: How is it that some who come to the Mother with a clear aspiration and call go away from her after some time? What is it that takes them away?*

A: Through the suggestions of the hostile forces, because of pride, egoism, ambition, sexual desire, vanity, greed or any other vital impulse urged by the hostile Powers.

*

> *Q: Are the vital forces so strong that in spite of a clear aspiration and Divine call in a person they can draw him away from the Mother?*

A: Every man is free at every moment to consent to the Divine call or not to consent, to follow the lower nature or to follow his soul.

*

> *Q: Does their leaving the path not mean that they were unable to judge by their knowledge whether their call for the Divine was true or not?*

A: All this about judging is nonsense. You feel the call or you do not and if you feel the call, you follow it without calculating or counting risks or asking whether you are fit or not.

*

> *Q: When people strongly feel the urge to leave the Sadhana and go away from the Mother, what is the best way for them to counteract this urge and stick on to the Mother?*

A: By understanding that it is the Devil who tempts them and not listening to the Devil.

*

> *Q: Can those Sadhaks, who have lived in the Ashram
> for many years, forget the Mother's Grace after leaving
> it?*

A: Some of them seem to forget.

*

> *Q: Is there any possibility of their returning to do the
> Sadhana under the Mother?*

A: It depends on the person.

6-9-1933

*

When the psychic being has been once fully awake, then it is not
possible for the Sadhak to revolt and go away; for if he does,
he leaves his soul behind with the Mother and it is only the outer
being that lives for a while elsewhere. But that is too painful a
condition; one has either to come back or life becomes hardly
worth living.

20-11-1935

*

What you have written is quite correct. To say that the Divine
is defeated when a Sadhak goes away is an absurdity. If the
Sadhak allows his lower nature to get the better of him, it is his
defeat, not the Divine's. The Sadhak comes here not because
the Divine has need of him, but because he has need of the
Divine. If he carries out the conditions of the spiritual life and
gives himself to the Mother's leading, he will attain his goal, but
if he wants to lay down his own conditions and impose his own
ideas and his own desires on the Divine, then all the difficulty
comes. That is what happened to X and Y and several others.
Because the Divine does not yield to them they go away; but
how is that a defeat for the Divine?

27-5-1937

WORKING OF THE CONSCIOUS FORCE IN THE ASHRAM

What seems to me of more importance is to try to explain how things are worked out here. Indeed very few are the people who understand it and still fewer those who realise it.

There has never been, at any time, a mental plan, a fixed programme or an organisation decided beforehand. The whole thing has taken birth, grown and developed as a living being by a movement of consciousness (Chit-Tapas) constantly maintained, increased and fortified. As the Conscious Force descends in matter and radiates, it seeks for fit instruments to express and manifest it. It goes without saying that the more the instrument is open, receptive and plastic, the better are the results. The two obstacles that stand in the way of a smooth and harmonious working in and through the Sadhaks are:

(1) the preconceived ideas and mental constructions which block the way to the influence and the working of the Conscious Force.

(2) the preferences and impulses of the vital which distort and falsify the expression.

Both these things are the natural output of the ego. Without the interference of these two elements my physical intervention would not be necessary.

You are quite right when you do not believe in "Mother likes", "Mother dislikes": it is quite a childish interpretation.

There is a clear precise perception of the Force and the Consciousness at work, and whenever this Force gets distorted or the Consciousness is obscured in their action, I have to interfere and rectify the movement. In most cases things are mixed up and there again I have to intervene to separate the distorted transcription from the pure one.

Otherwise a great freedom of action is left to all, because the Conscious Force can express itself in innumerable ways and for the perfection and integrality of the manifestation no ways are to be *a priori* excluded, a trial is very often given before the selection is made.

22-8-1939

THE MOTHER AND THE ASHRAM'S DISCIPLINE

...He said, according to X, that the absence of discipline was the great bane in India: neither individuals nor groups had any discipline. Then why did he weep merely because he was not allowed to put his hand-bag in a place not intended for it? I do not agree myself with him in the idea that there is perfect discipline in the Ashram; on the contrary, there is a great lack of it, much indiscipline, quarrelling and self-assertion. What there is is organisation and order which the Mother has been able to establish and maintain in spite of all that. That organisation and order is necessary for all collective work; it has been an object of admiration and surprise for all from outside who have observed the Ashram; it is the reason why the Ashram has been able to survive and outlive the malignant attacks of many people who would otherwise have got it dissolved long ago. The Mother knew very well what she was doing and what was necessary for the work she has to do.

Discipline itself is not something especially Western; in Oriental countries like Japan, China and India it was at one time all-regulating and supported by severe sanctions in a way that Westerners would not tolerate. Socially whatever objections we may make to it, it is a fact that it preserved Hindu religion and Hindu society through the ages and through all vicissitudes. In the political field there was, on the contrary, indiscipline, individualism and strife; that is one reason why India collapsed and entered into servitude. Organisation and order were attempted but failed to endure. Even in the spiritual life India has had not only the free wandering ascetic, a law to himself, but has felt impelled to create orders of Sannyasins with their rules and governing bodies and there have also been monastic institutions with a strict discipline. Since no work can be done successfully without these things — even the individual worker, the artist for instance, has to go through a severe discipline in order to become efficient — why should the Mother be held to blame if she insists on discipline in the exceedingly difficult work she has put in her charge?

I don't see on what ground you expect order and organisation to be carried on without rules and without discipline. You seem to say that people should be allowed complete freedom with only such discipline as they choose to impose upon themselves; that might do if the only thing to be done were for each individual to get some inner realisation and life did not matter or if there were no collective life or work or none that had any importance. But this is not the case here. We have undertaken a work which includes life and action and the physical world. In what I am trying to do, the spiritual realisation is the first necessity, but it cannot be complete without an outer realisation also in life, in men, in this world. Spiritual consciousness within but also spiritual life without. The Ashram as it is now is not that ideal, for that all its members have to live in a spiritual consciousness and not in the ordinary egoistic mind and mainly rajasic vital nature. But, all the same, the Ashram is a first form which our effort has taken, a field in which the preparatory work has to be done. The Mother has to maintain it and for that all this order and organisation has to be there and it cannot be done without rules and discipline. Discipline is even necessary for the overcoming of the ego and the mental preferences and the rajasic vital nature, as a help to it at any rate. If these were overcome outward rules etc. would be less necessary; spontaneous agreement, unity, harmony and spontaneous right action might take its place. But while the present state of things exists, by the abandonment or leaving out of discipline except such as people choose or not choose to impose upon themselves, the result would be failure and disaster. ...On that principle the work also would have gone to pot, there would have been nothing but strife, assertion by each worker of his own idea and self-will and constant clashes; even as it is, that has abounded and it is only the Mother's authority, the frame of work she has given and her skill in getting incompatibilities to act together that has kept things going.

I do not find that Mother is a rigid disciplinarian. On the contrary, I have seen with what a constant leniency, tolerant patience and kindness she has met the huge mass of indiscipline, disobedience, self-assertion, revolt that has surrounded her, even revolt to her very face and violent letters overwhelming her with the worst kind of vituperation. A rigid disciplinarian would not have treated these things like that.

I do not know what ill-treatment visitors have received, apart from the insistence on rules of which you complain; but it cannot be a general complaint, otherwise the number of visitors would not be constantly increasing nor would so many people want to come back again or even come every time or so many want to stay on if the Mother allowed them. After all, they do not come here on the basis of a social occasion but for Darshan of those whom they regard to be spiritually great or, in the case of constant visitors, for a share in the life of the Ashram and for spiritual advantage, and for both of these motives one would expect them to submit willingly to the conditions imposed and not to mind a little inconvenience.

As regards Golconde and its rules — they are not imposed elsewhere — there is a reason for them and they are not imposed for nothing. In Golconde Mother has worked out her own idea through Raymond, Sammer and others. First, Mother believes in beauty as a part of spirituality and divine living; secondly, she believes that physical things have the Divine Consciousness underlying them as much as living things; and thirdly that they have an individuality of their own and ought to be properly treated, used in the right way, not misused or improperly handled or hurt or neglected so that they perish soon and lose their full beauty or value; she feels the consciousness in them and is so much in sympathy with them that what in other hands may be spoilt or wasted in a short time last with her for years or decades. It is on this basis that she planned the Golconde. First, she wanted a high architectural beauty, and in this she succeeded — architects and people with architectural knowledge have admired it with enthusiasm as a remarkable achievement; one spoke of it as the finest building of its kind he had seen, with no equal in all Europe or America; and a French architect, pupil of a great master, said it executed superbly the idea which his master had been seeking for but failed to realise; but also she wanted all the objects in it, the rooms, the fitting, the furniture to be individually artistic and to form a harmonious whole. This, too, was done with great care. Moreover, each thing was arranged to have its own use, for each thing there was a place, and there should be no mixing up, or confused or wrong use. But all this had to be kept up and carried out in practice; for it was easy for people living there to create a complete confusion and misuse and to bring everything to disorder and ruination in a short time. That was why the rules were made and for no other purpose. The Mother hoped that if right people were accommodated there or others trained to a less rough and ready living than is common, her idea could be preserved and the wasting of all the labour and expense avoided.

Unfortunately, the crisis of accommodation came and we were forced to house people in Golconde who could not be accommodated elsewhere and a careful choice could not be made. So, often there was damage and misuse and the Mother had to spend 200/300 Rupees after Darshan to repair things and restore what had been realised. Y has taken the responsibility of the house and of keeping things right as much as possible. That was why she interfered in the hand-bag affair — it was as much a tragedy for the table as for the doctor, for it got scratched and spoiled by the hand-bag — and tried to keep both the bag and shaving utensils in the places that had been assigned for them. If I had been in the doctor's place, I would have been grateful to her for her care and solicitude instead of being upset by what ought to have been for him trifles, although, because of her responsibility, they had for her their importance. Anyhow, this is the rationale for the rules and they do not seem to me to be meaningless regulation and discipline.

Finally, about financial arrangements. It has been an arduous and trying work for the Mother and myself to keep up this Ashram, with its ever-increasing numbers, to make both ends meet and at times to prevent deficit budgets and their results; specially in this war time, when the expenses have climbed to a dizzy and fantastic height, only one accustomed to these things or who had similar responsibilities can understand what we have gone through. Carrying on anything of this magnitude without any settled income could not have been done if there had not been the working of a divine Force. Works of charity are not part of our work, there are other people who can see to that. We have to spend all on the work we have taken in hand and what we get is nothing compared to what is needed. We cannot undertake

things that would bring in money in the ordinary ways. We
have to use whatever means are possible. There is no general
rule that spiritual men must do works of charity or they should
receive and care for whatever visitors come or house and feed
them. If we do it, it is because it has become part of our work.
The Mother charges visitors for accommodation and food because she has expenses to meet and cannot make money out of
air; she charges in fact less than her expense. It is quite natural
that she should not like people to take advantage of her and
allow those who try to take meals in the Dining Room under
false pretences; even if they are a few at first, yet if this were
allowed, a few would soon become a legion. As for people being
allowed to come in freely for Darshan without permission, which
would soon convert me into a thing for show and an object of
curiosity, often critical or hostile curiosity, it is I who would be
the first to cry "stop".

I have tried to explain our standpoint and have gone to some
length to do it. Whether it is agreed with or not, at any rate it is
a standpoint and I think a rational one. I am writing only on the
surface and I do not speak of what is behind or from the Yogic
standpoint, the standpoint of the Yogic consciousness from
which we act; that would be more difficult to express. This is
merely for intellectual satisfaction and there there is always room
for dispute.

25-2-1945

*

It is very true that physical things have a consciousness within
them which feels and responds to care and is sensitive to careless
touch and rough handling. To know or feel that and learn to be
careful of them is a great progress of consciousness. It is always
so that the Mother has felt and dealt with physical things and
they remain with her much longer and in a better condition than
with others and give their full use.

16-4-1936

*

The Mother has never objected to people who "cannot pay" residing or visiting the Ashram without paying; she expects payment only from visitors who can pay. She did object strongly to the action of some rich visitors (on one occasion) who came here, spent money lavishly on purchases etc. and went off without giving anything to the Ashram or even the smallest offering to the Mother — that is all.

21-10-1943

TWO FOUNDATIONS OF THE ASHRAM'S MATERIAL LIFE

What your vital being seems to have kept all along is the "bargain" or the "mess" attitude in these matters. One gives some kind of commodity which he calls devotion or surrender and in return the Mother is under obligation to supply satisfaction for all demands and desires spiritual, mental, vital and physical, and, if she falls short in her task, she has broken her contract. The Ashram is a sort of communal hotel or mess, the Mother is the hotel-keeper or mess-manager. One gives what one can or chooses to give, or it may be nothing at all except the aforesaid commodity; in return the palate, the stomach and all the physical demands have to be satisfied to the full; if not, one has every right to keep one's money and to abuse the defaulting hotel-keeper or mess-manager. This attitude has nothing whatever to do with Sadhana or Yoga and I absolutely repudiate the right of anyone to impose it as a basis for my work or for the life of the Ashram.

There are only two possible foundations for the material life here. One is that one is a member of an Ashram founded on the principle of self-giving and surrender. One belongs to the Divine and all one has belongs to the Divine; in giving one gives not what is one's own but what already belongs to the Divine. There is no question of payment or return, no bargain, no room for demand and desire. The Mother is in sole charge and arranges things as best they can be arranged within the means at her disposal and the capacities of her instruments. She is under no obligation to act according to the mental standards or vital desires and claims of the Sadhaks; she is not obliged to use a democratic equality in her dealings with them. She is free to deal with each according to what she sees to be his true need or what is best for him in his spiritual progress. No one can be her judge or impose on her his own rule and standard; she alone can make rules, and she can depart from them too if she thinks fit, but no one can demand that she shall do so. Personal demands and desires cannot be imposed on her. If anyone has what he finds to be a real need or a suggestion to make which is within the province assigned to him, he can do so; but if she gives no sanction, he must remain satisfied and drop the matter. This is the spiritual discipline of which the one who represents or embodies the Divine Truth is the centre. Either she is that and all this is the plain common sense of the matter; or she is not and then no one need stay here. Each can go his own way and there is no Ashram and no Yoga.

If on the other hand one is not ready to be a member of the Ashram or bear the discipline and is still admitted to some place in the Yoga, he remains apart and meets his own expenses. There is no discipline for him on the material plane, except the rules necessary for the safety of the work; there is no material responsibility for the Mother.

                                                               11-4-1930

THE MOTHER'S PRINCIPLE OF ACTION AND WASTE

I did not consider it necessary to say anything about the question of waste beyond assuring you that the undertaking of useless and unnecessary work only in order to keep the men employed was no part of the Mother's principle of action. The Mother did not know to what pipe you referred and had no time or inclination to make enquiries about it. It is quite true that, so long at least as the Sadhaks are not Siddha Yogis, self-control is the law; they have to learn to refrain from indulgence of excess in any direction — the provision made for them being ample for a Sadhak and much more than is allowed elsewhere — and from negligence, greed or the pursuit of individual fancy. When they do these things, the Mother does not intervene at every moment to check them; a standard has been set, they have been warned against waste, a framework has been created, for the rest they are expected to learn and grow out of their weaknesses by their own consciousness and will with the Mother's inner force to aid them. In the organisation of work there was formerly a formidable waste due to the workers and Sadhaks following their own fancy almost entirely without respect for the Mother's will; that was largely checked by reorganisation. But waste to a certain extent continues and is almost inevitable so long as the Sadhaks and workers are imperfect in their will and consciousness, do not follow in spirit or detail the Mother's recommendations or think themselves wiser than herself and make undue room for their "independent" ideas. Here too the Mother does not always insist, she watches and observes, intervenes outwardly more than in the individual lives of the Sadhaks, but still leaves room for them to grow by consciousness and experience and the lesson of their own mistakes and often employs an inner in preference to an outer pressure. In these matters she must exercise her own judgment and vision and there is no use in anybody offering his approval or censure — for she works from a different centre of vision than theirs and they have not a superior light by which they can judge or guide her.

As regards waste, I must point out that in our view free expenditure is not always waste, to have a higher standard than is current in this very tamasic and backward place is not necessarily waste. In matters of building and maintenance of buildings as in others of the same order the Mother has from the beginning set up a standard which is not that current here — the usual system being to use the cheapest possible materials, the cheapest labour and to disregard appearance, allowing things to go shabby or making only patchwork to keep them up. I suppose "thrifty" minds would consider the local principle to be sound and a higher standard to be waste. If the higher standard has been kept, it is not for the glory of anyone, the Ashram or the Mother — the principle of glory being foreign to Yoga, but from another point of view which is not mental and can only be fully appreciated when the consciousness is capable of understanding the vision of things with which the Mother started her work. I do not consider it useful to write about that now, — the general misunderstanding in these subjects can only disappear when the Sadhaks have got rid of the ordinary mind and vital and are able to look at things from the same vision level as that from which the conception of the Yoga and the work took its rise....

For the same reason I refuse to answer criticisms, attacks and questionings directed against the Mother. Whether in work or in Yoga, the Mother acts not from the mind or from the level of consciousness from which these criticisms arise but from quite another vision and consciousness. It is perfectly useless therefore and it is inconsistent with the position she ought to occupy to accept the ordinary mind and consciousness as judge and tribunal and allow her to appear before it and defend her. Such a procedure is itself illogical and inconsequent and can lead nowhere; it can only create or prolong a false atmosphere wholly inimical to success in the Sadhana. For that reason if these doubts are raised, I no longer answer them or answer in such a way as to discourage a repetition of any such challenge. If people want to understand why the Mother does things, let them get into the same inner consciousness from which she sees and acts. As to what she is, that also can only be seen either with the eye of faith or of a deeper vision. That too is the reason why we keep here people who have not yet acquired the necessary faith or vision; we leave them to acquire it from within as they will do if their will of Sadhana is sincere.

I have written at length on this question once for all; I do not propose to repeat it. People no longer expect it from me; even those who did expect it formerly have ceased to do so. On other questions, so far as they are not connected or mixed up with those things, I may answer hereafter as I find time.

26-12-1936

*

The Mother does not provide the Sadhaks with comforts because she thinks that the desires, fancies, likings, preferences should be satisfied — in Yoga people have to overcome these things. In any other Ashram they would not get one tenth of what they get here, they would have to put up with all possible discomforts, privations, hard and rigorous austerities, and if they complained, they would be told they were not fit for Yoga. If there is a different rule here, it is not because the desires have to be indulged, but because they have to be overcome in the presence of the objects of desire and not in their absence. The first rule of Yoga is that the Sadhak must be content with what comes to him, much or little; if things are there, he must be able to use them without attachment or desire; if they are not he must be indifferent to their absence.

7-1-1937

DEMAND AND DESIRE

Q: What sort of things can come under the category of "demand and desire"? What is the exact form of "demand and desire"?

A: There are no special sort of things — demand and desire can cover all things whatsoever — they are subjective, not objective and have no special form. Demand is when you claim something to get or possess, desire is a general term. If one expects that the Mother shall smile at him at the Pranam and feels wronged if one does not get it, that is a demand. If one wants it and grieves at not getting it, but without revolt or sense of an unjust deprivation that shows desire. If one feels joy at her smile, but remains calm in its absence knowing that all the Mother does is good, then there is no demand or desire.

*

Q: You have said about the Divine: "He may give all that is truly needed — but people usually interpret this idea in the sense that He gives all that they think or feel they need. He may do that — but also He may not." But it is said that He supplies all our psychic needs.

A: In the end, yes; but here too people expect Him to supply them constantly, which does not always happen.

30-1-1936

*

Q: If our desires are to be rejected, why does Mother sometimes satisfy them?

A: It is you who have to get rid of them. If the Mother does not satisfy at all and the Sadhak keeps them, they will get stronger by suggestion from outside. Each one has to deal with them from within.

4-9-1933

*

Q: X told me that if anything comes to us without our asking for it we should not reject it. For example, someone offers us sweetmeat: we may accept it. But we should not be depressed when things desired by us are not given to us. What do you say about that?

A: How can such a rule stand? Supposing someone comes and offers you meat or wine, can you accept it? Obviously not. A hundred other instances could be given where the rule would not stand. What the Mother gives or allows you, you can take.

24-3-1933

THE MOTHER'S SOLE AUTHORITY OVER
THE ASHRAM WORK

If anybody in the Ashram tries to establish a supremacy or dominating influence over others, he is in the wrong. For it is bound to be a wrong vital influence and come in the way of the Mother's work.

All the work should be done under the Mother's sole authority. All must be arranged according to her free decision. She must be free to use the capacities of each separately or together according to what is best for the work and best for the worker. None should regard or treat another member of the Ashram as his subordinate. If he is in charge, he should regard the others as his associates and helpers in the work, and he should not try to dominate or impose on them his own ideas and personal fancies, but only see to the execution of the will of the Mother. None should regard himself as a subordinate, even if he has to carry out instructions given through another or to execute under supervision the work he has to do.

All should try to work in harmony, thinking only of how best to make the work a success; personal feelings should not be allowed to interfere, for this is a most frequent cause of disturbance in the work, failure or disorder.

If you keep this truth of the work in mind and always abide by it, difficulties are likely to disappear; for others will be influenced by the rightness of your attitude and work smoothly with you or, if through any weakness or perversity in them, they create difficulties, the effects will fall back on them and you will feel no disturbance or trouble.

*

There is one thing everybody should remember that everything should be done from the point of view of Yoga, of Sadhana, of growing into a divine life in the Mother's consciousness. To insist upon one's own mind and its ideas, to allow oneself to be governed by one's own vital feelings and reactions should not be the rule of life here. One has to stand back from these, to be detached, to get in their place the true knowledge from above, the true feelings from the psychic within. This cannot be done if the mind and vital do not surrender, if they do not renounce their attachment to their own ignorance which they call truth, right, justice. All the trouble rises from that; if that were overcome, the true basis of life, of work, of harmony of all in the union with the Divine would more and more replace the trouble and difficulty of the present.

*

In your letter to the Mother I note that you profess to be writing a confession, but the tone of it is rather a justification of your faultless self accompanied by an accusation against the Mother of favouritism, bad temper, and injustice. I observe also that your statement of facts is incorrect and as far as it concerns the Mother, grotesque. You lay stress too on a point in which you can justify yourself, and you ignore all the rest in which you were in fault. I will assume, however, that all this was unintentional and that, in writing such a letter, you were unconscious of the movements of your vital being which inspired its spirit and tone.

I would suggest that in your relations with others, — which seem always to have been full of disharmony, — when incidents occur, it would be much better for you not to take the standpoint that you are all in the right and they are all in the wrong. It would be wiser to be fair and just in reflection, seeing where you have gone astray, and even laying stress on your own fault and not on theirs. This would probably lead to more harmony in your relations with others; at any rate, it would be more conducive to your inner progress, which is more important than to be the top-dog in a quarrel. Neither is it well to cherish a spirit of self-justification and self-righteousness and a wish to conceal either from yourself or from the Mother your faults or your errors.

As for your doubts about the Mother, they are not likely to disappear so long as you think you can read the Mother's mind by the light of your own and pass your mental judgments on her and her action from those erroneous data. Nor can they easily disappear if your faith breaks down every time that she does something which your limited intelligence cannot understand or which is displeasing to the feelings and demands of your vital nature. If you do not believe that she has a consciousness greater and wider than yours and not measurable by ordinary standards and judgments, at the very least a Yogic consciousness, I do not see on what ground you are practising Yoga here under her guidance. Those who constantly doubt and criticise and blame or attribute her actions to the most common and vulgar human feelings and motives and yet pretend to accept her or to accept myself and my Yoga, are guilty of a stupid and irrational inconsequence. As for understanding, that is another matter. I would suggest that you must grow out of the ordinary mind and become conscious with the true consciousness before you can hope to do it. And for that faith and surrender and fidelity and openness are conditions of some importance.

6-11-1929

*

How can you do like the Mother or do the work that she can do? That is the ambition and vanity coming up.

5-11-1932

*

There is no reason for your seeing the Mother nor is this the time for it. Nor is there any room for discussion in this matter.

There are two things that must be clearly understood. The work here is the Mother's and she has the right to give her orders in whatever way she pleases and they must be obeyed. No one can be allowed to flout her orders, however conveyed, or insist on his own ideas, will or fancies. If you are prepared to respect and obey her orders without making conditions, you can be allowed to continue the work, otherwise you must discontinue.

Secondly, all violence must stop. If you want to remain in the Ashram, this kind of conduct must cease.

18-7-1937

THE MOTHER'S WORK IN THE VITAL PLANE

Your dream was evidently a symbolic representation of some part of the vital plane (corresponding to a part of human nature also) in which the Mother had made her house (established something of her consciousness). The village represented some formation of human life in which there is outward beauty and harmony as in certain parts of European life, but no touch of the Divine. The jungle represented the surroundings in which this formation has been made — it is made in the midst of a vital nature which is wild and savage and full of dangerous things — the village, the formation is therefore something quite insecure and artificial. That is indeed the nature of much of human civilisation, an artificial construction in the midst of a dangerously unregenerated vital nature, and it can collapse at any moment. The sea is the vital consciousness itself, for water is often a symbol of the vital. The footpath seems to indicate something the Mother wants the Sadhaks to build, to form in that part of the vital, but which is not easy to make and only can be made by constant perseverance which will finally prevail against the instability of the vital. Vital dreams of this kind are often very interesting and instructive if one can get the clue to their symbols, but to get the clue is not always easy.

13-2-1936

*

My description of the vital applied to that part of it which you saw in dream — it does not describe the vital in the Ashram but of certain sides of ordinary human existence. Nevertheless the human vital everywhere, in the Ashram also, is full of unruly and violent forces — anger, pride, jealousy, desire to dominate, selfishness, insistence on one's own will, ideas, preferences, indiscipline — and it is these things that are the cause of the disorder and difficulty in the Ashram work. The rule established in order to control or combat these tendencies is that the Mother's will and the rule and discipline established by her shall be followed and not each worker be led by his own ego. But there are many who insist on their own ego and resent discipline. They are ready to follow the Mother's will and rule and discipline only in name and so far as it agrees with their own ideas and preferences. There is no cure for this except by an inner change. In outside life discipline is enforced because refusal of discipline is visited by severe penalties or else results in so much discomfort of various kinds that the indisciplined man has either to submit or to go. But here in the Ashram it is not possible to enforce the rule in this way. An inner obedience has to be given as the source of the outer obedience. The only remedy is the descent into the consciousness of that golden lotus which you saw in your vision. Everyone in whom it is established or even who feels its influence will become a centre of the true consciousness and true action which will change life in the Ashram.

14-2-1936

NECESSITY OF DEPARTMENTAL HEADS

It is not physically possible for the Mother to give the work direct to each worker and exercise a direct control, so that physically as well as inwardly he may offer it to her. For every department there must be a head who consults her in all important matters and reports everything to her, but in minor matters he need not always come for a previous decision — that is not possible. X is there in the Building Department as the head because he is a qualified engineer. That is a necessity of outward organisation which is unavoidable here as elsewhere and has to be accepted if the work is to be done. But it does not mean that X or any other head is to be considered as a superior person or that one has to surrender to his ego. One has to get rid of his own ego as far as possible and regard the work done under whatever conditions as an offering to the Mother.

20-8-1936

*

It is quite impossible for the Mother to see to every detail of the organisation of the Ashram in person; even as it is, she has no time free at all. It is understood that you can have..., but it is with those who have charge that you must insist on the execution of any arrangement.

20-7-1933

*

It was the Mother who selected the heads [of departments] for her purpose in order to organise the whole; all the lines of the work, all the details were arranged by her and the heads trained to observe her methods and it was only afterwards that she stepped back and let the whole thing go on on her lines but with a watchful eye always. The heads are carrying out her policy and instructions and report everything to her and she often modifies what they do when she thinks fit. Their action is not perfect, because they themselves are not yet perfect and they are also hampered by the ego of the workers and the Sadhaks. But nothing can be perfect so long as the Sadhaks and workers do not come to the realisation that they are not here for their ego and self-indulgence of their vital and physical demands but for a high and exacting Yoga of which the first aim is the destruction of desire and the substitution for it of the Divine Truth and the Divine Will.

9-1-1936

*

What I meant in my letter was that the Mother does not usually think about these things herself, take the initiative and direct each one in each instance what they shall do or how, unless there is some special occasion for doing so. This she does not do, in fact, in any department of work. She keeps her eye generally on the work, sanctions or corrects or refuses sanction, intervenes when she thinks necessary. It is only a few matters in which she takes the initiative, plans and designs, gives special and detailed orders. In the line of embroidery, X refers to her anything necessary or any of the workers undertakes something and informs the Mother that she would like to do something for her, handkerchief, apron, cover or sari. The Mother approves or disapproves what is suggested or suggests something herself or changes what is proposed. Work done in this way is as much work done according to the Mother's will as anything initiated, thought of and planned in whole and detail by her alone. I do not quite understand why you should consider that this way of work implies an absence of unity with the Mother's will or of surrender on your part. It is the offering within you that is important and brings in time the full completeness of surrender.

17-9-1936

*

I do not quite understand on what you want the *anumati*. If it is about embroidery, I have said that to follow the existing arrangement, viz., when you have the will or the inspiration to do some work of embroidery, then to put it before the Mother and take her sanction or ask for her decision, is quite a right way to work according to the Mother's will; it is not at all inconsistent with surrender. But if you prefer to leave everything to the Mother and not suggest or propose anything yourself, you can do that.

Mother only asked me to write to you about the way things are usually done, because as she is not in the habit of thinking herself about these things, it is not as easy for her to remember and think out something as to decide upon suggestions put before her.

18-9-1936

NEED OF LEARNING SUBORDINATION AND CO-OPERATION

The Mother has her own reasons for her decisions; she has to look at the work as a whole without regard to one department or branch alone and with a view to the necessities of the work and the management. Whatever work is done here, one has always to learn to subordinate or put aside one's own ideas and preferences about things concerning it and work for the best under the conditions and decisions laid down by her. This is one of the main difficulties throughout the Ashram, as each worker wants to do according to his own ideas, on his own lines according to what he thinks to be the right or convenient thing and expects that to be sanctioned. It is one of the principal reasons of difficulty, clash or disorder in the work, creating conflict between the workers themselves, conflict between the workers and the heads of departments, conflict between the idea of the Sadhaks and the will of the Mother. Harmony can only exist if all accept the will of the Mother without grudge and personal reaction.

Independent work does not exist in the Ashram. All is organised and interrelated, neither the heads of departments nor the workers are independent. To learn subordination and co-operation is necessary for all collective work; without it there will be chaos.

10-3-1936

*

It is impossible for the Mother to arrange the work according to personal considerations as then all work would become impossible.

25-7-1934

IMPORTANT POINTS FOR WORKING IN THE RIGHT SPIRIT

There are certain things that A must fix in his mind and feel and act in their spirit, if he is to get rid of his depression and unrest and feel happy and at home. You will explain clearly to him what I write here.

1. He is not here as B's nephew, but as a child of the Mother.

2. He is not here under the care, guardianship and control of B, but under the Mother's control and care and he owes allegiance to her alone.

3. The work given to him in the stores is the Mother's work and not B's; he must do it with that idea, as the Mother's work, and no other.

4. B is at the head of the stores, garden, granary and receives his directions from the Mother or reports his arrangements to her for approval — just as C in the B.D.[1] or D in the Dining Room or E or F in their departments. Others in these departments are supposed to receive their directions from the head and act in accordance. But this is because it is necessary for the discipline and good order of the work; it does not mean that the work is B's or the building work is C's or the Dining Room work is D's — all is the Mother's work and must be done by each, by the head as by the others, for her. It would not be possible to

---

[1] Building Department.

get the work done if each and every worker insisted on being independent and directly responsible to her or on doing things in his own way; there is too much of this spirit and it is the cause of much confusion and disorder. The Mother cannot see to the whole work herself physically and give orders direct to each worker; therefore the arrangement made is indispensable. On the other hand, the head of a department is also supposed to act according to the Mother's directions — or in their spirit when he is left free — and not otherwise; if he does according to his mere fancy or obeys his own personal likes and dislikes or misuses his trust for his personal satisfaction or convenience, he is answerable for any failure in the work that may result or wrong spirit or clash or confusion or false atmosphere.

5. Any work done personally for B or another (not for the Ashram) is not part of the Mother's work and the Mother has nothing to do with that; if such work is asked, A may do it if he likes or not do it if he thinks it improper.

6. A has been given one work at least by the Mother direct — that is the cleaning of the kitchen vessels. Let him do it according to the Mother's directions and with scrupulousness and perfection; it will be an opportunity for him to show what he can do and the rest can be seen to hereafter.

7. He is not bound to accept food from G and B or presents etc. ; if he does not like it, why does he receive these things? He is perfectly free to refuse. His staying here and everything else does not depend on B, but on the Mother alone — so he has no reason to fear.

8. Finally, he should clear his vital of restlessness and desires — for that in him as in everybody is the root cause of depression and, if he were elsewhere and under other circumstances, the depression would still come because the root cause would still be there. Here if he turns entirely to the Mother, opens to her and works and lives turning towards her, he will get release and happiness and grow into light and peace and become in all his being a child of the Divine.

19-3-1932

*

It is very good that you have spoken and cleared up things. Certainly, it is quite true that the inner being should be turned to the Mother and to her alone.

As for the work, the inner development, psychic and spiritual, is surely of the first importance and work merely as work is something quite minor. But work done as an offering to the Mother becomes itself a part of Sadhana and a means and a part of the inner development. That you will see more as the psychic grows within you. Apart from that the work is important because necessary to the maintenance of the Ashram, which is the frame of the Mother's action here.

A is not wrong in giving importance to persons. It is quite true that the work would go on if the persons now in charge were not there and others were in their place, but in most cases it would go on badly or at least worse than now and there would be no certainty that those others would be adequate instruments of the Mother's will. For the work of the charge of departments for instance done by men like A, B, C, there is needed a combination of qualities, a special capacity, a personality and the power of control called organisation and above all fidelity and obedience to the Mother's will, the faith in her perceptions and the desire to carry them out. It is not many in the Ashram who have that combination. Before the Mother took up directly through A the work, now concentrated in Aroumé and the granaries, all was confusion, disorder, waste, self-indulgence, disregard of the Mother's will. Now though things are far from perfect, because the workers are not at all perfect, still all that is changed. In that change your presence in the kitchen and D's in the granary has counted for much; without you there it would have been far more difficult to realise the organisation of things the Mother wanted and in those two parts of the work it might even have been impossible. The Divine Will is there but it works through persons and there is a great difference between one instrument and another — that is why the person can be of so much importance.

*

Certainly, I cannot say that the ideas you put forward in this letter are true. They are errors of the physical mind which seldom gets hold of the real truth of things. It is not a fact that the Mother got displeased and frowned on you every time you wrote about A. That is the kind of thing the Sadhaks are always thinking and saying about the Mother, that she is frowning on them in displeasure for this reason or smiling on them for that, and the reasons they assign are those suggested by their own physical minds, but have nothing to do with anything in the consciousness of the Mother which is not in a constant bubbling of human pleasure and displeasure. I have tried to explain that to the Sadhaks again and again but they prefer to believe that their own minds are infallible and that what I say is untrue. So I will only say that your idea is mistaken.

It is also not a fact that you cannot do Sadhana, for you were doing it for a time and doing it very well. But your physical mind came across and took you outside and is trying to keep you outside instead of allowing you to go and remain within. That is why I have been trying to persuade you to go within and not live in these outside ideas and reactions of the physical being which prevent Sadhana and only give trouble.

It is not a fact that the Mother wants you to be a puppet of A. As regards the work it is not at all clear that all you think is right and all A does is wrong. You speak of your personality and what you seem to say is that A is in the work trying to impose his personality and that you want to affirm yours against it and the Mother ought to have supported you, but she does not regard your personality at all but insists on your subordinating it to A's. But the Mother does not at all look at it from that standpoint or regard anybody's personality. In her view people's personalities which means their ego ought to have no place in the work. It is not your work or A's work, but the Divine work, the Mother's work and it is not to be governed by your ideas or feelings or A's ideas or feelings or B's or C's or D's or anybody else's, but by the vision, perception and will of the Mother which does not express any human personality (if it did there would be no justification for the existence of this Ashram) but proceeds from a deeper consciousness. It has been the great obstacle to the full success and harmony of the work that everybody almost has had this idea of his own personality, ideas, feelings etc. and more or less tried to insist on them — this has been the cause of most of the difficulties and of all the disharmony and quarrel. We want all this to stop; for when it stops altogether then there will be some possibility of the differences and turmoil ceasing and the work will better serve the purpose for which the Mother created it. That is why I have been trying to explain to you about the necessity of subordinating the personality and doing the work for the Divine, not insisting on one's own personality, ego, ideas, feelings as the important thing. There remains the question what is to be the relation between A and yourself in the work — this, as there is no more time today, I will write in another letter.

4-7-1937

P.S. When I say that you are mistaken or do not agree with you, you seem to think my letters show displeasure and that my disagreeing with you means that I am vexed with you for writing your views; but that is not so. If I answer what you write, it must be to tell you what seems to myself and to the Mother the true way of seeing things and acting. That does not imply any displeasure.

*

I do not think I said anywhere you had done anything contrary to A's instructions in your work. I was speaking of what you had written in criticism of his way of doing things, and especially I wanted to remove your idea that the necessity of acting under his instructions meant a disregard of your personality or a desire on the Mother's part to make you a puppet of A. Where there is a big work with several people working together for a purpose which is common to all and not personal to any, it cannot be done unless there is a fixed arrangement involving subordination and discipline in each worker. That is so everywhere, not here alone. A has to act under the Mother, carry out her instructions, work according to ideas she has given him. She has laid down the lines on which he must work, and whatever he does must be on those lines. He is not free to change them or do anything contrary to the ideas given him. Where he makes decisions in details of the work, they must be in consonance with these lines and ideas. He has to report to the Mother, to take her sanction and accept her decisions on all matters. If the Mother's decisions are contrary to his proposals or contradict his own ideas of what should be done, he has still to accept them and carry them out. The idea that the D.R. work is done according to his ideas and not the Mother's is an error. But all that is simply the necessity of the work, it is not a disregard of A's personality. In the same way you have to carry out A's instructions because he is charged by the Mother with the work and given authority by her. All the D.R. workers are in the same position and are supposed to carry out his instructions and keep him informed, because he is directly responsible to the Mother for everything and unless he has this authority he cannot carry out his responsibility. In the same way B has been asked to carry out your instructions in the kitchen because you are at the head of the kitchen. All that is not a disregard of your personality or of B's personality or an assertion of A's — it is the necessity of the work which cannot be smoothly done if there is not this arrangement. That is what I wanted you to understand so that you might see why the Mother wanted you to do like that, not for any other reason, but for the necessity of the work and so that it may be smoothly done.

On the other hand as you are at the head of the work and the practical working is in your hands, you have every right to put any difficulties before A and ask for a solution. He on his side will often need information from you and may need also to know what you think should be done. But if even after knowing, he thinks it right to follow his own idea of what should be done and not yours, you should not mind that. He has the responsibility and must act according to his lights subject to the sanction of the Mother. Your responsibility finishes when you have informed him and told him your idea. If his decision is wrong, it is for the Mother to change it.

I hope I have made the conditions clear. There is no necessity for you to agree with A's ideas nor outside the work are you under any obligation to do what he wants you to do. There you are quite free. It is only in the work that there is this necessity in action — for the sake of the work.

I have written so much because you wanted to know what the Mother expected you to do. It is not meant as a pressure upon you, but only to explain things and show you the way and the reason for which they have to be done.

5-7-1937

*

For the Sadhana, it is not true that some are here only because they give money and others because they are workers only. What is true is that there are many who can prepare themselves only by work, their consciousness not being yet ready for meditation of the more intense kind. But even for those who can do intense meditation from the beginning, Sadhana by work is also necessary in this Yoga. One cannot arrive at its goal by meditation alone. As for your own capacity, it was evident when for a fairly long period an active Sadhana was proceeding within you. Everybody's capacity however is limited — little can be done by one's own strength alone. It is reliance on the Divine Force, the Mother's Force and Light and openness to it that is the real capacity. This you had for a time, but as with many others it got clouded over by the coming up of the physical nature in its full force. This clouding happens to almost everybody at that stage, but it need not be lasting. If the physical consciousness resolves to open itself, then nothing more is needed for progress in the Sadhana.

10-7-1937

*

If you leave it to the Mother entirely, then what the Mother would want you to do is to go on with the work as best you can without allowing yourself to be disturbed or troubled by these things which you enumerate in your letters, without insisting on your own ideas or vital feelings. That is indeed the rule that all ought to follow, to do their work here as the Mother's work, not their own; the worker must not insist on the work being done according to his own ideas; for that is to treat it as his own work, not the Mother's. If there are inconveniences, troubles, things done not as he would like them to be, still he should go on doing his work as best he can under the circumstances. That is a rule of the Sadhana, to remain unconcerned by outward circumstances and quietly do what one has to do, what one can do, leaving the rest to the Mother. It is not possible to have everything perfect at present, even supposing that what one thinks to be right is the best. There is much in the Ashram and the work that is not as perfect as the Mother would like it to be, but she knows that the perfection she would like is not yet possible because of circumstances and the imperfection of her instruments; she arranges all for the best according to what is now possible. The worker should do his work in this spirit according to the Mother's arrangements and he should use his work as a means for growing spiritually in devotion, obedience, self-offering to the Mother, not insisting on himself, his ideas, his feelings and preferences. To be able to do that makes the consciousness ready for inner experience and progress in Sadhana.

I have tried to explain what the Mother wants and why she wants it. She wants you to do her work quietly, taking all inconveniences, defects and difficulties quietly, and doing your best; what X does or arranges should not disturb you — if he makes mistakes he is responsible for it to the Mother and it is for the Mother to see what is to be done. That is what she wants from you — if you can do it, then things will go more smoothly and she will be able more easily to lead things in the direction she wants. It is also, as I have tried to explain to you, the best thing for your own Sadhana.

5-7-1937

*

You must remember what I wrote to you before that the Mother wants you to remain quiet and do your work as well as you can under the circumstances without allowing yourself to be upset by these things. Any improvement in the conditions of life and work in the Ashram depends on each one trying to progress and open within to the true consciousness, growing spiritually within and not minding about the faults or conduct of others. No change can come by outer means; for this reason the Mother has long ceased to intervene outwardly in the clashes and disagreements between Sadhaks. Let each progress inwardly and then only the outer difficulties will disappear or become negligible.

21-4-1938

*

It is quite impossible to take you away from the kitchen and leave the others to work in your place. Such a solution would be very bad for you; for it would mean your losing a work in which the Mother's force has been long with you and sitting in your room with your thoughts which will not be helpful or according to your active nature. It would be very bad too for the kitchen; your place cannot be filled by anyone else there however well they may work in their own limits — none of them could be trusted with the responsibility the Mother has given to you.

The difficulties you have are the difficulties which are met in each department and office of the Ashram. It is due to the imperfections of the Sadhaks, to their vital nature. You are mistaken in thinking that it is due to your presence there and that if you withdrew all would go smoothly. The same state of things would go on among themselves, disagreements, quarrels, jealousies, hard words, harsh criticisms of each other. A's or any other's complaints against you are because you are firm and careful in your management; there are the same or similar complaints against B and others who discharge their trust given to them by the Mother scrupulously and well. There are against them the same murmurs and jealousies as are directed against you in the kitchen because of their position and their exercise of it. It would be no solution for B or others trusted by the Mother to withdraw and leave the place to those who would discharge the duty less scrupulously and less well. It is the same with you and the kitchen work; it is not the way out. The way out can only come by a change in the character of the Sadhaks brought about by the process of the Sadhana. Till then you should understand and be patient and not allow yourself to be disturbed by the wrong behaviour of the others, but remain quietly doing your best, sustaining yourself on the trust and support given you by B and the Mother. It is the Mother's work and the Mother is there to support you in doing it; put your reliance on that and do not allow the rest to affect you.

14-7-1935

*

I am rather surprised at your description of the people who show contempt towards you. Leaving aside A who is not in question, there is nobody working with you who is far advanced in Sadhana or is regarded by the Mother as more specially her own than are others. You are certainly as much her own as anybody else in the kitchen; she has always owned you as her child and little star and what can anybody be more than that? I see no reason therefore why you should care so much if anybody is not behaving well with you. I have told you already that people in the Ashram — it is true even of those who have inner experiences and some opening — are not yet free in their outer selves from ego and wrong ideas and wrong movements. It is no use getting distressed or depressed by that. What you must do is to be turned only to the Mother and relying on her go forward quietly with your work and Sadhana until the time when the Sadhaks are sufficiently awakened and changed to feel the need of greater harmony and union with each other. Let only your spiritual change and progress matter for you and for that trust wholly in the Mother's force and her grace which is with you — do not let things or people disturb you, — for compared with the truth within and the journey to the full Light of the Mother's Consciousness these things have no importance.

6-12-1935

*

I do not know why you suppose that the Mother was displeased with you for your letter. I think my answer was quite kind and without any touch of displeasure in it. I was silent about most of what you had written, because when there are letters of this kind I take it as an unburdening of the mind and always either remain silent in so far as it concerns others or else I say that we must rely on the growth of inner consciousness to get rid of the faults and deficiencies and mistakes of the Sadhaks. Silence does not imply that these defects and mistakes do not exist. But all have defects in various forms and make mistakes and the best Sadhaks are not exempt. The human way is to get angry and rebuke and condemn and, if the Mother does not do the same or is not severe, to think she is unjust or partial or unseeing or wilfully blind to the defects of her favourites. But the Mother is not blind; she knows very well the nature of all the Sadhaks, their faults as well as their merits; she knows too what human nature is and how these things come and that the human way of dealing with them is not the true way and changes nothing. It is why she has patience and love and charity for all, not for some alone, who are sincere in their work or their Sadhana.

It is strange also that you should conclude that she puts no value on you. From the first the Mother has had a special kindness for you; she has appreciated and supported you so steadily that people have accused her of blind partiality towards you just as they accuse her with regard to A. When you were in trouble and difficulty with suggestions and revolts, she was love and patience itself and helped and supported you through all. Afterwards since your Sadhana opened, we have been watching solicitously over it, — I have been spending time daily writing answers, giving you knowledge of what you should know, trying to lead you forward with love and care. Why should all this have been done, if we had no value for you?

You know these things but your physical mind has become too active and clouded your perception for a time. You must get back from it into your inner self.

30-8-1936

*

I wrote that your letter showed an attack of the old consciousness because of its tone "I will not bear these things — it is better for me to go away from here etc." These are the old suggestions, not the attitude of your inner being which was to give yourself and leave all to the Mother. The attitude of your inner being must also extend to your attitude to these outer things — knowing that whatever imperfections there are have to be worked out from within by each one, just as your own imperfections have to be worked out from within yourself by the Mother's aid and working in you.

That is with regard to your former letter. As to the present — to say what you see is all right but there is also in what you write a judgment passed upon what you see. These judgments you have expressed in a statement of what you think to be X's wrong motives, actions and mistakes. You put these statements and judgments before the Mother — for what? That she may take some action? But for that she must form her own judgment, and this she cannot do without facts, precise facts — she cannot act on a general statement by anyone. It is only if the person whom X blindly trusts is named that she can judge whether X is making a mistake in trusting him. If he listens to certain people and not to others, she must know who these people are and what are the circumstances in which he did that; then only can she judge whether he is right or wrong in doing so. So with everything. Many general statements have been made against X by others, but whenever it has come to particulars in dispute, the Mother has seen that it is only sometimes in details that she had to change what he decided, his general management was in accordance with what she had laid down for him as the lines to follow. Ways of speech, defects of character, errors of judgment in particulars, these are a different matter. Each one has them and, as I have often said, they must be changed from within; but I am speaking of outer things, particular actions, particular ways of doing things. There she must be told with precise facts what is complained of in his action.

If it is not a general complaint you make about the D.R. and Aroumé work but in regard to yourself and your work particularly, there too you must give the precise facts of what he has done or failed to do before the Mother can judge or say or do anything. What is it that he has not reported to her or has stated wrongly to her about your work or you? What are the conveniences that he has not conceded to you?

I write all that because you seem to expect the Mother to do something. But she must know what it is, what it is based on and whether she can do it or not with benefit to the work. Quarrels and clashes of ego there have been plenty in the D.R. and Aroumé, but that she cannot accept as a base of her action; she does not side with one or against another in these things. What is proper or necessary for the work is the thing she has to consider.

3-10-1936

*

All that has happened between you and X, as described by you, are trifles and a little good sense and good will on both sides should be enough to deprive them of importance and to get over any slight disturbance they may create. Quarrels take place and endure because both sides think the other is in the wrong and has behaved ill; but neither side can be in the right in a vital quarrel. The very fact of quarrelling like that puts both in the wrong. Moreover, it is not right to be so sensitive about being dominated or controlled. In the work especially one must accept the control of anyone whom the Mother puts in charge, so far as the work goes. In other matters, one can keep one's due independence without breaking off relations or any kind of quarrel.

There would be no use in changing your work or your residence, even if it were possible under the circumstances. It is the inner attitude that has to be kept right, the will to harmony must be fully established. A change of work is not the remedy. The idea of a good atmosphere or bad atmosphere in the house is also a thing not to be indulged. One must create one's own atmosphere not penetrable by other influences and one can always do that by union and closeness to the Mother.

2-10-1935

*

What you write is no doubt correct. These are very wrong ideas in the minds of the workers and not at all the right attitude. But we have not to do the work for the satisfaction of the Sadhaks, but rather because it is the Mother's work, the divine work and it has to be done well and in the right way. If the workers or others are not satisfied, it has still to be done well and in the right way. When their nature changes and they see their mistake, then they will recognise the truth and change their attitude. Some have good will and have only to learn to see more clearly and get free from their mental misjudgments. Others are more obscure and egoistic and will take more time to get the right poise. Till that happens we must go on with a quiet firmness and resolution and a great patience.

WORK IN THE ASHRAM AND THE MOTHER'S WORK

Whose work is it if it is not the Mother's work? All that you do, you have to do as the Mother's work. All the work done in the Ashram is the Mother's.

All those works, meditation, reading *Conversations*, studying English, etc. are good. You can do any of them dedicating them to the Mother.

Meditation means opening yourself to the Mother, concentrating on aspiration and calling in her force to work and transform you.

18-9-1932

REASONS FOR ALLOWING WORK

Yes, that is correct. Mother does not care for the food for itself; but she allows X to do it as an offering. So with the work — although the work has its own importance. Y and Z are not given physical or practical external work because their energy cannot run in that direction and they cannot do it — not because training in physical and practical work is not good for all. In ideal circumstances a many-sided activity of the being would be the best — but as yet it is not always practicable.

26-9-1933

KARTAVYAM KARMA AND WORK SANCTIONED BY
THE MOTHER

Q: Can it be said that all the work sanctioned by the Mother is "kartavyam karma"?

A: If the Sadhak has a strong insistence or a strong desire, the Mother may say "Yes" or "Do as you like" or give her sanction to the thing requested or demanded. That does not make it a *"kartavyam karma"*, but simply a thing which the Sadhak can do. Again if a thing is indifferent or unobjectionable and the Mother is asked by somebody if he can do it, and she agrees, that does not exalt it into a *"kartavyam karma"*.

31-7-1937

*

Q: So far I had the belief that all work sanctioned by the Mother was her work and work done for her is our "kartavyam karma". Is this not so? If a person gives up all duties to his family, country and society and sincerely does work only for the Divine, as an offering to the Mother, is he not doing the Mother's work and is it not his "kartavyam karma"? Outside it may be difficult to decide this, but here, under the living Presence of the Mother, is this not an assured fact? If not, then what is really meant by "kartavyam karma"?

A: I was asked whether everything done that had the Mother's permission was not a *"kartavyam karma"*. People ask for permission to a host of things dictated by various reasons — it does not follow that the Mother's permission to all these things are her dictates. What work is given by the Mother is her work — also whatever work is done with sincerity as an offering to the Mother is her work also — that goes without saying. But Karma covers all kinds of actions and not work only.

31-7-1937

PROPAGANDA WORK FOR THE MOTHER

Mother does not set much value on propaganda, but still work of that kind can be her work. Only it has to come from her impulsion, be done with quietude, with measure, in the way she wants it to be done. It is from the inner being that it should be done in union with the Mother's will, not from the vital mind's eager impulse. To concentrate most on one's own spiritual growth and experience is the first necessity of the Sadhak — to be eager to help others draws away from the inner work. To grow in the spirit is the greatest help one can give to others, for then something flows out naturally to those around that helps them.

9-4-1937

THE MOTHER'S APPROVAL AND POSSIBILITIES OF SUCCESS

Approval or permission! People get it into their heads that they would like to do some music, because it is the fashion or because they like it so much and the Mother may tolerate it and say "All right, try." That does not mean they are predestined or doomed to be musicians — or poets or painters according to the case. Perhaps one of them who try may bloom, others drop off. X starts painting and shows only a fanciful dash at first, after a time he brings out remarkable work. Y does clever facile things; one day he begins to deepen and a possible painter in the making outlines; others — well, they don't. But they can try — they will learn something about painting at least.

May, 1935

THE MOTHER'S ATTITUDE TO ERRORS IN WORK

Q: From what Mother said yesterday it seems that one should attach little importance to one's errors in work and not mind or correct those of others. Also, since

> *the material world is only one of the several worlds, only a small portion of the total manifestation, should we not attach very little importance to material things, material work and its details?*

A: What Mother said was that she was perfectly aware of errors done in the work, but as she had to work out a certain Force in these things looking at them from an inner viewpoint, not with the external intellect, she found it often necesary to pass over imperfections and errors. This does not at all mean that the Sadhak-worker has not to care whether there are errors in his work where he is responsible. If other Sadhaks commit errors that is their responsibility, one can observe and avoid similar mistakes in oneself, but one Sadhak cannot correct the errors of others unless that comes within his responsibility — each has to correct himself and his own defects and mistakes.

We are here in this material world and not in the others except by an inner connection. Also our life and action lie here, so it will not do to neglect the material world and things, though we should not be attached and bound to them by *āsakti* and desire. We have to acquire a knowledge of the nature and powers of other worlds (planes) so far as they are connected with this one and we can use them to help and uplift the action here. But still the field of action is here and not elsewhere.

21-8-1936

EXTERNAL ORGANISATION AND INNER HARMONY

Mistakes come from people bringing their ego, their personal feeling (likes and dislikes), their sense of prestige or their convenience, pride, sense of possession, etc. into the work. The right way is to feel that the work is the Mother's — not only yours, but the work of others — and to carry it out in such a spirit that there shall be general harmony. Harmony cannot be brought about by external organisation only, though a more and more perfect external organisation is necessary; inner harmony there must be or else there will always be clash and disorder.

*

Q: You have written "Harmony cannot be brought about by external organisation only...inner harmony there must be or else there will always be clash and disorder." What is that inner harmony?

A: Union in the Mother.

21-4-1933

*

The Mother's victory is essentially a victory of each Sadhak over himself. It can only be then that any external form of work can come to a harmonious perfection.

12-11-1937

*

The remedy for these things is to think more and more of the Mother and less and less of the relations of others with yourself apart from the Mother. As X is trying, so you should try to meet others in the Mother, in your consciousness of unity with the Mother and not in a separate personal relation. Then these difficulties disappear and harmony can be established — for then it is not necessary to try and please others — but both or all meet in their love for the Mother and their work for her.

THE MOST NEEDED THING

The one thing that is most needed for this Sadhana is peace, calm, especially in the vital — a peace which depends not on circumstances or surroundings but on the inner contact with a higher consciousness which is the consciousness of the Divine, of the Mother. Those who have not that or do not aspire to get it can come here and live in the Ashram for ten or twenty years and yet be as restless and full of struggle as ever, — those who open their mind and vital to the Mother's strength and peace get it even in the hardest and most unpleasant work and the worst circumstances.

October, 1933

ORDINARY FELLOWSHIP AND UNITY IN THE NEW CONSCIOUSNESS

The Mother has not laid stress on human fellowship of the ordinary kind between the inmates (though good feeling, consideration and courtesy should always be there), because that is not the aim; it is a unity in a new consciousness that is the aim, and the first thing is for each to do his Sadhana to arrive at that new consciousness and realise oneness there.

31-10-1935

NO PLACE FOR VITAL RELATIONS IN YOGA

The whole principle of this Yoga is to give oneself entirely to the Divine alone and to nobody and nothing else, and to bring down into ourselves by union with the Divine Mother-Power all the transcendent light, force, wideness, peace, purity, Truth-Consciousness and Ananda of the supramental Divine. In this Yoga, therefore, there can be no place for vital relations or interchanges with others; any such relation or interchange immediately ties down the soul to the lower consciousness and its lower nature, prevents the true and full union with the Divine and hampers both the ascent to the supramental Truth-Consciousness and the descent of the supramental Ishwari Shakti.

*

The Mother is pressing for the sex-trouble to go out of the Sadhaks — as it is a great obstacle. So it must go.

29-10-1934

LEARNING TO LIVE WITHIN

You have to learn to live in yourself with the Mother, in contact with her consciousness, and meet others only with your exterior surface.

*

If it is like that, it is probably because you are living outside, allowing yourself to be disturbed by outward contacts. One cannot find happiness of a lasting character unless one lives within. Work, action must be offered to the Mother, done for her sake only, without any thought for yourself, your own ideas, preferences, feelings, likes, dislikes. If one's eyes are fixed on these latter things, then at every step one gets some friction either in the mind or vital or if these are comparatively quiet on the body and nerves. Peace and joy can only become stable if one lives within with the Mother.

2-1-1937

*

That is all right. But what I wrote was not put down as a rule for you alone. It is one which everyone ought to follow, X and everybody else. For it is only when work and action are done in that way, without insistence on one's personal ideas and personal feelings but only for the Divine's sake without thought of self that work becomes fully a Sadhana and the internal and the external nature can arrive at a harmony. It makes it more possible for the inner being to take up and enlighten the outer action and grow conscious of the Mother's force behind it guiding it in its works.

3-1-1937

*

To fix times is not possible or desirable — you must yourself organise your day in such a manner as to make the best use of it and let the Mother know how you do it.

The most important thing is to be turned inwardly towards the Mother and to Her alone, to avoid too many outward contacts is necessary only to help in this — but it is not necessary nor desirable to avoid all contact with people. What is necessary is to meet these contacts with the right mind and consciousness, not throwing yourself out — treating them as things of the surface, not getting attached to them or absorbed by them in any way.

Yes, of course, it was an inner concentrated condition in which you could come in contact with the Mother. The flowers indicate always an opening (usually psychic) in some part of the consciousness.

28-10-1933

MOTHER'S DISAPPROVAL OF COMPLETE RETIREMENT

Mother does not at all approve of the idea of a complete retirement. It does not bring the control, only an illusion of a control because the untoward causes are removed for a time. It is a control established while in contact with the outward things that is alone genuine. You must establish that from within by a fixed resolution and practice. Too much mixing and too much talk should be avoided, but a complete retirement is not the thing. It has not had the required result with anyone so far.

27-11-1936

DIFFERENCES IN THE MOTHER'S WAY OF DEALING
WITH SADHAKS

You have spoken of your singing. You know well that we approve of it, and I have constantly stressed its necessity for you as well as that of your poetry. But the Mother absolutely forbade A's singing. So you see that to music for some she is indifferent or even discourages it, for others she approves as for B, C and others. For some time she encouraged the concerts, afterwards she stopped them. You drew from the prohibition to A and the stopping of the concerts the conclusion that the Mother did not like music or did not like Indian music or considered music bad for Sadhana, and all sorts of strange mental reasons like that. Mother prohibited A because while music was good for you, it was spiritual poison to A — the moment he began to think of it and of audiences, all the vulgarity and unspirituality in his nature rose to the surface. You can see what he is doing with it now. So, again, with concerts though in a different way: she stopped them because she had seen that wrong forces were coming into the atmosphere, which had nothing to do with music in itself: her motives were not mental. It was for similar reasons that she drew back from big public displays like D's. On the other hand, she favoured and herself planned the exhibition of painting at the Town Hall. So you will see that there is no mental rule, but in each case the guidance is determined by spiritual reasons which are of a flexible character. There is no other consideration, no rule; music, painting, poetry and many other activities which are of the mind and vital can be used as part of spiritual development or of the work and for a spiritual purpose: "it depends on the spirit in which they are done."

That being established, these things depend on the spirit, the nature of the person, its needs, the conditions and circumstances.

*

The Sadhana is done by the Mother according to the Truth and necessity of each nature and of each plane of Nature. It is not one fixed process.

13-9-1933

*

Concern yourself with your own progress and follow there the lead the Mother gives you. Leave others to do the same; the Mother is there to guide and help them according to their need and their nature. It does not in the least matter if the way she follows with him seems different or the opposite of that which she takes with you. That is the right one for him, as this is the right one for you.

*

The Mother speaks or writes much more pointedly and sharply to those whom she wishes to push rapidly on the way because they are capable of it, and they do not resent or suffer but are glad of the pressure and the plainness because they know by experience that it helps them to see their obstacles and change. If you wish to progress rapidly you must get rid of this vital reaction of *abhimāna*, suffering, wounded feeling, seeking for argument of self-justification, outcry against the touch that is intended to liberate — for so long as you have these, it is difficult for us to deal openly and firmly with the obstacles created by the vital nature.

In regard to the difference between you and X: The Mother's warning to you against the undesirability of too much talk, loose chat and gossip, social self-dispersion was entirely meant and stands; when you indulge in these things, you throw yourself out into a very small and ignorant consciousness in which your vital defects get free play and this is likely to bring you out of what you have developed in your inner consciousness. That was why we said that if you felt a reaction against these things when you went to X's, it was a sign of your (psychic) sensitiveness coming into you — into your vital and nervous being, and we meant that it was all for the good. But in dealing with others, in withdrawing from these things you should not allow any sense of superiority to creep in, or force on them by your manner or spirit a sense of disapproval or condemnation or pressure on them to change. It is for your personal inward need that you draw back from these things, that is all. As for them, what they do in these matters, right or wrong, is their affair, and ours; we will deal with them according to what we see as necessary and possible for them at the moment, and for that purpose we can not only deal quite differently with different people, allowing for one what we forbid for another, but we may deal differently with the same person at different times, allowing or even encouraging today what we shall forbid tomorrow.... A human soul and nature cannot be dealt with by a set of mental rules applicable to everybody in the same way; if it were so, there would be no need of a Guru, each could set his chart of Yogic rules before him like the rules of Sandow's exercise and follow them till he became the perfect Siddha!

25-10-1932

*

Q: The Mother does not seem to turn away from people who are not faithful. She often allows them to do what they like.

A: It is the Mother's business. She alone can say what is the right way to deal with people. If she were to deal with people only according to their defects, there would be hardly half a dozen people left in the Ashram.

26-3-1933

*

Whatever is done by the Mother is for the good of the Sadhak and the Sadhana.

9-12-1935

*

Q: How can one make the vital being understand that the Mother is never partial?

A: One way is to have entire faith in the Mother — the other is to believe that she is wiser than yourself and must have reasons for everything she does which are better than your mind's judgments.

22-3-1934

*

Q: I am sure that for everything the Mother does there is a reason, and that what she does is according to the

> *need of each one, but the vital does not believe it, and it
> is not yet well established in the mental. How can this
> be firmly established in the mental so that it does not
> yield to any temptation?*

A: It should be established — that is all. So long as the vital
or mental think themselves wiser than the Mother and able to
judge her how do you expect these stupidities to disappear?

22-3-1934

*

> *Q: Can the physical mind have a correct understanding
> of the Mother's dealings?*

A: Not until it is enlightened by the true consciousness and
knowledge from above.

4-7-1936

THE MOTHER'S USE OF THE MAHAKALI METHOD

All these things depend on the person, the condition, the circumstances. The Mother uses the method you speak of, the Mahakali method,

  (1) with those in whom there is a great eagerness and a
fundamental sincerity somewhere even in the vital,

  (2) with those whom she meets intimately and who, she
knows, will not resent or misunderstand her severity or take it
for a withdrawal of kindness or grace, but will regard it as a true
grace and a help to their Sadhana.

  There are others who cannot bear this method — if it was
continued they would run a thousand miles away in misunder
standing and revolt and despair. What the Mother wants is for
people to have their full chance for their souls, be the method
short and swift or long and tortuous. Each she must treat according to his nature.

9-5-1933

*

If you are afraid of the Mother's scoldings, how will you progress? Those who want to progress quickly, welcome even the blows of Mahakali, because that pushes them more rapidly on the way.

*

Q: Is it possible to have that relation with the Mother in which she would feel free to correct me and tell me, without any kind of consideration for my feelings, what I must do and must not do?

A: Certainly, when the Divine Consciousness is fully realised, there will be no difference between the Mother's will and the Sadhak's.

For a relation to exist in which Mother can do as you say, the Sadhak must not be afraid of the Mahakali aspect and ask only for sweetness. He must be able to take the blows of Mahakali as a blessing. He must also believe in her vision and judgment and word, otherwise when she says or does something unpleasant to his ego that ego will go sulking, justifying itself, calling her names etc. as is the habit with so many in the Ashram when she does not do what they like. There are very few here who can take this attitude even imperfectly, but it is with them that the Mother has this relation. With others who have a different nature, she cannot but behave differently — for she has to act with each according to his nature.

THE MOTHER'S WAY OF WORKING

The difficulty about meeting your demand that the Mother should plan out and fix a routine for you in everything which you must follow is that this is quite contrary to the Mother's way of working in most matters. In the most physical things you have to fix a programme in order to deal with time, otherwise all becomes a sea of confusion and haphazard. Fixed rules have also to be made for the management of material things so long as people are not sufficiently developed to deal with them in the right way without rules. But these things of which you write are different; they are concerned with your inner development, your Sadhana. In fact, even in outward things the Mother does not plan with her mind and make a mental map and rule of what is to be done; she sees what is to be done in each case and organises and develops it according to the nature of each case. In matters of the inner development and the Sadhana it is still more impossible to map out a plan fixed in every detail and say, "Every time you shall step here, there, in this way, or that line and no other." Things would become so tied up and rigid that nothing could be done; there would be no true and effective movement.

If the Mother asked you to tell her everything, it was not in order that she might give you directions in every detail which you must obey. It was in order, first, that there might grow up the complete intimacy in which you would be entirely open to her, so that she might pour more and more and continuously and at every point the Divine Force into you which would increase the Light in you, perfect your action, deliver and develop your nature. It is this that was important; all else is secondary, important only so far as it helps this or hinders. In addition, it would help her to give whenever needed the necessary direction, the necessary help or warning, not always by words, more often by a silent intervention and pressure. This is her way of dealing with those who are open to her; it is not necessary to give express orders at every moment and in every detail. Especially, if the psychic consciousness is open and one lives fully in that, it gets the intimation at once and sees things clearly and receives the help, the intervention, the necessary direction or warning. That was what was happening to a great extent when your psychic consciousness was very active, but there was a vital part in which you were not open and which was coming up repeatedly, and it is this that has created the confusion and the trouble.

Everything depends on the inner condition, and the outward action is only useful as a means and a help for expressing or confirming the inner condition and making it dynamic and effective. If you do or say a thing with the psychic uppermost or with the right inner touch, it will be effective; if you do or say the same thing out of the mind or the vital or with a wrong or mixed atmosphere, it may be quite ineffective. To do the right thing in the right way in each case and at each moment one must be in the right consciousness — it can't be done by following a fixed mental rule which under some circumstances might fit in and under others might not fit in at all. A general principle can be laid down if it is in consonance with the Truth, but its application must be determined by the inner consciousness seeing at each step what is to be done or not done. If the psychic is uppermost, if the being is entirely turned towards the Mother and follows the psychic, this can be increasingly done.

All depends therefore not on a mental rule to follow in practice, but in getting the psychic consciousness back and putting its light into this vital part and making that part turn wholly to the Mother. It is not that the question of your going too much to X is of no importance, — it is of considerable importance — but to limit the contact is effective only as a means of helping your vital part to withdraw from this servitude to old movements. It is the same everywhere.

The kind of outward obedience you lay stress on, asking for a direction in every detail, is not the essence of surrender, although obedience is the natural fruit and outward body of surrender. Surrender is from within, opening and giving the mind, vital, physical, all to the Mother for her to take them as her own and re-create them in their true being which is a portion of the Divine; all the rest follows as a consequence. It would not then be necessary to ask her word and order outwardly in every detail, the being would feel and act according to her will; her sanction would be sought as the seal of that inner unity, receptiveness of her will and obedience.

11-6-1932

THE MOTHER'S REGARD FOR TRUTH

Mother heard that X had objected to your working in her room, but she brushed it aside at once saying that that could have no importance. It has nothing to do with her decision which was made on other grounds quite independently of it.

P.S. A lie is a lie whoever speaks it. If you give credit to what someone or another thinks or says as Mother's motive in an action, take her statement of her motive as untrue and somebody else's who cannot know as sound and true and on that challenge Mother for want of frankness, is the resulting upset our fault? It is a question of greater confidence in the Mother than in the statements or interpretations of Sadhaks or the hasty assumptions or inferences of your mind or the feelings of your vital made without having the needed information. If you could get rid of that movement, things would be easier.

15-5-1936

*

Q: How can the maxim "a lie is a lie" apply to all? It can apply only to those who are bound by moral and social codes, or as a principle only if the intention behind is wrong. If a higher motive demands a concealing or misrepresenting something by words I would hardly call it a lie. The motive, the basis, are all superhuman and cannot fall in the same category. I think Krishna did not always speak the exact truth and his half-lies always provoke an understanding smile in all who listen to his stories.

A: If the Mother did a thing for one reason and said that she did it for quite another she did not have, I fail to see how it can be anything but a falsehood. No superhuman motive can make a falsehood not a falsehood. Moreover, if you really believe that the Divine can speak what is not true without being untrue and that that is a part of divinity, why do you resent when you think the Mother has done it and grow sorrowful and indignant over her supposed unfair and uncandid treatment of you and cry she ought to have been frank, etc.? You ought rather to think she is acting from superhuman motives and accept gladly whatever she does. At least that seems to be the logic of such a position. You base yourself evidently on the position that the Divine Consciousness is above good and evil. But that does not mean that it does evil and good impartially. It can only mean that it acts from a light that is beyond that level of human consciousness which makes the human standard of these things. It acts for and from a greater good than the apparent good men follow after. It acts also according to a greater truth than men conceive. It is for this reason that the human mind cannot understand the divine action and its motives — he must first rise into a higher consciousness and be in spiritual contact or union with the Divine. But if anyone recognises that, he can no longer judge the divine action with his human mind and from his human point of view. The two things would be quite incompatible.

But this does not fall under any such explanation. To allege a false motive cannot be a movement of a greater Truth and consciousness. To keep silence and not reveal one's motive is one thing — to say I did not act from that motive when I actually did so, is not silence, it is falsehood. It is a matter not of moral, but spiritual importance. The Mother cares for the Truth and she has always said that lying and falsehood create a serious obstacle to realisation. How then can she herself do that?

I do not remember any lies or half-lies told by Krishna, so I can say nothing on that point. But if he did according to the Mahabharata or the Bhagawata, we are not bound either by that record or by that example. I think Rama and Buddha told none.

17-5-1936

*

It is good if you have freed yourself from this bondage. Love of Truth is divine, but this kind of truth is a very mixed product accompanied as it is by hardness or a fierce anger. Truth does not insist on a blind adherence to the spoken word — as for instance, if a man says that he will kill another under the impression that that other has done him a grievous wrong and afterwards carries out his word even when he has found out that the other was innocent and no wrong done. That is what literal adhesion to the spoken word would come to, if scrupulously held as a principle. Truth, on the contrary, demands that a man shall cleave to the principle of Truth in things only, and in the case above the principle of Truth would demand that he should break his vow and not keep it. If a man pledges himself to something that is against the principle of Love and Compassion, or against that of obedience and surrender to the Divine, it is not Truth to keep that pledge — for it would be a pledge to follow falsehood — and how can Truth be held in allegiance to falsehood? That would be an Asuric, not a divine Truthfulness.

As for the Mother, one will not find in her this blind adherence to an arrangement once made. If, for instance, she told someone, next time you yield to sex-passion in any way, you will have to leave the Ashram, and if the man did it and repented, she too might relent and not insist in following out her menace. These matters or interviews are not promises, contracts or engagements, — they are arrangements only and can be altered. If she has arranged for half an hour she can make it instead three-quarters of an hour — or diminish it to twenty minutes. There is a plasticity needed in the movement of time and the habit of life cannot afford to be rigid in its movements, otherwise life would either be turned into a mere mechanism or break to pieces. But in this case there was no intention; it was a pure accident; by some oversight your name had not been written in the morning list and Mother came to the door when those on the list were finished. She could not go back because it was extremely late and it had been a long and exhausting morning spent in a continual struggle with adverse forces and she had to come in, do what still she had to do and come to me to report what had happened.

But even if she had intended it for some reason not known to you, your reaction was not the right one. For the basis you have taken for your Yoga is to obey the Will whatever it may be. These things — seemingly accidental — happen when they are predestined and they come in as an ordeal for something in the vital which has by this painful process to accept change.

28-9-1933

FUTILITY OF JUDGING MOTHER'S ACTIONS BY MIND

Obviously. Neither Nature nor Destiny nor the Divine work in the mental way or by the law of the mind or according to its standards — that is why even to the scientist and the philosopher Nature, Destiny, the way of the Divine all seem a mystery. The Mother does not act by the mind, so to judge her action with the mind is futile.

5-5-1936

*

The Mother does not discuss these mental problems with her disciples. It is quite useless trying to reconcile these things with the intellect. For there are two things, the Ignorance from which the struggle and discord comes and the secret Light, Unity, Bliss and Harmony. The Intellect belongs to the Ignorance. It is only by getting into a better consciousness that one can live in the Light and Bliss and Unity and not be touched by the outward discord and struggle. That change of consciousness therefore is the only thing that matters, to reconcile with the intellect would make no difference.

MISREPRESENTATION OF THE MOTHER'S WORDS

It is not X alone, but many or most who turn things [spoken by the Mother] in that way — the tendency is almost universal in human nature. It is not from dishonesty that he or others do it — it is because when they listen, their minds are not silent but active and the thought of their minds mixes with what they have heard and gives it another turn or shape or colour. Often also the vital interferes and exaggerates or reshapes according to the desire or the convenience. This is much more often unconsciously than consciously done.

In the present instance, the Mother spoke quite generally, not about Y or what had happened in Z's case, and she meant that what ought to be remembered is not remembered because of some strong immediate desire which pushes the memory behind until the desire is fulfilled and then only, if at all, the recollection comes. X evidently added his own ideas, applied it specially to Y's action and thought that the Mother had said it was consciously done — that Y remembered and yet went against her conscious sense of right in order to fulfil her desire. That was not what the Mother said or meant by her general statement.

30-3-1933

*

It is only when the Mother speaks directly that you can say "The Mother has said".

9-7-1933

DANGERS OF "ALL FROM THE MOTHER" THEORY

What you write is in itself unexceptionable — it is indeed what was offered to the Sadhaks at the beginning — but the difficulty is precisely there, in the complete sincerity of the nature. Few have been able to rise to it and only a distant approximation (if the phrase can be accepted) has been attained by some. Apart from incomplete sincerity, there is the difficulty that the brain is clouded by egoism and desire and imagines it is doing the very thing when it is doing something else. That is why I spoke of the danger of the theory of all from the Mother. There are people who have taken it that all that comes from the ego or the vital comes from the Mother, is her inspiration or what she has given them. There are others who have taken it as an excuse for going on in the old rut independently, saying that when the Mother wants she will change things! There were even some who on this basis created a subjective Mother in themselves whose dictates, flattering to their ego and desire, they pitted against the contrary dictates of the Mother here, and came to think that this external Mother is after all new and the real thing is the inner one or that she was putting them through an ordeal by contradicting the inner dictates and seeing what they would do! The

truth remains the truth, but this power of twisting by the mind
and other parts of the nature has to be kept in sight also.

17-10-1936

THE MOTHER'S WORK AND TIME

It is not because your French is full of mistakes that Mother does
not correct it, but because I will not allow her to take more work
on herself so far as I can help it. Already she has no time to rest
sufficiently at night and most of the night she is working at the
books, reports and letters that pour on her in masses. Even so
she cannot finish in time in the morning. If she has to correct all
the letters of the people who have just begun writing in French
as well as the others, it means another hour or two of work — she
will be able to finish only at nine in the morning and come down
at 10-30. I am therefore trying to stop it.

*

Mother never avoids opening letters or any other work because
of absence of time: she deals with all the work that comes to her
even if she is ill or if she has no time for rest.

15-2-1936

*

Mother prefers that when she walks on the terrace people should
not be looking at her because it is the only time when she can concentrate a little on herself — apart from the necessity of taking
some fresh air and movement for the health of the body. If she
has to attend to the pull of so many people, that cannot be done.
The interview she gives you is a different matter; she has to arrange it herself and it is part of her work, so there is no need to
change. What was said was only for the walk on the terrace.

*

Mother has a very limited time for seeing people — she has so much to do. So it is only when there is a strong necessity that she sees except for those who have work to do with her.

1933

THE RIGHT WAY OF MEETING THE MOTHER

The right attitude to approach the Mother when she sees one is to keep the being perfectly quiet and open to receive, without any activity of the mind or desire in the vital, with only the surrender and the psychic readiness to accept whatever is given.

23-2-1932

*

When one comes to the Mother, one must not come with these things in the mind — but in quietude and light solely to receive from her what one can assimilate.

10-4-1934

*

The Mother does not usually speak with those who come for an interview before starting. If she had to speak, she would not give an interview at all to most, for she would have no time. Moreover it is not by speech or instruction or answering questions that Mother works on the consciousness of the Sadhaks, it is by a silent influence to which they have to learn to open themselves.

As for your readiness for the Ashram life, it should be evident to yourself from your reactions especially about your family that you are not ready — you would have been pulled away by these feelings and it would have been a serious fall for you. To be told the truth about themselves and get the guidance unasked — that is a grace which Sadhaks accept with gladness — to weep and feel hurt is a reaction of the vital which must be got over. Psychic weeping, a weeping from the soul deep within, tears of the soul's yearning, of sorrow for the resistance of Nature, of joy or love or Bhakti does not cause a fall, it can help and open up the inner soul from its veils; but this weeping has no strain or suffering in it, it is something very deep and quiet and brings a sense of purification and release. That is not so with the weeping which comes from the vital and is born of hurt or *abhimāna* or disappointment or shakes or disturbs the nature.

16-3-1937

*

Q: I intend to sweep out the lower forces before meeting the Mother tomorrow. Failing it I do not like to show my face to her.

A: That is the suggestion of the lower forces. They want to create an excuse for your remaining aloof like that.

*

Q: It seems I have learnt a lot about myself during yesterday, my birthday, on which Mother had given me an interview. It may be perhaps a kind of experienced knowledge aided by Her Force. I no more feel myself so weak, helpless or a slave to my defects and imperfections. Rather there is a growing surety that I shall be able to get rid of my whole lower nature.

A: It is what we call growing conscious — a perception of which the base is the psychic though it may take place in the mind or vital or physical. No doubt the Force that woke it up came from the Mother.

9-9-1937

*

Why should you decide beforehand that your birthday is spoiled? You have only to throw off all these undesirable ideas and feelings which proceed from a still imperfectly purified part of the external being and take the right attitude which you should always have when you come to the Mother. There should be no idea of what others have or have not — your relation is between the Mother and yourself and has nothing to do with others. Nothing should exist for you but yourself and the Divine — yourself receiving her Force flowing into you.

To secure that better, do not spend your time at your disposal in speech — especially if anything of the depression remains with you, it will waste the time in discussing things which cannot help the true consciousness to predominate. Concentrate, open yourself and let the Mother bring you back to the psychic condition by what she will pour into you in meditation and silence.

16-5-1933

SIGNIFICANCE OF BIRTHDAY MEETING

Q: Is there any special significance in the Mother's seeing the Sadhaks on their birthdays?

A: About the birthdays. There is a rhythm (one among many) in the play of the world-forces which is connected with the sun and the planets. That makes the birthday a day of possible renewal when the being is likely to be more plastic. It is for this reason that Mother sees people on their birthdays.

18-5-1934

*

Q: You wrote once that on birthdays the physical is more open and receptive to the Mother than on other days. Is that why she gives special blessings to us on our birthdays?

A: It is not a question of a physical birthday or of the body — it is taken as an occasion for opening a new year of life with a growing new birth within. That is the meaning in which the Mother takes the birthday.

7-10-1936

MEETING THE MOTHER IN DREAM

Q: For a long time I was thinking of meeting the Mother but was hesitating to ask for an interview. Last night in dream I met her and had a talk with her. Was it the real Mother I met or some constructed figure of my dream-mind?

A: Of course, it was the Mother you met and the meeting must have been due to your thought about meeting her.

9-6-1935

*

Q: Kindly let me know the significance of my frequently coming to the Mother on the supraphysical plane. Did my vital come to the Mother for refreshing its energy, for purification, etc.?

A: This kind of vital coming to the Mother all the Sadhaks have in their sleep and dream, if they are a little conscious there. Even those who are not Sadhaks or others who do not know her come, but they are not aware of it. The vital plane is a supraphysical plane. The vital moves about in its own plane and is not limited by the physical mind or its consciousness or experience.

13-7-1937

*

It [coming to the Mother on a supraphysical plane] may be for any object or without any specific object — there is no rule in such matters.

14-7-1937

*

Q: I saw twice in dream that the Mother was giving me soup with her hand and I was bowing down at her feet.

> *Why did I see like this? What is the spiritual meaning*
> *of the soup which the Mother was giving us?*

A: The soup was instituted in order to establish a means by which the Sadhak might receive something from the Mother by an interchange in the material consciousness. Owing to the past association probably you see like that when your material consciousness in dream receives something from the Mother.

27-7-1933

THE MOTHER'S ACTION IN MEDITATION

When I spoke of the inner mind of the Ashram, I was only using a succinct expression for the "minds of the members of the Ashram" and I was not thinking of the collective mind of the group. But the action of the Mother in the meditation is at once collective and individual. She is trying to bring down the right consciousness in the atmosphere of the Ashram — for the action of the minds and vital of the Sadhaks does create a general atmosphere. She has taken this meditation in the evening as a brief period in which all is concentrated in the sole force of the descending Power. The Sadhaks must feel that they are there only to concentrate, only to receive, only to be open to the Mother and nothing else matters.

November, 1934

*

About the meditation and the seat, the Mother gives this meditation *only* for bringing down the true light and consciousness into the Sadhaks. She does not want it to be turned into a formality and she does not want any personal questions to arise there. It should solely be a meditation and concentration without personal or other desires or claims or ideas rising there and interfering with her object.

2-11-1934

*

It is not by the physical presence but the Mother's concentration at the time of meditation which brings the quiet to those who can receive it.

6-3-1937

*

It is only Mother who can give orders here.

What Mother would like you to do is to come to the Meditation and Pranam putting aside all feelings of ego, anger, quarrel with others, demand for this or that, thinking only of your Sadhana and making yourself quiet to receive from her the only things that are really precious and needful.

22-9-1936

*

Q: When I try to meditate in the presence of the Mother, there is always a disturbing rush of thoughts as to what she is bringing down etc.

A: It is simply a bad habit of the mind, a wrong activity. It is not in the least useful for the mind to ask or try to determine what the Mother wills or is bringing — that only interferes. It has simply to remain quiet and concentrated and leave the Power to act.

11-1-1934

*

Q: During the period of concentration I get all sorts of useless thoughts and desires, which I forget afterwards. How am I to remember them and open them to the Mother?

A: Aspire at the time — they will of themselves be open to the Mother.

26-6-1933

*

> *Q: During the general meditation with the Mother,*
> *my consciousness rose upwards in an utter passivity.*
> *I became unaware of my body up to the neck.*

A: It means the whole mind was liberated for a while from imprisonment in the body sense and became free in the passivity of the wider self.

16-8-1834

*

> *Q: I feel that when the Mother comes down to give*
> *meditation in the Meditation Hall, the atmosphere of*
> *the Hall extends to all the Ashram houses. Am I right in*
> *my feeling?*

A: It is natural that it should be so as the Mother, when she concentrates on the inner work, is accustomed spontaneously to spread her consciousness over the whole Ashram. So to anyone who is sensitive, it must be felt anywhere in the Ashram, though perhaps more strongly in the nearer houses on an occasion like the evening meditation.

7-11-1934

THE MOTHER'S ACTION DURING PRANAM

> *Q: During Pranam does Mother work from Overmind?*

A: Not from the ordinary Overmind, but from the Power above it. Naturally the Overmind has to be used as a channel.

22-11-1933

RIGHT USE OF DARSHAN AND PRANAM

Physical means [like Darshan and touch in the Pranam] can be and are used in the approach to divine love and worship; they have not been allowed merely as a concession to human weakness, nor is it the fact that in the psychic way there is no place for such things. On the contrary, they are one means of approaching the Divine and receiving the Light and materialising the psychic contact, and so long as it is done in the right spirit and they are used for the true purpose they have their place. It is only if they are misused or the approach is not right because tainted by indifference and inertia, or revolt or hostility, or some gross desire, that they are out of place and can have a contrary effect — as the Mother has always warned people and has assigned it as the reason why she does not like lightly to open them to everyone.

*

No one should look upon the Pranam either as a formal routine or an obligatory ceremony or think himself under any compulsion to come there. The object of the Pranam is not that Sadhaks should offer a formal or ritual daily homage to the Mother, but that the Sadhaks may receive along with the Mother's blessings whatever spiritual help or influence they are in a condition to receive or assimilate. It is important to maintain a quiet and collected atmosphere for that purpose.

*

If you attach any value to the Darshan it is better to be *recueilli*. If her coming is only one incident of the day's routine like taking dinner, then of course it does not matter.

Recueilli means drawn back, quiet and collected in oneself.

24-7-1933

*

The best way for Darshan is to keep oneself very collected and quiet and open to receive whatever the Mother gives.

12-2-1937

INADVISABILITY OF BRINGING SICK AND INSANE PEOPLE
FOR DARSHAN

Mother cannot see her. The most we can concede is that she may be brought for Darshan in the way proposed, but she must simply take the blessing and pass, there must be no lingering. It is a mistake to bring sick people or the insane to the Darshan for cure — the Darshan is not meant for that. If anything is to be done or can be done for them, it can be done at a distance. The Force that acts at the time of Darshan is of another kind and one deranged or feeble in mind cannot receive or cannot assimilate it — it may produce a contrary effect owing to this incapacity if received at all. If the Force is withheld, the Darshan is useless, if received by such people it is unsafe. It is similar reasons which dictate the rule prohibiting children of tender years to be brought to the Darshan.

13-8-1937

WRONG SUGGESTION OF MAKING PRANAM TO OTHERS

It [the wish to make Pranam to others] is a wrong suggestion from somewhere. It is very necessary not to take the attitude of Pranam to others or to give even in thought a place at all approaching or similar to the Mother's.

27-7-1934

PRANAM AND THE MOTHER'S CONTACT

Mother's contact is there all the day and the night also. If one keeps the right contact with her inwardly all day, the Pranam will bear its right fruit, for you will be in the right condition to receive. To make the whole day depend upon the Pranam, the whole inner attitude depend on the most outer aspect of the outer contact is to turn the whole thing topsy-turvy. It is the fundamental mistake made by the physical mind and vital which is the cause of the whole trouble.

16-3-1935

*

It is only if one can feel the inward touch of the Mother without the necessity of the physical contact that the true value of the latter can be really active. Otherwise there is a danger of its becoming like a mere artificial stimulant or a pulling of vital force from her for one's own benefit.

2-3-1937

*

If they are so dependent on the physical touch that they cannot feel anything when it is not there, this means that they have not used it at all for developing the inner connection; if they had, the inner connection after so many years would already be there. The inner connection can only be developed by an inner concentration and aspiration, not by a mere outward Pranam every day. What most people do is simply to pull vital force from the Mother and live on it — but that is not the object of the Pranam.

4-3-1937

*

Yes, but the vital's test is very foolish. If the Sadhana goes on whether you see the Mother or not, that would rather show that the psychic connection is permanently there and active always and does not depend on the physical contact. The vital seems to think the Sadhana ought to cease if you do not see the Mother but that would only mean that the love and devotion need the stimulus of physical contact. The greatest test of love and devotion is on the contrary when it burns as strongly in long absence as in the presence. If your Sadhana went on as well on non-Pranam as on Pranam days it would not prove that love and devotion are not there, but that they are so strong as to be self-existent in all circumstances.

8-6-1936

*

Q: It is curious that I feel Mother nearer at Pranam

time than when she meets us and speaks to us familiarly.
Is it because of a defect of the physical mind?

A: Yes — or at least of some part of the physical consciousness.

30-4-1934

*

Q: Just after making my Pranam to the Mother I experienced an unimaginable depth in the heart and a fire bursting out.

A: That is of course the psychic depth and the psychic fire.

5-5-1936

*

Q: When the Mother pressed her hand on X's head to bless, I felt her touch concretely on my head! How does this happen?

A: It shows that the subtle physical is growing conscious and felt the touch and blessings of the Mother which is always there.

20-3-1935

*

There is always a touch coming from Mother at Pranam, one has to be conscious and open to receive it.

14-11-1933

*

Q: Is it possible to receive the Mother's influence at a distance in the Ashram in the same way as we receive it at Pranam?

A: It is possible to receive, but not in the same way. There is an element, a touch on the physical consciousness that is wanting.

30-5-1933

*

Q: In the evening when I am late and miss the Mother, do I receive Her Light as I would if I were present?

A: You can receive the Light at all times — even if less concretely than in the physical presence.

1-9-1933

*

Q: You wrote: "Without the inner touch the inner being cannot work." I do not understand how this explained my question. The Mother's inner or subtle touch felt before had not the same effect as her physical touch during the Pranam. The former came and disappeared within a few seconds, leaving practically no effect, whilst the latter left its impress for a long time even in spite of depression and resistance.

A: It is because you lived in your outer and not in your inner being that it is like that. But unless you open to the inner touch, the inner being cannot develop.

3-2-1937

*

The inner touch is the Mother's influence felt in the inner being.

6-2-1936

*

Q: When I had experiences and realisations why did I not feel the inner touch, since it is said that none can

*have experiences (which are the fruits of the inner being's
development) without it?*

A: You did not feel it because the inner being was not awake to
it — it felt only the results — and these results were not experiences in the inner being itself but the self above.

6-2-1937

THE INNER AND THE OUTER CONTACT

Let the inner contact with the Mother increase — unless that is
there, the outer contacts if too much multiplied easily degenerate
into a routine.

*

I mean the inner contact in which one either feels one with her
or in contact with her or aware of her presence or at the very
least turned towards her always.

16-3-1935

*

*Q: Today I had an intense desire to go in the Mother's
rooms upstairs so as to be near and close to her.*

A: But the coming near to the Mother should be in the inner
rooms, not the outer. For in the inner rooms one can always
enter and even arrange to stay there permanently.

8-3-1935

*

*Q: How is it that in writing a letter to you the higher
things increase and become stronger?*

A: I suppose it is because in the act of writing or rather in its beginning you enter into contact with the Mother and the Force.

10-5-1936

TWO WAYS OF THE MOTHER'S GIVING

The Mother gives in both ways. Through the eyes it is to the psychic, through the hand to the material.

29-9-1932

*

Obviously, the time has nothing to do with it. One hour's touch or a moment's touch — as much can be given by the one as by the other.

18-4-1935

*

It was not because of any fault of yours that the Mother gave only a short blessing; she has to do that for all who come at the beginning because they need to go quickly to their work. If you want a longer blessing, you must come afterwards. But, when you have to come early, you can get as much out of the Mother's short blessing, if you are quiet and open.

SIGNIFICANCE OF THE MOTHER'S GIVING OF FLOWERS

Q: What is the significance of the Mother's giving us flowers at Pranam every day?

A: It is meant to help the realisation of the thing the flower stands for.

28-4-1933

*

Q: Are flowers mere symbols and nothing more? Can

*the flower symbolizing silence, for example, help in the
realisation of silence?*

A: It is when the Mother puts her force into the flower that it
becomes more than a symbol. It then can become very effective
if there is receptivity in the one who receives.

19-7-1937

*

*Q: We do not get from the Mother the flowers which our
mind thinks we should get.*

A: Obviously not — the mind chooses according to likings or
fancies or else to some mental idea of what should be; the
Mother chooses by intuitive observation of what is needed.

9-7-1934

PHYSICAL NEARNESS TO THE MOTHER AND PROGRESS IN SADHANA

It is a mistake to think that those who meet the Mother physically
are any nearer the goal of perfection than those who do not meet
her except at Pranam and meditation. All depends on the inner
being and how it can meet her from within and receive her force
and profit by it. Of course, if people meet her with their psychic
prominent, and not with the outer consciousness only, it should
be different, but —

29-7-1936

*

*Q: Many people believe that those whom the Mother
gives frequent interviews and sends things often are very
near to her and are progressing rapidly while those whom
she does not see often or to whom she does not send
things are only given a chance to do their Sadhana. Is
this belief true?*

A: It is all nonsense. Some of the best Sadhaks are among those whom the Mother seldom or never calls and she sends them nothing. Nor do they expect it — they feel the Mother always with them and are satisfied and ask for nothing else.

27-7-1933

*

Q: You have said that those who do Sadhana outside the Ashram cannot do it fully because the physical nearness to the Mother in the Ashram alone can bring a possibility of transformation. Carrying this idea a little further, it naturally follows that even in the Ashram, those who live physically nearer to the Mother and meet her more often are of the inner circle, more intimate even outwardly, and therefore nearer transformation. Q.E.D.?

A: Living in the Ashram is one thing, living with the Mother in close proximity is another. Your Q.E.D. like most mental logic is contradicted by the facts of life. One could argue on that basis that A who lives in the same house as the Mother is nearer perfection than B and much nearer than C or D who live outside. E never meets the Mother except at Pranam and on her birthday, so she must be an utterly backward person and F who meets the Mother daily for five, ten, fifteen or twenty minutes must be far ahead of her, well on towards perfection. But these things are not so. So the argument breaks down at every point. Progress in Sadhana or superior capacity is not dependent on one's being near the Mother or meeting her more often. Q.E.D.

30-7-1936

*

Q: People who approach the Mother often must be very fortunate, is it not so?

A: If one has the desire or the claim, one brings in all sorts of demands, angers, jealousies, despairs, revolts, etc. which spoil

the Sadhana and do not help it. To others the nearness of the
Mother becomes a mixture.

*

The Mother was giving freely of her physical contact in former
years. If the Sadhaks had had the right reactions, do you think
she would have drawn back and reduced it to a minimum? Of
course if people know in what spirit to receive from her the physical touch is a great thing, but for that the constant physical
nearness is not necessary. That rather creates a pressure of the
highest forces which how many can meet?

22-4-1933

*

It is the ego that wants the satisfaction of being the first or specially singled out. It is this egoistic vital demand with all its
consequent results and disturbances that made it necessary for
Mother to limit the physical manifestation of nearness to a
minimum.

17-4-1935

*

The one thing important is to keep the inner attitude and establish the inner connection with the Mother independent of all
outward circumstances. It is that that brings all that is needed.
Those who are most deep in the Yoga are not those who physically see most of the Mother. There are some who are in constant nearness or union with her, who apart from the Pranam and
the evening meditation come to her only once a year.

13-11-1934

*

There is more profit to be had by being open to the Mother than
by coming physically to her at the present stage. Some even who
make a point of her calling them go backward rather than for-

ward — because they make a point of it, introducing thus a basis of vital demand which makes a very shaky foundation for relations with the Mother.

*

Q: Is it not true that one who sees the Mother more often and talks with her receives more Light by being in her presence?

A: No. It depends entirely on the condition of the person and his attitude. Especially, if they insist on seeing her or on remaining when she wants them to go or are in a bad mood and throw it on her, it is very harmful for them to see her. Each should be contented with what the Mother gives them, for she alone feels what they can or cannot receive. Mental constructions of this kind and vital demands are always false.

3-4-1933

*

There is a confusion here. The Mother's grace is one thing, the call to change another, the pressure of nearness to her is yet another. Those who are physically near to her are not so by any special grace or favour, but by the necessity of their work, — that is what everybody here refuses to understand or believe, but it is the fact: that nearness acts automatically as a pressure, if for nothing else, to adapt their consciousness to hers which means change, but it is difficult for them because the difference between the two consciousnesses is enormous especially on the physical level and it is on the physical level that they are meeting her in the work.

27-4-1944

*

Q: Is it not true that those who are bodily nearest to the Mother are those who are open to her, one with her

will and close to her in their inner being? Is it not also
a fact that there are certain special advantages in being
bodily near to the Mother?

A: It is not so easy to be "one with the will" of the Mother or to be entirely open. To be bodily close imposes a constant pressure for progress, for perfection, which no one yet has been able to meet. People have romantic ideas in this matter which are not true.

The demand [of A] was to live inside or have free access (to the Mother's rooms) at all times (which is not allowed to anybody, neither to B or C nor anyone else) and to be on an equality with or superiority over those who were admitted. Such a demand shows a total ignorance of the reasons which are behind the admission (it has nothing to do with special grace or favour) and also of the fitness of things. If she had been allowed, she would not have been able to bear it even for a few days.... B and C are different — they have special work to do which makes it necessary for them to come close to the Mother or see her often. It has nothing at all to do with any superiority in Sadhana, as you have yourself pointed out by quoting the examples of D etc.

7-3-1935

*

What I meant was not that bodily closeness is important but that it is not easily bearable. The touch at Pranam and bodily closeness do not mean the same thing. By bodily closeness I meant living with the Mother or in continued and frequent physical contact with her.... As for bearing the closeness, most people do that usually by shutting themselves as much as possible to the pressure, — when they can't do that they get upset by it. That is the whole fact of the matter.

5-8-1935

*

I am afraid all these are mental constructions. You are constructing in your mind what X ought to feel. But as a matter of fact neither X's nor anybody's difficulties are removed by their coming to Mother or by their sitting one hour or two hours or even three hours with her. Plenty of people have done that and gone away as glum, desperate and revolted as they came. Among the people who see the Mother like Y are some who have crises as bad as yours...and as frequent.... It is also not true that those who have talked much with Mother (about houses, repairs, servants, etc.) understood her better. In former days some people used to see much of Mother in another way, i.e., to talk with her on all sorts of subjects — but even those did not really understand her. I repeat that all that is mental building and constructed inference and does not square with the facts. It is only when one is inwardly open to her that one profits by the "contact" with her, not the physical but the spiritual or inner contact, and then the mere thought of her or a mere thought from her can set right anything wrong; then the physical contact also can help, but it is not indispensable. And as for understanding her, it is only by entering into the spiritual consciousness that one can understand her, or if not understand in the mind, at least feel and respond to what she is through an increasing oneness.

4-8-1935

*

It would be most foolish to call back this meaningless delusion — for nothing can be farther from the actual and practical truth than to suppose that those who are in physical nearness to the Mother or have frequent physical approach are happier or more satisfied than others — it is not in the least true — or to allow it to prevent the progress of the inner peace. If you would only get rid of this delusion, nothing would be able to prevent the growth of the Peace and that inner nearness which alone makes people in this Ashram divinely happy. Happiness comes from the soul's satisfaction, not from the vital's or the body's. The vital is never satisfied; the body soon ceases to be moved at all by what it easily or always has. Only the psychic being brings the real joy and felicity.

8-9-1934

*

Quite so. None need be jealous of anything or anybody, since each has his own point of contact [with the Mother] which nobody else has — apart from what all have.

4-1-1934

WRONG IDEAS ABOUT THE MOTHER'S SMILE
AND TOUCH AT PRANAM

The Mother deals with each one in a different way, according to their need and their nature, not according to any fixed mental rule. It would be absurd for her to do the same thing with everybody as if all were machines which had to be touched and handled in the same way. It does not at all mean that she has more affection for one than for another, or those she touches in a particular way are better Sadhaks or less so. The Sadhaks think in that way because they are full of ignorance and ego. Instead of thinking whether the Mother favours one more or the other less, comparing and watching what she does, they ought to be concerned at Pranam with only their own spiritual reception of her influence. Pranam is for that and not for these other things which have nothing to do with Sadhana.

Jealousy and envy are things common to human nature, but these are the very things that a Sadhak ought to throw out of himself. Otherwise why is he a Sadhak at all? He is supposed to be here for seeking the Divine — but in the seeking for the Divine jealousy, envy, anger, etc., have no place. They are movements of the ego and can only create obstacles to the union with the Divine.

It is much better to remember that one is seeking for the Divine and make that the whole governing Idea and aim of the life. It is that which pleases the Mother more than anything else; these jealousies and envies and competitions for her favour can only displease and distress her.

31-10-1935

*

Q: At the Pranam ceremony I am not able to fathom

the mystery of the Mother's working: what she gives and how I receive it. What is the inner meaning of her touch on my head or her look into my eyes.

A: You have to develop the inner intuitive response first — i.e. to think and perceive less with the mind and more with the inner consciousness. Most people do everything with the mind and how can the mind know? The mind depends on the senses for its knowledge.

10-7-1936

*

All this idea about the Mother's looks and her hand in the blessing which is current in the Ashram is perfectly irrational, false, even imbecile. I have a hundred times written to people that the whole thing is wrong and rests on a false suggestion of the adverse forces made in order to create a disturbance. The Mother does not refrain from smiling or vary her smile or her manner of blessing in order to show displeasure or because of anything the Sadhak has done. She does not, as certain people annoyingly believe, dose out her smiles or blessings in such a way as to assign a number of marks for each Sadhak according to his good behaviour or bad behaviour. These variations are not intended to assign a competitive place to each Sadhak, as to schoolboys in a class. All these ideas are absolutely absurd, trivial and unspiritual. The Ashram is not a schoolboys' class nor is the Yoga a competitive examination. All this is the creation of the narrow physical mind and vital ego and desire. If the Sadhaks want to get a true basis and make true progress, they must get these ideas out of their minds altogether. Yet they cling obstinately to it in spite of all I can write, so dear is this falsehood to their mind. You must get rid of it altogether. At the Pranam the Mother puts her force to help the Sadhak — what he ought to do is to receive quietly and simply, not to spoil the occasion by these foolish ideas and by watching who gets more of her hand and smile and who gets less. All that must go.

8-12-1936

*

Q: During Pranam what does the Mother want to show us by her special expression? Does it express her liking or disliking any action of the persons concerned?

A: She wants to show you nothing; it has nothing to do with the doings or misdoings of the Sadhaks. Pranam is not intended for watching the Mother's expression or what she does with this one or that one or in what way she smiles or with how much of her hand she blesses — the Sadhaks' preoccupation with these things is childish and for the most part full of mistaken inferences, imaginations, often curiosity, desire for gossip, criticism etc. Such a state of mind is a hindrance, not a help to Sadhana. The proper attitude is one of self-dedication and simple and straightforward receptivity to what the Mother wishes to give, an undisturbed and undisturbing openness to her working in the being.

*

Understand once for all that the Mother is not using the Pranam to show her pleasure and displeasure; it is not meant for that purpose. The only circumstance under which the Mother's attitude at Pranam is likely to be influenced by the actions of the Sadhak is when there is some great betrayal or a violent breach of the main rules of spiritual life...or when the Sadhak has become positively hostile to the Mother and the Yoga. But then it is not a special show of displeasure at Pranam, but a withdrawal of the gift of grace which is quite a different matter.

*

Many of the Sadhaks are in the habit of thinking the Mother is displeased, not smiling at them, angry when it is quite otherwise. This usually happens when their own consciousness is not at peace or when they are thinking or conscious of faults or wrong movements or wrong acts that they may have done. The idea that the Mother is angry is an imagination; if there is anything not as usual, it is in the Sadhak himself and not in the Mother.

*

The Mother's force can come down quite nicely and gently — there is no need of palpitations, giddiness or nausea for that. The Mother was not at all angry with you. I suppose you expected her to be angry and see like that?

All the Sadhaks do that — and I have not yet been able to cure them of this seeing their own imaginations in the Mother's face or manner.

*

Q: We depend very much on finding in the Mother's ways a manifestation of her love for us. We feel we can progress when we get it.

A: This demand for physical manifestation of love must go. It is a dangerous stumbling-block on the way of Sadhana. A progress made by indulgence of this demand is an insecure progress which may any moment be thrown down by the same force that produced it.

8-10-1935

*

Q: I have heard that many Sadhikas love the Mother so much that they are ready to die for her. But if there is no physical expression of the Mother's love for them, they can't love her and some go so far as to revolt, weep or fast.

A: It is self-love that makes them do it. It is just the same kind of vital love that people have outside (loving someone for one's own sake, not for the sake of the beloved). What is the use of that in the Sadhana here? It can only be an obstacle.

15-10-1935

*

It is not the mind but the lower vital that gets troubled after Pranam — all the rest comes in as suggestions because the gate has been opened to them by this trouble. There are certain stock tricks of the adverse Force to disturb the Sadhana and one of them is this notion in the lower vital of not having been perfectly blessed at Pranam or not having got a smile or not the proper kind of smile or of the Mother's face being serious and severe. Whoever lets in that feeling, immediately suggestions of revolt, depression or dissatisfaction pour in into his mind. The only thing to be done for that is to cast off patiently all acceptance of this feeling, knowing that it is a drop of poison from the Adversary.

28-7-1936

*

It is certainly your imagination which makes you think that the Mother was "indifferent" or "hard" to you at Pranam. The Mother, on the contrary, made a special concentration in her blessing to help you. There are a certain number of Sadhaks who, when she does that, invariably ask, "Why were you displeased and hard with me today?", while there are others who cry out if there is the slightest departure from the ordinary movements, assuming that the Mother must have had a deliberate intention in it and that intention necessarily unfavourable to them, an intention of indifference or displeasure, and very often when she smiles more than usual in order to give them courage, they write to her that she was very serious that day and did not smile at all. Do not allow yourself to catch the infection and become one of them; for it creates a great obstacle to the help given and opens the door to serious vital troubles. Open yourself simply to the Mother's help with trust and confidence, that is the best way of not feeling far from her.

The Mother did not know at that time of your having spoken to X. So your conjecture of that being the cause of her fancied displeasure is quite groundless. It is quite wrong to think that the Mother gets displeased and angry with the Sadhaks and shows it with her actions at Pranam. This kind of idea of the Divine or of the Mother is a very mistaken one and you should not allow it to get hold of you.

5-7-1935

*

When the Mother does not smile at Pranam, it is not from displeasure but in almost every case from some reason not connected with any action of the Sadhak, — either from absorption or concentration on something that is being done. As you say, it does not matter — what is important is to receive what has to be received.

4-11-1934

*

It is a mistake to think that the Mother's not smiling means either displeasure or disapproval of something wrong in the Sadhak. It is very often merely a sign of absorption or of inner concentration. On this occasion the Mother was putting a question to your soul.

31-7-1938

*

It is a great pity you allowed the thought that the Mother was severe with you to come in and throw you down. These thoughts are never true and whenever a Sadhak indulges it, he is always invaded by the old movements. The Mother's love and kindness have always been the same and will always remain the same to you, so you should never accept this idea that she is displeased or severe. But whatever the mistakes or difficulties, our help will be with you and the Mother's force will work to bring you out and get you back the psychic openness and peace which you had for many days this time and which is bound to return and become permanent after a while.

19-11-1935

*

Q: People get troubled when they see the Mother looking serious instead of smiling. They find it difficult not to feel that they have displeased her in some way or other.

A: The whole foundation of the difficulty is erroneous. It is the wrong idea that if Mother is serious it must be because of some personal displeasure against "me" — each Sadhak who complains of being the "me". I have repeated a hundred times to complaints that it is not so, but nobody will give up this idea — it is too precious to the ego. The Mother's seriousness is due to some absorption in some work she is doing or, very often, to some strong attack of hostile forces in the atmosphere.

19-4-1935

*

Q: *Sometimes the Mother looks at us with a smile as if she were pleased; at other times quite differently, in a rather serious way.*

A: Why not? The Mother cannot be serious, absorbed in herself? Or do you think it is only displeasure against the Sadhaks that can make her so?

18-6-1933

*

Q: *One sometimes catches from the atmosphere a depression when people are passing before the Mother for Pranam; it is chiefly connected with her smiling or not smiling.*

A: That is because many Sadhaks are full of this idea. They are looking to see if the Mother smiles or how she smiles or what she does, instead of being quiet and concentrated to receive from her. So the atmosphere is full of that.

6-10-1933

*

Q: *The physical being feels the need of the Mother's smile when it meets her look. Is it a kind of desire?*

A: Yes. There has to be no disturbance when it does not come (knowing that its absence is not a sign of displeasure or anything of the kind) — then the Ananda of receiving it will be purer.

11-12-1933

*

You should certainly throw away the vital demand and the disturbance which it creates in your Sadhana. Mother gives her smile to all and she does not withhold it from some and give it to others. When people think otherwise, it is because some vital disturbance, depression or demand or some movement of jealousy, envy or competition distorts their vision.

27-2-1933

*

On that day the Mother did not smile at anybody. It was not personal to you. A particular Power was acting in her which did not act in the ordinary way.

10-4-1934

*

If the Mother does not put her hand on the head in Pranam, it does not mean that she is displeased — it may have quite other causes. People have this idea but they are quite mistaken. Sometime ago the Mother failed to put her hand on the head of a Sadhika at Pranam for two days. People mocked at her and looked down at her. As a matter of fact she was having remarkable realisations and getting more power from the Mother at Pranam than on ordinary days. The whole idea is an error.

2-8-1933

*

Q: *If the ego determines its revolt according to the Mother's failing to smile or to put her hand on our head,*

> *how is it that at times it can remain quiescent in spite of*
> *her failing to do so?*

A: The ego acts according to these things when it dominates;
when it does not dominate or is not present then these
motives can have no effect. The whole question is whether the
ego leads or something else leads. If the higher consciousness
leads, then even if the Mother does not smile or put her hand at
all, there will be no egoistic reaction. Once the Mother did that
with a Sadhika, being herself in trance — the result was that the
Sadhika got a greater force and Ananda than she had ever got
when the Mother put her hand fully.

11-11-1935

*

> *Q: Yesterday it happened that the Mother did not bless*
> *me with her hand during Pranam. But I was more de-*
> *lighted and cheerful than usual. Why did this bring me*
> *more happiness? Why does it take place with me alone?*

A: That is not so. It has taken place with others. One of them
at least found that she felt on such an occasion even more force
of the Mother than usual flowing through her than on ordinary
occasions.

It is not true. There are instances in which Mother did not smile
or put her hand at all (being in trance) but the Sadhak being in a
right and receptive attitude received far more than ever before.

*

Your idea about Mother's mysterious smile is your own imagination — Mother says that she smiled with the utmost kindness
and took the most helpful attitude possible towards you. I had
written to you already that you must not put these imaginations

between yourself and the Mother; for they push the help given away from you. These imaginations and their effect on you are suggested by the same vital forces that are disturbing you so that you may not get free from the disturbance.

My help and the Mother's help are there — you have only to keep yourself open to it to recover.

27-3-1933

*

Why should you think that the Mother will be angry? We have ourselves told you to write everything frankly and conceal nothing — so there is not the least likelihood that she will resent what you write. Moreover, she knows perfectly well the difficulties of the Sadhana and of human nature and if there is a goodwill and a sincere aspiration such as you have, any stumblings or falterings of the moment will not make any difference in her attitude to the Sadhak. The Mother thinks you must have had a wrong impression about her putting her hand just a little only — for she was just the same with you as always and there has been no reason why there should be any change.

17-4-1933

*

I do not at all understand why you should think that the Mother was displeased with you for any reason whatever. She was just as she is always with you. Even if you had made any mistake, the Mother now is disposed to overlook mistakes and leave it to the pressure of the Light and the psychic being of the Sadhak to set things right. But why on earth should she be displeased because you wanted to stop the French lessons with X or for any such trivial reason! Whether you continue or suspend your lessons is a detail which has to be settled in accordance with the condition of your mind and the needs of your Sadhana and it can be settled either way. It is surprising that you should think Mother could show displeasure over so slight a matter. You must get over a nervousness of this kind and not disturb your good condition by

imaginations — for it is an imagination since it had no reality
behind it. Have a more perfect confidence and do not let your
mind create difficulties where there are none.

*

Mother was not in the least displeased about the tea, why should
she be? Nor was she angry with you at all. She smiled at you
as usual — you must have been thinking of something else
and not observed it. There is no reason at all for your sadness
therefore — you should throw these ideas aside, Mother does not
get displeased about such trifles.

30-11-1933

*

Exactly, I say "the Mother's smiling or not smiling has nothing
to do with anything in you." I say also "It is yourself becoming
conscious, it is not any displeasure of the Mother that makes
you conscious — it is her mere presence that makes it possible
for you to become conscious of yourself, it is not any displeasure,
it is not any sad looking that does it."

*

There is no chance of the Mother giving you the "look" you
fear. On your side do not imagine one when it is not there —
any number of people are still doing that!

*

It is, of course, the resistance of the old vital in the past that is
being redeemed which creates this irritation and these imaginations about the Mother's displeasure. For, as a matter of fact,
there was no dissatisfaction against you in the Mother's mind
and this idea is usually a suggestion to the Sadhak's mind from
the Force that wants to create the wish to go or any other kind of
discontent or depression. It is a curious form of delusion that
has taken root, as it were, in the Ashram atmosphere and is che-

rished not so much by the individual vital as by the forces that work upon it to break, if possible, the Sadhana. You must not allow any harbourage to that or else it will create any amount of trouble. The absence of proper sleep naturally brings a state of fatigue in the nerves which helps these things to come — for it is through the physical consciousness that they attack and if it can make that consciousness tamasic in any way, their entry is more easy.

15-9-1936

*

The Mother has in no way changed towards you nor is she disappointed with you — that is the suggestion drawn from your own state of mind and putting its wrong sense of disappointment and unfitness on to the Mother. She has no reason to change or be disappointed, as she has always been aware of the vital obstacles in you and still expected and expects you to overcome them. The call to change certain things that seem to be in the grain of character is proving difficult even for the best Sadhaks, but the difficulty is no proof of incompetence. It is precisely this impulse to go that you must refuse to admit — for so long as these forces think they can bring it about, they will press as much as they can on this point. You must also open yourself more to the Mother's Force in that part and for that it is necessary to get rid of this suggestion about the Mother's disappointment or lack of love, for it is this which creates the reaction at the time of Pranam. Our help, support, love are there always as before — keep yourself open to them and with their aid drive out these suggestions.

26-1-1937

*

Mother put her hand just as usual. Not only so, but as she saw your condition needed special help, she tried to give it. But when you are in this condition, it is unfortunate that you are so much occupied with the feeling of misery as to feel nothing else, nothing that does not minister to or increase the misery. Support you always have; there is absolutely no reason why we should withhold it. If anyone is in serious trouble in the Ashram, that falls on us and most on the Mother — so it is absurd to suppose that we can take pleasure in anyone suffering. Suffering, illness, vital storms (lusts, revolts, angers) are so many contradictions of what we are striving for and therefore obstacles to our work. To end them as soon as possible is the only will we can have, not to keep them in existence.

If you could only acquire the power to detach yourself somewhere in you when these storms come, not to be swept away by the push or the thoughts that rise! Then there would be something that could feel the support and be able to react against these forces.

28-6-1935

*

It is entirely untrue that Mother was pushing you away today. There may be days when she is absorbed and therefore physically inattentive to what her hand is doing. But today she was specially attentive to you and at the Pranam she was putting force on you for peace, tranquillity and the removal of difficulty. If she at all acted by the palm or anything else, it was for that she was acting. About this there can be no mistake, for she was specially conscious of her action and purpose today. What must have happened was that something must have felt the pressure and intervened and persuaded your physical mind by suggestion that it was *you* she was pushing away, not the difficulty. This is a very clear instance of how easy it is for the Sadhaks to make a wrong inference and think that the Mother is doing the very opposite of what she is doing. Very often when she has concentrated most to help them by pressing out their difficulties, they have written to her "You were very severe and displeased with me this morning." The only way to avoid these wrong reactions is to have full psychic confidence in the Mother, believing that all she does is for their good and out of the Divine Mother's care for them and not against them. Then nothing of this kind will happen. Those who do that, can get the full help of her concentration even if in her absorption she does not touch the hand or smile. That is why I have constantly told the Sadhaks not to put their own interpretations on the Mother's appearance or actions at the Pranam — because these interpretations may always be wrong and make an opening for an unfounded depression and an attack.

23-1-1935

*

The obsession about the smile and touch has to be overcome and rejected because it has become an instrument of the contrary Forces to upset the Sadhaks and hamper their progress. I have seen any number of cases in which the Sadhak is going on well or even having high experiences and change of consciousness and suddenly this imagination comes across and all is confusion, revolt, sorrow, despair and the inner work is interrupted and endangered. In most cases this attack brings with it a sensory delusion so that even if the Mother smiles more than usual or gives the blessing with all her force she is told "you did not smile, you did not touch" or "you hardly touched". There have been any number of instances of that also — the Mother telling me, "I saw X disturbed or else a suggestion coming towards him and I gave him my kindest smile and blessing", and yet afterwards we get a letter affirming just the contrary, "you did not smile, etc." And you are all ready to give the Mother the lie, because you felt you saw and your senses cannot be deceived! as if a mind disturbed does not twist the sense observation also! as if it were not a common fact of psychology that one constantly gets an impression according to his mood or thought! Even if the smile or touch were less, it should not be the cause of such reproaches, if there is not an intention in it and there is no intention at all as we have constantly warned all of you. Of course, the cause is that the Sadhaks apply the movements of a vital human love to the Mother and the ordinary vital human love is full of contrary movements of distrust, misunderstanding, jealousy, anger, despair. But in Yoga this is most undesirable — for here trust in the Mother, faith in her divine Love is of great importance;

anything that denies or disturbs it opens the door to obstacles and wrong reactions. It is not that there should be no love in the vital, but it must purify itself of these reactions and fix itself on the psychic being's trust and confident self-giving. Then there can be the full progress.

30-6-1935

*

These things ought to be entirely rejected. When they rise they often twist the consciousness so much as to falsify sometimes the vision itself and always the feeling. The Mother has observed constantly that the people on whom she has smiled tell her she has been glowering and severe or that she has been displeased when there was no displeasure in her and then on the strength of that they go wrong altogether.

10-4-1933

*

Q: I see that every evening some being throws false suggestions upon me, saying, "The Divine does not like you." Lately their force of insistence has increased. I try my best to reject them but without any success. May the Mother prevent this being from approaching me ever! What is that being? From some vital world?

A: Yes, it is a being of falsehood from the vital world which tries to make one take its false suggestions for the truth and disturb the consciousness, and get it to leave the straight path and either get depressed or turned against the Mother. If you reject and refuse to listen or believe always, it will disappear.

30-3-1933

INADVISABILITY OF LISTENING TO FALSE
CRITICISM OF THE MOTHER

It might be charitable to warn X not to listen to imbecile remarks of this kind [against the Mother] from whomsoever they may come, and, if he hears them, to do nothing to propagate them. He had been progressing extremely well because he opened himself to the Mother; but if he allows stupidities like that to enter his mind, it may influence him, close him to the Mother and stop his progress.

As for Y, if he said and thought a thing like that [about the Mother] it explains why he has been suffering in health so much lately. If one makes oneself a mouthpiece of the hostile forces and lends oneself to their falsehoods, it is not surprising that something in him should get out of order.

7-1-1932

CAUSES OF THE MOTHER'S ILLNESS

The Mother has had a very severe attack and she must absolutely husband her forces in view of the strain the 24th November will mean for her. It is quite out of the question for her to begin seeing everybody and receiving them meanwhile — a single morning of that kind of thing would exhaust her altogether. You must remember that for her a physical contact of this kind with others is not a mere social or domestic meeting with a few superficial movements which make no great difference one way or the other. It means for her an interchange, a pouring out of her forces and a receiving of things good, bad and mixed from them which often involves a great labour of adjustment and elimination and in many cases, though not in all, a severe strain on the body. If it had been only a question of two or three people, it would have been a different matter; but there is the whole Ashram here ready to enforce each one his claim the moment she opens her doors. You surely do not want to put all that upon her before she has recovered her health and strength! In the interests of the work itself — the Mother has never cared in the least for her body or her health for its own sake and that indifference has been one reason, though only an outward one, for the damage done — I must insist on her going slowly in the resumption of the work and doing only so much at first as her health can bear.

It seems to me that all who care for her ought to feel in the way
I do.

*

I had hoped to write shortly, but I have not been able to do so.
Therefore, for the moment, since I have promised you this letter
in the morning, I can only repeat, on the other matter, that I
have not said that you in any degree or the Sadhaks generally
were the cause of the Mother's illness. To another who wrote
something of the kind from the same personal standpoint, I
replied that the Mother's illness was due to a struggle with
universal forces which far overpassed the scope of any individual
or group of individuals. What I wrote about the strain thrown
on the Mother by the physical contact was in connection with
her resumption of work — and it concerns the conditions under
which the work can best be done, so that these forces may not in
future have the advantage. Conditions have been particularly
arduous in the past owing to the perhaps inevitable development
of things, for which I do not hold anyone responsible; but now
that the Sadhana has come down to the most material plane on
which blows can still be given by the adverse forces, it is necessary to make a change which can best be done by a change
in the inner attitude of the Sadhaks; for that alone now can
make — until the decisive descent of the supramental Light and
Force — the external conditions easier. But of this I cannot
write at the tail-end of a letter.

16-11-1931

*

I have not yet said anything about the Mother's illness because
to do so would have needed a long consideration of what those
who are at the centre of a work like this have to be, what they
have to take upon themselves of human or terrestrial nature and
its limitations and how much they have to bear of the difficulties
of transformation. All that is not only difficult in itself for the

mind to understand but difficult for me to write in such a way
as to bring it home to those who have not our consciousness or
our experience. I suppose it has to be written but I have not yet
found the necessary form or the necessary leisure.

19-11-1931

*

It is much easier for the Sadhak by faith in the Mother to get
free from illness than for the Mother to keep free — because the
Mother by the very nature of her work had to identify herself
with the Sadhaks, to support all their difficulties, to receive into
herself all the poison in their nature, to take up besides all the
difficulties of the universal earth-Nature, including the possibility
of death and disease in order to fight them out. If she had not
done that, not a single Sadhak would have been able to practise
this Yoga. The Divine has to put on humanity in order that the
human being may rise to the Divine. It is a simple truth, but
nobody in the Ashram seems able to understand that the Divine
can do that and yet remain different from them — can still remain the Divine.

8-5-1933

*

*Q: People in the Ashram believe that their difficulties
and illnesses are taken by the Mother on herself and therefore she has sometimes to suffer. But at that rate there
would be too much onrush of these things on her from
many Sadhaks. An idea comes to me of taking upon
myself some of these difficulties and illnesses so that
I can also suffer with her pleasantly?*

A: Pleasantly? It would be anything but pleasant either for you
or for us.

It is rather a crude statement of a fact. The Mother in order
to do her work had to take all the Sadhaks inside her personal
being and consciousness; thus personally (not merely imper-

sonally) taken inside, all the disturbances and difficulties in them including illnesses could throw themselves upon her in a way that could not have happened if she had not renounced the self-protection of separateness. Not only illnesses of others could translate themselves into attacks on her body — these she could generally throw off as soon as she knew from what quarter and why it came — but their inner difficulties, revolts, outbursts of anger and hatred against her could have the same and a worse effect. That was the only danger for her (because inner difficulties are easily surmountable), but matter and the body are the weak point or crucial point of our Yoga, since this province has never been conquered by the spiritual Power, the old Yogas having either left it alone or used on it only a detail mental and vital force, not the general spiritual force. It was the reason why after a serious illness caused by a terribly bad state of the Ashram atmosphere, I had to insist on her partial retirement so as to minimise the most concrete part of the pressure upon her. Naturally, the full conquest of the physical would revolutionise matters, but as yet it is the struggle.

                                                                31-3-1934

*

> Q: Is it not inevitable that in the process of conversion
> and transformation all these resistances, disturbances,
> revolts should arise in every Sadhak? Could they be
> eliminated by anyone from the very beginning of his
> Sadhana so that there would be less of these things for
> the Mother to take upon her own self?

A: The nature of the terrestrial consciousness and of humanity being what it is, these things were to some extent inevitable. It is only a very few who escape with the slighter adverse movements only. But after a time these things should disappear. It does so disappear in individuals — but there seems to be a great difficulty in getting it to disappear from the atmosphere of the Ashram — somebody or other always takes it up and from him it tries to spread to others. It is, of course, because there is behind it one of the principles of life according to the Ignorance — a deeply rooted tendency of vital Nature. But it is the very aim of Sadhana to overcome that and substitute a truer and diviner vital Force.

1-4-1934

*

What you saw is correct, but if the attitude of the Sadhak is the true psychic attitude, then the Mother has not to suffer; she can act on them without anything falling on her.

22-1-1937

*

It is due to the impurities of the Sadhaks thrown on the Mother.

There seems to be no remedy possible before the physical change. If the Mother puts an inner wall between her and the Sadhaks, it would not happen, but then they would be unable to receive anything from her. If all were more careful to come to her with their deepest and highest consciousness, then there would be less chance of these things happening.

*

The danger of helping others is the danger of taking upon oneself their difficulties. If one can keep oneself separate and help, this does not occur. But the tendency in helping is to take the person partially or completely into one's larger self. This is what the Mother has had to do with the Sadhaks and the reason why she has sometimes to suffer — for one cannot always be on guard against any backwash when one is absorbed or in action. There is also the difficulty that the persons helped get the habit of drawing and pulling on your forces instead of leaving it to you to give just what you can and ought to give. And many other smaller possibilities one who helps others has to face.

29-1-1935

*

There are many who did that in the past. I don't know that he does it now. But all bad thoughts upon the Mother or throwing of impurities on her may affect her body as she has taken the Sadhaks into her consciousness nor can she send these things back to them as it might hurt them.

17-3-1936

*

There is not the slightest necessity for the Mother drawing impurities into herself — any more than for the Sadhak inviting impurity to come into himself. Impurity has to be thrown away, not drawn in.

18-3-1936

*

The idea of unburdening desires, imperfections, impurities, illnesses on the Mother so that she may bear the results instead of the Sadhaks is a curious one. I suppose it is an imitation of the Christian ideal of a Christ suffering on the cross for the sake of humanity. But it has nothing to do with the Yoga of transformation.

1-11-1936

REASONS OF THE MOTHER'S TEMPORARY RETIREMENT

There will always be doubts, upsettings and confusion of the physical mind and vital, so long as the vital approaches the Mother from the wrong standpoint, — e.g. if it insists on judging her by her response to its demands and ideas of what she ought to give it. Not to impose one's mind or vital will on the Divine but to receive the Divine's Will and follow it, is the true attitude of Sadhana. Not to say "This is my right, want, claim, need, requirement, why do I not get it?", but to give oneself, to surrender and to receive with joy whatever the Divine gives, not grieving or revolting, is the right way. Then what one receives will be the right thing for one. All this you know very well; why do you constantly allow your outer vital to forget it and drag you back towards the old wrong attitude?

As for the Mother drawing back from the old course, routine etc. of her action with regard to the Sadhaks, it was a sheer necessity of the work and the Sadhana. Everything had got into a wrong groove, was full of mixed movements and a mistaken attitude — and consequently things were going on in the same rajaso-tamasic round without any chance of issue — like a squirrel in a cage. The Mother's illness was an emphatic warning that this could not be allowed to go on any longer. A new basis of action and relations has to be built up in which no further sanction will ever seem to be given to the past mistaken movements of the Sadhaks which were standing in the way of the descent of the Truth into the physical (material) nature. The basis cannot be built in a day, but the Mother had to stand back, otherwise to build it at all would be impossible.

7-12-1931

*

It is not a fact that the Mother is retiring more and more or that she has any intention of going inside entirely like me. Your remarks about the privileged few are incomprehensible to me; we are not confiding in a few at the expense of others or telling them what is happening while keeping silent to you. This is an old complaint of yours and it has no foundation. If anybody claims to have the special confidence of the Mother, he is making an egoistic claim which is not justifiable. Your real point seems to be about the Mother's not taking up the soup and its accompaniments again. I have told you already why she was compelled by the experience of her illness to stand back from the old routine — which had become for most of the Sadhaks a sort of semi-ecclesiastical routine and nothing more. It was because of the mistaken attitude of the Sadhaks which had brought about an atmosphere full of movements contrary to the Yoga and likely to lead to disaster — as it had already begun to do. To resume the soup on the old footing would be to bring back the old condi-

tions and end in a repetition of the same round of wrong movements and the same results. The Mother has been slowly and
carefully taking steps to renew on another footing her control
of things after her illness, but she can take no step which will
allow the old dark movements to return — movements of some
of which I think you yourself were beginning to take notice. The
next step is for the Sadhaks themselves to take; they must make
it possible (by their change of attitude, by their resolution to rise
on the lower vital and physical plane into the true consciousness)
for a union with the Mother on that plane *in the right way and
with the right result* to become possible. More I cannot say just
now; but I fully intend to be more explicit hereafter — so far
as I can without special reference to individuals; for there are
things personal to people's Yoga that can often be spoken of only
to themselves and not to others.

As for your other questions I shall consider them in another
letter. I will only say that what happens is for the "best" in this
sense only that the end will be a divine victory in spite of all difficulties — that has been and always will be my seeing, my faith
and my assurance — if you are willing to accept it from me.
But that does not mean that your sadness and depression are
necessary to the movement! The sooner they disappear never to
recur again, the more joyously the Mother and I will advance on
the steep road to the summits, and the easier it will be for you to
realise what you want, the complete Bhakti and Ananda.

28-12-1931

X

THE MOTHER'S HELP IN DIFFICULTIES

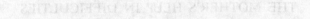

THE MOTHER'S HELP IN DIFFICULTIES

ASSURANCE OF VICTORY

Be sure that the Mother will always be with you to carry you upon the path. Difficulties come and difficulties go, but, she being with you, the victory is sure.

18-7-1936

*

The path you have now taken — to cleave to the Mother through all circumstances and let nothing shake you from that will bring the true solution of difficulties for you. For it seems the psychic being has started its work in you.

24-12-1935

*

Remain firm and turned in the one direction — towards the Mother.

*

THE DESCENT AND THE DIFFICULTIES

> *Q: Is it true that the nearer the descent of the Supermind the greater will be the difficulties of those in whom it is to come down first?*

A: It is true, unless they are so surrendered to the Mother, so psychic, so plastic, free from ego that the difficulties are spared to them.

FAITH IN THE MOTHER'S WORKING

It is the true attitude to leave all to the Mother and trust entirely in her and let her lead you on the path to the goal.

2-3-1936

*

It is not by his own strength or good qualities that anyone can attain the divine change; there are only two things that matter, the Mother's force at work and the Sadhak's will to open to it and trust in her working. Keep your will and your trust and care nothing for the rest — they are only difficulties that all meet in their Sadhana.

13-5-1936

*

Nothing is impossible if the nature of the psychic being is awake and leading you with the Mother's consciousness and force behind it and working in you.

19-10-1935

*

If one remains in full confidence in the Mother and psychically open, then the Mother's force will do all and one has only to give consent and keep oneself open and aspire.

12-11-1935

*

All faults and errors are redeemed by repentance. Confidence in the Mother, self-giving to the Mother, these if you increase them will bring the change in the nature.

*

Whether the progress is rapid or slow, the attitude should always be an entire faith and reliance on the Mother; just as you do not think that the progress was the result of your own effort or merit but of your taking the right attitude of reliance and the Mother's Force working, so you should not think that any slowness or difficulty was due to your own demerit but only seek to keep this attitude of reliance and let the Mother's Force work — slowly or rapidly does not matter.

14-11-1935

*

No. It is perhaps how some part of the vital or physical consciousness figured it. But the path is not a desert nor are you alone, since the Mother is with you.

2-11-1933

THE MOTHER'S POSITIVE ATTITUDE

Mother never thinks of future difficulties, falls or dangers. Her concentration is always on love and light, not on difficulties and downfalls.

*

It is the higher reality that Mother brings into the world — without it all else is ignorant and false.

3-8-1934

THE ONE THING TO DO ALWAYS

Once one has entered the path of Yoga, there is only one thing to do, to fix oneself in the resolution to go to the end whatever happens, whatever difficulties arise. None really gets the fulfilment in Yoga by his own capacity — it is by the greater Force that stands over you that it will come — and it is the call, persistent

through all vicissitudes, to that Force, by which the fulfilment
will come. Even when you cannot aspire actively, keep yourself
turned to the Mother for the help to come — that is the one thing
to do always.

                                                            3-1-1934

TRUST IN THE MOTHER'S FORCE IN DIFFICULTY

What is needed is perseverance — to go on without discourage-
ment, recognising that the process of the nature and the action
of the Mother's force is working through the difficulty even and
will do all that is needed. Our incapacity does not matter —
there is no human being who is not in his parts of nature in-
capable — but the Divine Force is also there. If one puts one's
trust in that, incapacity will be changed into capacity. Difficulty
and struggle themselves then become a means towards the
achievement.

                                                            27-5-1936

                                *

Do not brood over your difficulties. Leave them to the Mother
and let her Force work them out of you.

                                                            22-3-1935

                                *

Never allow this idea "I am not able", "I am not doing enough"
to come and vex you; it is a tamasic suggestion and brings depression and depression opens the way to the attacks of the wrong
forces. Your position should be, "Let me do what I can, the
Mother's force is there, the Divine is there to see that in due time
all will be done."

                                                            4-11-1935

                                *

Not to be disturbed, to remain quiet and confident is the right
attitude, but it is necessary also to receive the help of the Mother

and not to stand back for any reason from her solicitude. One ought not to indulge ideas of incapacity, inability to respond, dwelling too much on defects and failures and allowing the mind to be in pain and shame on their account; for these ideas and feelings become in the end weakening things. If there are difficulties, stumblings or failures, one has to look at them quietly and call in tranquilly and persistently the Divine help for their removal, but not to allow oneself to be upset or pained or discouraged. Yoga is not an easy path and the total change of the nature cannot be done in a day.

*

All this is of no utility — complainings, questionings, etc. of this kind should be put aside. You have to go on quietly, without depression or trouble, receiving the Mother's forces, allowing them to work, rejecting all that stands in their way but not troubled by difficulty or defects in yourself or by any delay or slowness in the working.

                                                                    25-10-1933

*

Do not admit these suggestions of despair or impatience. Give time for the Mother's force to act.

                                                                    12-6-1937

*

This kind of grief and despondency are the worst obstacles one can raise up in the Sadhana — they ought not to be indulged in. What one cannot do oneself one can get done by calling the Mother's force. To receive that and let it work in you is the true means of success in the Sadhana.

*

Whatever difficulties still remain, be sure that they will be surmounted. There is no need for the outer being to be nervous —

the Mother's Force and the devotion within you will be sufficient to overcome all that stands in the way.

*

There is no reason to be discouraged. Three years is not too much for the preparation of the nature and it is usually through fluctuations that it gradually grows nearer to the point where a continuous progress becomes possible. One has to cleave firmly to the faith in the Mother's working behind all appearances and you will find that that will carry you through.

31-8-1935

*

You should not yield to sorrow or despair — there is no reason why you should. The Mother's grace has not been withdrawn from you for a moment. Do not allow the attacks of others to shake you like this — you know well the motives from which they act — and for the rest they are not going to pursue any farther the course which a fit of passion dictated to them. The protection will be with you and you need not fear or sorrow any longer. Put your trust in the Divine and shake off all this like a nightmare that has passed. Believe that our love and grace are with you.

*

There has always been too much reliance on the action of your own mind and will — that is why you cannot progress. If you could once get the habit of silent reliance on the power of the Mother — not merely calling it in to support your own effort — the obstacle would diminish and eventually disappear.

*

The more one is open to the Mother's action, the more easily difficulties get solved and the right thing is done.

21-9-1934

*

It was by your personal efforts without guidance that you got into difficulties and into a heated condition in which you could not meditate etc. I asked you to drop the effort and remain quiet and you did so. My intention was that by your remaining quiet, it would be possible for the Mother's Force to work in you and establish a better starting-point and a course of initial experiences. It was what was beginning to come; but if your mind again becomes active and tries to arrange the Sadhana for itself, then disturbances are likely to come. The Divine Guidance works best when the psychic is open and in front (yours was beginning to open), but it can also work even when the Sadhak is either not conscious of it, or else knows it only by its results.

DIFFICULTIES AND THE MOTHER'S GRACE

Q: Can it be believed that the Mother's Grace is acting even when the difficulties do not disappear?

A: In that case everybody might say, "All my difficulties must disappear at once, I must attain to perfection immediately and without difficulties, otherwise it proves that the Mother's Grace is not with me."

20-7-1933

*

You must throw all that away. Such depressions can make you shut to what Mother is giving you. There is absolutely no good reason for such an attitude. The existence of difficulties is a known thing in the Yoga. That is no reason for questioning the final victory or the effectuality of the Divine Grace.

4-2-1933

PSYCHIC DEVELOPMENT AND THE MOTHER'S GRACE

Q: What is the Law of the working of the Mother's Grace?

A: The more one develops the psychic, the more is it possible
for the Grace to act.

13-8-1933

*

What has to be gained is the constant prominence of that part
which is always aware of the Mother — it is of course the psychic
— for that though it can be covered over for the time being cannot be misled by the contrary suggestions. Once it is awake, it
always re-emerges from obscuration — that is the guarantee of
the final arrival at the goal, but if it can be maintained in front
or even consciously felt behind in all conditions, then the stages
of the way also become comparatively safe and can be passed
with greater ease and security.

6-2-1937

*

It is when there is no attachment to outward things for their own
sake and all is only for the Mother and the life through the inner
psychic being is centred in her that the best condition is created
for the spiritual realisation.

11-11-1935

*

Never mind about the purity of the body. The love of the Mother
purifies both heart and body — if the soul's aspiration is there,
the body also is pure. What happened in the past does not in the
least matter.

THE MOTHER'S CONSTANT HELP

The Mother's help is always there but you are not conscious of
it except when the psychic is active and the consciousness not
clouded. The coming of suggestions is not a proof that the help
is not there. Suggestions come to all, even to the greatest Sadhaks
or to the Avatars — as they came to Buddha or Christ. Obstacles
are there — they are part of Nature and they have to be over-

come. What has to be attained is not to accept the suggestions, not to admit them as the truth or as one's own thoughts, to see them for what they are and keep oneself separate. Obstacles have to be looked at as something wrong in the machinery of human nature which has to be changed — they should not be regarded as sins or wrong doings which make one despair of oneself and of the Sadhana.

*

Q: Today while engaged in work I felt a peaceful energy and something like ice touching my head. Then the knowledge came to me with a strong feeling and vision that though the Mother is not physically near us, she is always present near and around us and is constantly removing all kinds of difficulties with the touch of her affectionate hand. Was this a vision or realisation? Through what consciousness did it come to me?

A: It is a realisation attended with vision and feeling. It is psychic and the mental together that produced it.

11-6-1933

STRAIGHTFORWARDNESS AND THE MOTHER'S HELP

Those who are not straightforward cannot profit by the Mother's help, for they themselves turn it away. Unless they change, they cannot hope for the descent of the supramental Light and Truth into the lower vital and physical nature; they remain stuck in their own self-created mud and cannot progress.

November, 1928

CHANGE OF THE VITAL WITH THE MOTHER'S HELP

The Mother's help is always there for those who are willing to receive it. But you must be conscious of your vital nature, and the vital nature must consent to change. It is no use merely observing that it is unwilling and that, when thwarted, it creates depression in you. Always the vital nature is not at first willing and always when it is thwarted or asked to change, it creates this depression by its revolt or refusal of consent. You have to insist till it recognises the truth and is willing to be transformed and to accept the Mother's help and grace. If the mind is sincere and the psychic aspiration complete and true, the vital can always be made to change.

15-7-1932

*

It is this idea that you are helpless because the vital consents to the wrong movement that comes in the way. You have to put your inner will and the Mother's light on the vital so that it shall change, not leave it to do what it likes. If one is to be "helpless" and moved by any part of the instrumental being, how is change possible? The Mother's force or the psychic can act, but on condition that the assent of the being is there. If the vital is left to do what it likes, it will always go after its old habits; it has to be made to feel that it must change.

*

What is still restless in the vital has to quiet down for the peace of mind to be even and constant. It has to be controlled, but only control will not be enough. The Mother's Power has to be called always.

10-4-1934

*

Put the Mother's notice henceforth at the door of your vital being, "No falsehood hereafter shall ever enter here", and station a sentry there to see that it is put into execution.

18-5-1933

*

The Mother cannot tell you to go because there is no true cause why you should go and it would be very bad for you to do so as well as bad for the work and everything else. The reasons for your not giving up the work are just the same as before and not in the least changed by anything that has happened. Jealousy is no doubt a great defect of the nature, but many here have it; almost everyone has some serious defect in his nature which stands in his way and gives trouble. But it is not a remedy for this to give up work and Sadhana and abandon the Mother. You have to go on working and doing the Sadhana with the Mother's aid behind you until this and all other obstacles are got rid of. We have told you already that these things cannot be got rid of in a day, but if you persevere and rely on the Mother they will yet disappear. Do not allow an adverse Force to mislead you; reject all depression and go straight forward till you reach the goal.

17-7-1935

*

We are very glad to hear that you are better and that X has helped you out of the crisis. Surely this jealousy must go and no trace of it remain. Do not doubt that the Mother's love is and will be always with you. Trust in her grace and all this will go out of you and leave you the true child of the Mother which in your mind and heart you always are.

18-7-1935

*

Mother has no wish to abandon you and it has never been her will that you should go away from her. You must put yourself in harmony with her will and then all will go right. Her love will guide you and her protection will be effective.

Rest until you are well. Do not be in a hurry to go to work before you have recovered your strength.

19-7-1935

CALLING THE MOTHER IN DIFFICULTY

When difficulties arise, remain quiet within and call down the Mother's force to remove them.

26-8-1933

*

To call to the Mother always is the main thing and with that to aspire and assent to the Light when it comes, to reject and detach oneself from desire and any dark movement. But if one cannot do these other things successfully, then call and still call.

The Mother's force is there with you even when you do not feel it; remain quiet and persevere.

15-9-1934

*

You should not allow yourself to get upset by these small things. If when the movements you complain of come, you remain quiet and open to the Mother and call her, after a time you will find a change beginning to come in you. Meditation is not enough; think of the Mother and offer your work and action to her, that will help you better.

7-4-1932

*

There is only one way if you cannot exert your will — it is to call the Force; even the call only with the mind or the mental word is better than being extremely passive and submitted to the attack, — for although it may not succeed instantaneously, the mental call even ends by bringing the Force and opening up the consciousness again. For everything depends upon that. In the externalised consciousness obscurity and suffering can always be there; the more the internalised consciousness reigns, the more these things are pushed back and out, and with the full internalised consciousness they cannot remain — if they come, it is as outside touches unable to lodge themselves in the being.

21-8-1933

*

Even when one cannot call in actively the Mother's Force one must keep the reliance that it will come.

26-8-1936

*

It is the physical mind that feels too inert — but if some part of the being turns to the Mother, that is enough to bring the help.

25-1-1934

*

It is an obsession from the subconscient physical bringing back the habitual thoughts, "I can't call rightly — I have no real aspiration, etc."; the depression, the memory, etc. are from the same source. It is no use indulging in these ideas. If you cannot call the Mother in what you think the right way, call her in any way — if you can't call her, think of her with the will to be rid of these things. Don't worry yourself with the idea whether you have true aspiration or not — the psychic being wants and that is sufficient. The rest is for the Divine Grace on which one must steadfastly rely — one's own merit, virtue or capacity is not the thing that brings the realisation.

I shall send the force to rid you of this obsession in any case, but if you can abandon these habitual ideas, it will make the disappearance of the attack easier.

4-1-1937

*

It is always best in these difficulties to tell the Mother and call for her help. It is probably something in his vital that needs somebody to protect and care for — but you must accustom yourself to the idea that it is not needed and the best thing is to give the person to the care of the Mother — offer the object of your affection to her.

15-11-1937

PRAYER TO THE MOTHER FOR INNER AND OUTER THINGS

> *Q: You say, "when one is a Sadhak the prayer should be for the inner things belonging to the Sadhana and for outer things only so far as they are necessary for that and for the Divine work". This latter portion about prayer for outer things is not clear to me. Can you kindly explain?*

A: All depends on whether the outer things are sought for one's own convenience, pleasure, profit etc., or as part of the spiritual life, necessary for the success of the work, the development and fitness of the instruments etc. It is a question mainly of inner attitude. If for instance you pray for money for buying nice food to please the palate, that is not a proper thing for a Sadhak; if you pray for money to give to the Mother and help her work, then it is legitimate.

> *Q: I quote several types of prayers which I offer and shall be grateful to know which of them are outer or inner, right or wrong, helpful or hindrance, or what amendment to them can make them pure: —*
> *1. In the night-time when I sit to read and an untimely attack of sleep comes, I pray to the Mother to be freed from the attack.*

A: If your reading is part of the Sadhana, that is all right.

> *Q: 2. When I go to sleep I pray to the Mother for her force to take over my Sadhana during the sleep, to make my sleep conscious, luminous, to protect me during the sleep, to keep me conscious of the Mother.*
> *3. When I wake up any time in the sleep I pray to the Mother to be with me and protect me.*

A: These two are part of the Sadhana.

Q: 4. While going out for and during walk I pray to give me force to take more exercise and to gain more strength and health and thank the Mother for the help.

A: If strength and health are requested as being necessary for the Sadhana and the development of the perfection of the instrument it is all right.

Q: 5. When I see any dog on the way while walking I at once pray to the Mother to protect from its attack and remove my fear.

A: A call for protection is always permissible. The removal of fear is part of the Sadhana.

Q: 6. When I go for food I pray for the Mother's force to help me to offer every morsel to the Mother, to get everything easily digested, to make a growth of complete equality and detachment in my consciousness enabling me to take any food with equal Rasa of universal Ananda without any insistence or seeking or greed or desire.

A: This is again part of the Sadhana.

Q: 7. When I go for work I pray for the Mother's force to take over my work, help me and make me do it well and carefully with love, devotion and pleasure, with the remembrance of the Mother and feeling of being supported and helped by her without ego or desire.

A: This also.

Q: 8. During the work also when there is a pause I pray for force, help and constant remembrance.

A: This also.

> Q: 9. When any bad or impure thought, seeing and
> sensation come in me I pray for its removal and purity.

A: This also.

> Q: 10. When I am reading I try to pray when possible
> to understand all quickly, to grasp and absorb completely.

A: If it is as Sadhana or for the development of the instrument, it
is all right.

> Q: 11. When I commit any mistake in the work I pray
> to be more conscious, alert and unerring.

A: This also is part of the Sadhana.

> Q: 12. When I go to the post office to register a parcel
> of Prasad to my friend I pray to have the parcel accepted
> immediately and avoid any delay.

A: That can be done, if avoidance of waste of time is considered
as part of the right regulation of the life of Sadhana.

> Q: 13. When I sit down for meditation I pray for
> Mother's juice to take over my meditation and make it
> deep, steady, concentrated and free from all attacks of
> troubling thoughts, vital restlessness, etc.

A: This is part of the Sadhana.

> Q: 14. In depression, difficulty, wrong suggestions,

> *doubt, inertia, on any occasion or happening I pray to*
> *the Mother to hold courage, keep faith, face them and*
> *overcome them.*

A: This also.

> *Q: 15. At all other times as far as I can I pray to the*
> *Mother to fill me with her peace, power, light etc., or*
> *offer any other kind of required prayer, and thank her for*
> *supporting, strengthening and sustaining me.*

A: This also.

REMOVAL OF RECURRING DIFFICULTIES

> *Q: What is the right way of meeting one's recurring*
> *difficulties?*

A: Equality, rejection, calling on the Mother's force.

1-8-1933

*

What stands in the way is the recurring circle of the old mixture. To break out of that is very necessary to arrive at an
inner Yogic calm and peace not disturbed by these things. If that
is established, it will be possible to feel in it the Mother's Presence, to open to her guidance, to get, not by occasional glimpses
but in a steady opening and flowering, the psychic perception
and the descent of the spiritual Light and Ananda. For that
help will be with you.

7-3-1937

*

Plenty of people have this condition (it is human nature) and there is naturally a way of coming out of it — having full faith in the Mother to quiet the inner mind (even if the outer continues to be troublesome) and call in it the Mother's Peace and Force, which is always there above you, into the *ādhāra*. Once that is there, consciously, to keep yourself open to it and let it go on working with a full adhesion, with a constant support of your consent, with a conscious rejection of all that is not that, till all the inner being is tranquillised and filled with the Mother's Force, Peace, Joy, Presence — then the outer nature will be obliged to follow suit in its turn.

8-5-1933

RECOVERY FROM BAD CONDITIONS

These bad conditions are a lapse (often due to a very slight cause) from the inner poise to the outer consciousness. When they happen do not get affected, but remain quiet, call the Mother and get back inward.

24-1-1936

*

An occasional sinking of the consciousness happens to every-body. The causes are various, some touch from outside, some-thing not yet changed or not sufficiently changed in the vital, especially the lower vital, some inertia or obscurity rising up from the physical parts of nature. When it comes, remain quiet, open yourself to the Mother and call back the true conditions and aspire for a clear and undisturbed discrimination showing you from within yourself the cause of the thing that needs to be set right.

4-3-1932

THE MOTHER'S HELP IN ATTACKS

It is the forces of the Ignorance that begin to lay siege and then make a mass attack. Every time such an attack can be defeated and cast out, there is a clearance in the *ādhāra*, a new field gained for the Mother in the mind, vital or physical or the adjacent parts of the being. That the place in the vital occupied by the Mother is increasing is shown by the fact that you are now offering a strong resistance to these sieges that used formerly to overpower you altogether.

To be able to call the Mother's presence or force at such times is the best way to meet the difficulty.

It is with the Mother who is always with you and in you that you converse. The only thing is to hear aright, so that no other voice can come in between.

7-12-1933

*

However strong the attack may be, and even if it overcomes you for the time being, still it will rapidly pass away if you have formed the habit of opening to the Mother. The peace will come back if you remain quiet and keep yourself open to it and to the Force. Once something of the Truth has shown itself within you, it will always, even if for a time heavily clouded over with wrong movements, shine out again like the sun in heaven. Therefore persevere with confidence and never lose courage.

14-3-1932

*

Q: What is the best means for the Sadhaks to avoid suffering due to the action of the hostile forces?

A: Faith in the Mother and complete surrender.

17-6-1933

*

Q: When the Sadhaks overlook some weakness of their nature in the process of transformation, is it not possible that it will be shown to them by the Divine Mother rather than through a painful wound at the weak point dealt by the hostile forces?

A: If they are sufficiently open to the Divine it can be done —
but most Sadhaks have too much egoism and lack of faith and
obscurity and self-will and vital desires, — it is that that shuts
them to the Mother and calls in the action of the hostile forces.

                                                    17-6-1933

*

The play of the mental and vital defects in the human nature
which belongs to the Ignorance is allowed — as also the attacks
and suggestions of the Asuric forces — so long as there is anything in the nature which responds to these things. If they rise
in you in the presence of the Mother, it is because then a strong
pressure is put on them so that they have either to go out or to
put up a fight for existence. The remedy is to open to the Mother
only and to reject entirely and at all times all other forces, and to
reject them most when they become most active. Faith, sincerity,
perseverance will do the rest.

                                                    16-11-1932

TESTING BY THE MOTHER

The idea of tests also is not a healthy idea and ought not to
be pushed too far. Tests are applied not by the Divine but by
the forces of the lower planes — mental, vital, physical — and
allowed by the Divine because that is part of the soul's training
and helps it to know itself, its powers and the limitations it has
to outgrow. The Mother is not testing you at every moment, but
rather helping you at every moment to rise beyond the necessity
of tests and difficulties which belong to the inferior consciousness. To be always conscious of that help will be your best safeguard against all attacks whether of adverse powers or of your
own lower nature.

THE MOTHER'S OCCULT ACTION FOR ANSWERING
CALLS FOR HELP

As to the experience, certainly X's call for help did reach the

Mother, even though all the details she relates in her letter might not have been present to the Mother's physical mind. Always calls of this kind are coming to the Mother, sometimes a hundred close upon each other and always the answer is given. The occasions are of all kinds, but whatever the need that occasions the call, the Force is there to answer it. That is the principle of this action on the occult plane. It is not of the same kind as an ordinary human action and does not need a written or oral communication on the one who calls; an interchange of psychic communication is quite sufficient to set the Force at work. At the same time it is not an impersonal Force and the suggestion of a divine energy that is there ready to answer and satisfy anybody who calls it is not at all relevant here. It is something personal to the Mother and if she had not this power and this kind of action she would not be able to do her work; but this is quite different from the outside practical working on the material plane where the methods must, necessarily, be different, although the occult working and the material working can and do join and the occult power give to the material working its utmost efficacy. As for the one who is helped not feeling the force at work, his knowing might help very substantially the effective working, but it need not be indispensable; the effect can be there even if he does not know how the thing is done. For instance, in your work in Calcutta and elsewhere my help has always been with you and I don't think it can be said that it was ineffective; but it was of the same occult nature and could have had the same effect even if you had not been conscious in some way that my help was with you.

24-3-1949

*

Q: It was 1 a.m. at night when my brother in excruciating pain called me and asked if Sri Aurobindo could heal him. I took out some Prasad flowers that were with me and touched the affected part with them. And lo! the pain vanished and he began to recover. I want to know if you were aware of this and heard my prayer.

A: What happens in such cases is that when someone is accepted, the Mother sends out something of herself to him and this is with him wherever he goes and is always in connection with her being here. So when he does anything like what you did in this case with faith and *bhakti*, it reaches, through that emanation of herself which is with him, the Mother's consciousness inner or outer and the Force goes in return for the result.

WRONG IDEAS ABOUT THE MOTHER'S
LISTENING TO CALLS

Q: When X complained to me about her difficulty I told her that it could be removed by calling the Mother's help. But she argued that there was no hope for the calls of a newcomer like herself to be heard by the Mother. There were so many calls from the older and advanced Sadhaks that fresh calls from a beginner like herself would be but calls in the wilderness and would go unheard in that clamour. I replied that if the Mother does not come in answer to our calls she must have her reasons; and there can be no doubt that when she comes she will come to stay. In the meantime we should have faith and equanimity and prepare the necessary conditions. Possibly she has more important work to do than to act to our bidding, and why should we insist that she should leave that work and attend to us? The Mother has never been known to fail in answering when a real call is sent to her straight from the heart, for the very force in the call presupposes her presence. When I told this to X, I felt a strong pressure and vibrations from the centre of my forehead downwards between the eyebrows. What is the reason of this?

A: X's reasonings are not very sound; yours are better if not altogether flawless. The Mother is not limited by the physical mind, so even if she has "more important" work to do, that would not in the least stand in the way of her listening to a call from the wilderness or anywhere else. Also spiritual things do not go by seniority; so why should the clamour of "older cases" keep her? She can be and is with all who need her. So your "Mother does not come? will not come?" is not quite to the point, but the rest of your answer is. Mother is there even now and working in you, it is only your inner vision and feeling that are not opened so that you cannot see or feel her.

What came down to the centre of the forehead was the answer, let us say the touch of the Mother's presence — her consciousness, her force working on you to open the centre of the inner mind, inner will, the inner vision and when that opens one begins to see and know what is to the physical eye invisible and to the surface mind unknowable.

11-10-1935

UNFAILING HELP AND PROTECTION

The experience you had of the power of the Name and the protection is that of everyone who has used it with the same faith and reliance. To those who call from the heart for the protection, it cannot fail. Do not allow any outward circumstance to shake the faith in you; for nothing gives greater strength than this faith to go through and arrive at the goal. Knowledge and Tapasya, whatever their force, have a less sustaining power — faith is the strongest staff for the journey.

The protection is there over you and the watchful love of the Mother. Rely upon it and let your being open more and more to it — then it will repel attacks and always uphold you.

8-10-1936

CONDITIONS FOR THE WORKING OF
THE MOTHER'S PROTECTION

The Mother has made an arrangement with a view to all the occult forces and the best possible conditions for the protection of the Sadhaks from certain forces of death, disease, etc. It cannot work perfectly because the Sadhaks themselves have not the right attitude towards food and kindred vital physical things. But still there is a protection. If, however, the Sadhaks go outside her formation, it must be on their own responsibility.... But this arrangement is for the Ashram and not for those who are outside.

14-7-1933

*

Q: Is it not true that the Sadhaks observe the rules laid down by the Mother because they feel that by not observing them and disobeying her one goes out of her protection?

A: It is precisely that — one immediately goes out of the protection.

8-6-1933

*

Q: All would like to allow the Mother's protection to remain with them; but perhaps certain conditions have to be fulfilled?

A: There are very few who allow it. There is a general protection around all, but most go out of it by their attitude, thoughts or actions or open the way to other forces.

24-8-1933

*

It is not because the Mother has withdrawn her protection — she has not done that. It is more likely that it [the difficulty] came because you have been going too much out of your inner being and externalising yourself. It is better to draw back within again and recover the inner calm and peace.

*

Q: If people constantly have the Mother's protection around them, I don't think they will ever have depression and doubt or anything hostile to the Divine.

A: These things may try to come but they will not be able to enter or stay.

*

Q: If a boy comes here at an early age, will he be free from the difficulties that usually go with sex?

A: It is not automatically true — it is only possible — but on condition he gets fully into the influence of the Mother, is not too open to the atmosphere of other Sadhaks who have it, does not get upset at the initial age and also does not upset himself by reading erotic literature etc. There is no one who has been able to do all that yet.

8-11-1933

ACCIDENTS AND THE MOTHER'S PROTECTION

Q: X had a car accident this morning. Could Mother not see the possibility of this accident beforehand and prevent it? Or was it because X had in some manner gone out of the zone of her protection?

A: It was not possible to prevent the accident. When the danger comes a call to the Mother is the first thing to be done, that makes the general protection at once effective. X was in too externalised a state to do that and he did the very opposite thing to what should have been done — trying to get away in front of the car instead of behind it. But the true cause was something more internal — one of those choices made by the inner being (not necessarily known to the conscious mind) which bring these things as a response.

27-1-1936

THE MOTHER'S PROTECTION ON THE VITAL PLANE

It was a dream of the vital plane where all kinds of dangers occur until you get courage to face them. If there is no fear or if there is the protection of the Mother (which becomes manifest by remembering or calling her) then these dangers come to nothing. It is the fear of mad men that brought the thing in the vital; such things as this fear have to be thrown out of the nature.

8-9-1933

*

What happened in your experience was that the vital being got free from the body through its desire to unite with the Mother (you met the Mother on the borders between the vital and physical) and lived with its own life independent of the body. It entered into the vital world and, not being sheltered any longer in the body, felt helpless at first, till it called the Mother. The appearance of X there might possibly have been some part of the vital of X himself, but was more probably a vital being in his shape, perhaps the very vital being who has been troubling him. When you go into the vital world, you meet many such things, — the one sufficient protection is to call the Mother.

7-9-1933

REJECTION OF DIFFICULTIES BY INWARD SURRENDER

To come physically to the Mother for getting rid of a disturbance is unnecessary and useless; it is inwardly that you must take refuge in her and throw away the wrong movement, as you have seen on this occasion. To come physically would only create a habit of getting wrong and coming to her to get right and it would also lead to the wrong movement of throwing the difficulty on her instead of inwardly giving it up, rendering its surrender. But it is a general surrender that is needed which could prevent these useless disturbances over trifling matters, egoisms, insistences on one's own point of view, anger because one does not have one's own way or a due recognition of one's independence or importance.

*

It is the inner oneness that saves, not the outer nearness.

17-11-1933

WRITING TO THE MOTHER FOR HELP

You did well to speak to X and also to write to the Mother. Of course, Mother had observed X's difficulties; it is correct that the difficulty is the lack of a certain free opening — otherwise all that could be removed quickly and the necessary change of nature (mind, ego, etc.) carried on by smooth gradation. To write as you do is helpful for opening oneself and for receiving the precise touch. X's logic about the Mother's knowing and therefore there being no need to write is applicable if there is a free or at least a sufficient flow of giving and reception between the Mother and the Sadhak, but when a serious difficulty comes, this logic is not so applicable. Naturally, we shall do our best to help him in his struggle.

14-5-1936

LAYING ALL MOVEMENTS BARE BEFORE THE MOTHER

One rule for you I can lay down, "Do not do, say or think anything which you would want to conceal from the Mother." And that answers the objections that rose within you — from your vital, is it not? — against bringing "these petty things" to the Mother's notice. Why should you think that the Mother would be bothered by these things or regard them as petty? If *all* the life is to be Yoga, what is there that can be called petty or of no importance? Even if the Mother does not answer, to have brought any matter of your action and self-development before her in the right spirit means to have put it under her protection,

in the light of the Truth, under the rays of the Power that is working for the transformation — for immediately those rays begin
to play and to act on the thing brought to her notice. Anything
within that advises not to do it when the spirit in you moves you
to do it, may very well be a device of the vital to avoid the ray
of the Light and the working of the Force. It may also be observed that if you open yourself to the Mother by putting the
movements of any part of you under her observation, that of itself creates a relation, a personal closeness with her other than
that which her general silent or not directly invited action main-
tains with all the Sadhaks.

All this, of course, if you feel ready for this openness, if the
spirit moves you to lay what is in you bare before her. For it is
then it is fruitful — when it comes from within and is spontaneous and true.

18-5-1932

*

*Q: Today a thought has come to me: "Why are you
forcing yourself so much with regard to the control of
the vital being? Better not bother about opening your
thoughts and desires to the Mother; rather leave Her
to work on you."*

A: If you want the Mother to work through you, you must lay
before her your thoughts and desires and reject them.

3-9-1933

*

*Q: On reading my yesterday's letter to the Mother I
feel today as if She was not much pleased with my laying
before Her the wrong thoughts I had about X and Y.*

A: Your writing these things does not give any displeasure
to Mother. It is better to write if you have them, than to be silent
about it.

9-6-1933

WORKING OF THE MOTHER'S FORCE FOR PHYSICAL CURE

The inherent strength of the body does not do things like that. It is the Mother's force that does it, when one calls and opens oneself. Even people who never did Yoga and are conscious of nothing, get cured like that without knowing the reason or feeling the way in which it was done. The force comes from above or in descending it envelopes and comes from without inside or it comes out from inside after descending there. When you are conscious of the play of the forces, then you feel the working.

It (awakening) means the conscious action of the psychic from behind. When it comes to the front it invades the mind and vital and body and psychicises their movements. It comes best by aspiration and an unquestioning and entire turning and surrender to the Mother. But also it sometimes comes of itself when the *ādhāra* is ready.

5-5-1933

*

Q: When I got up from sleep I found that a cold had already entered. My consciousness brought down the Mother's Force and the cold disappeared. The same process was tried for other troubles too. I want to know if the method adopted for the Force was quite the right one.

A: It is quite the right way. It is very good that you are learning to use the Force.

27-8-1934

*

It is a fact of my experience that when the resistance in the body is too strong and persistent, it can help to take some aid of physical means as an instrumentation for the Force to work more directly on the body itself; for the body then feels itself supported against the resistance from both sides, by means both physical as well as supraphysical. The Mother's force can work through both together.

1-9-1936

*

Q: Since more than a fortnight every time I receive the Mother's touch at Pranam time I feel a sense of strong nourishment accompanied by joy and strength, as if a new substance is being poured down even in my physical body.

A: As you suffer from ill-health, Mother presses the nourishment of the divine strength and health into your physical being, renewing its substance with that.

4-11-1934

THE MOTHER'S ACTION IN CURING ILLNESS

Q: On what basis did the Mother's action proceed in the case recently submitted to her?

A: Mother acted on her inner perception about the whole affair; she does not act only on the outer facts but on what she feels or sees lying behind them.

29-8-1935

*

Q: X's letter to me about her hip joint pain was sent to the Mother by me not on the same day but on the next. Yet it seems from X's latest that her pain disappeared soon after that letter had reached me. Was there an automatic effect of the letter, even before the Mother was told of the letter's contents?

A: Y spoke to the Mother about X's pain on the same day —

so it is not necessary to suppose an automatic effect of the letter itself. But such an automatic effect does often take place either immediately after writing or when the letter enters the Mother's atmosphere.

so it is not necessary to suppose an automatic effect of the letter itself. But such an automatic effect does often take place either immediately after writing or when the letter enters the Mother's atmosphere.

XI

SOME EXPLANATIONS

SOME EXPLANATIONS

SIGNIFICANCE OF THE MOTHER'S SYMBOL

Q: I have been frequently thinking of the Mother's symbol of "Chakra" and its significance. I have understood it as follows:

Central circle — Transcendental power.

Four inner petals — Four powers working from the Supermind to Overmind.

Twelve outer petals — Division of four into twelve powers from Overmind to Intuition and mind.

Do you think I have understood the significance correctly?

A: Essentially (in general principle) the 12 powers are the vibrations that are necessary for the complete manifestation. These are the 12 seen from the beginning above the Mother's head. Thus there are really 12 rays from the sun not 7, 12 planets etc.

As to the exact interpretation of the detail of the powers, I see nothing against the arrangement you have made. It can stand very well.

15-4-1934

SIGNIFICANCE OF THE MOTHER'S FLAG

About the blue flag. I presume you mean the flag with the white lotus. If so, it is the Mother's flag, for the white lotus is her symbol as the red lotus is mine. The blue of the flag is meant to be the colour of Krishna and so represents the spiritual or divine consciousness which it is her work to establish so that it may reign upon earth. This is the meaning of the flag being used as the Ashram flag, that our work is to bring down this consciousness and make it the leader of the world's life.

14-3-1949

CONQUERING THE POWERS OF LIFE FOR THE MOTHER

This Yoga does not mean a rejection of the powers of life, but an inner transformation and a change of the spirit in the life and the use of the powers. These powers are now used in an egoistic spirit and for undivine ends; they have to be used in a spirit of surrender to the Divine and for the purposes of the divine Work. That is what is meant by conquering them back for the Mother.

USE OF EXTERNAL MEANS AS AID TO YOGIC FORCE

Of course, one must use these external means and there one must be careful so as to have as many factors as possible on one's side and give as little handle as possible to the adverse forces. But no outward action can be for us sure of success unless behind it is the growing Yogic vision and Yogic power.

We have had ourselves serious difficulties from the outside, petitions made against us to the Minister of Colonies in Paris and a report demanded from the Governor here which if acted on would have put the Ashram in serious jeopardy.

We used outward means of a very slight and simple character i.e. getting the Mother's brother (Governor in French Equatorial Africa) to intervene with the Ministry (and also an eminent writer in France, a disciple), but for the most part I used a strong inner Force to determine the action of the Colonial Office, to get a favourable report from the Governor here, to turn the minds of some who were against us here and to nullify the enmity of others. In all these respects I succeeded and our position here is made stronger than before; especially a new and favourable Governor has come. Nevertheless we have to remain vigilant that the situation may not be again threatened. Also one disadvantage has resulted, that we have been asked not to buy or rent more houses but to build instead. This is difficult without land and much money; so we are for the moment unable to expand.

In certain respects, however, this is not a disadvantage, as I have been long wishing to put off further expansion and consolidate the inward life of the Ashram in a more completely spiritual sense.

I give this as an example of how things have to be dealt with from the Yogic point of view.

20-3-1935

PHYSICAL EXPANSION AND INNER PROGRESS

Q: Is having more houses by the Mother a sign of progress of her work?

A: It is a sign of physical expansion. The progress depends upon what is behind; if the inner progress is not there, the physical expansion is of no great use.

7-7-1933

COMMERCE AND SPIRITUAL PROFIT

If you give the money to the Mother, that can't be commercial; commerce implies personal profit, and here your profit is only spiritual.

2-4-1944

THE MOTHER AND THE EXPRESSION OF BEAUTY

Q: Pourquoi la Mère s'habille-t-elle avec des vêtements riches et beaux?

A: Avez-vous donc pour conception que le Divin doit être représenté sur terre par la pauvreté et la laideur?[1]

Beauty is as much an expression of the Divine as Knowledge,

---

[1] Q: Why does the Mother put on rich and beautiful dresses?

A: Is it your notion that the Divine should be represented on earth by poverty and ugliness?

Power or Ananda. Does anyone ask why does the Mother want
to manifest the divine consciousness by knowledge or by power
and not by ignorance and weakness? It would not be a more
absurd or meaningless question than the one put by the vital
against her wearing artistic and beautiful dress.

27-2-1933

*

Q: Does it make any difference to the Mother's con-
sciousness whether she puts on the best saris or the old
ones, whether she lives in a palace or in a forest? What
do these outer things add to the inner reality? More pro-
bably they may be causing its diminution.

A: Outer things are the expression of something in the inner
reality. A fine sari or a palace are expressions of the principle
of beauty in things and that is their main value. The Divine
Consciousness is not bound by these things and has no attachment, but it is also not bound to abstain from them if beauty in
things is part of its intended action. The Mother, when the
Ashram was still unformed, was wearing patched cotton saris;
when she took up the work, it was necessary to change her
habits, so she did so.

22-10-1935

LIVING IN THE SUPERMIND AND INTEREST IN THE WORLD

Q: Is it at all possible for the Mother or anyone living
above the Overmind or even in the silence in have any
interest in the world, since the world would be felt from
there as a mere speck?

A: It all depends upon what basis one lives in the silence or
above. A speck can be of as much interest to the Divine Consciousness as an infinity.

8-8-1934

LIGHT-HEARTEDNESS AND YOGIC CHEERFULNESS

As for light-heartedness and *insouciance* — a light don't-care attitude is the last thing we would recommend to anybody. The Mother spoke of cheerfulness, and if she used the word light-hearted, it was not in the sense of anything lightly or frivolously gay and careless — although a deeper and finer gaiety can have its place as an element of the Yogic character. What she meant was a glad equanimity even in the face of difficulties and there is nothing in that contrary to Yogic teaching or to her own practice. The vital nature on the surface (the depths of the true vital are different) is attached on the one side to a superficial mirth and enjoyment, on the other to sorrow and despair and gloom and tragedy, — for these are for it the cherished lights and shades of life; but a bright or wide and free peace or an *ānandamaya* intensity or, best, a fusing of both in one is the true poise of both the soul and the mind — and of the true vital also — in Yoga. It is perfectly possible for a quite human Sadhak to get to such a poise, it is not necessary to be divine before one can attain it.

TRUE LOVE AND JEALOUSY

Only one thing I must note so that no wrong idea may linger in your understanding. You seem to say in one passage of a letter that the Mother had said to you that jealousy is inevitable in true love in ordinary life, and if it is not there when one sees the other loving elsewhere, then they don't love each other! You must have strangely misheard and misunderstood the Mother. It is just the opposite of what the Mother has always said and thought and the very contrary of all her knowledge and experience. It is the idea of the ordinary mind about jealousy and love, not hers. She remembers very well having told you just the opposite that, even in ordinary life, one is *not* jealous if one has the true love. Jealousy is the common movement of the human egoistic lower vital with its grasping possessive instinct and it cannot be anything else. I thought it better to make this clear so that there might be no misleading impression that such movements of the lower vital nature have any sanction or support in the truth of the soul; they belong to the vital Ignorance, they are fruits of the vital ego.

1-2-1933

ERROR OF EXTOLLING VITAL LOVE

Whatever may be the glamour of a vital love, once it falls away and one gets to a higher level, it should be seen to have been not the great thing one imagined. To keep this exaggerated estimate of it is to hold the consciousness back from the pull towards the greater thing with which that cannot for a moment compare. If one keeps a fervour like that for an inferior past it must make it more difficult to develop the entire person for a higher future. It is indeed not the Mother's wish that anybody should look back in a spirit of enthusiastic appreciation to the old vital love. It was indeed "so little" in any true estimate of things. It is not at all a question of comparison or of extolling the vital passion of one at the expense of that of the other. It is the whole thing that must dwindle in its proportions and recede into the shadowy constructions of the past that have no longer any importance.

1934

DECEPTIVE IDEA OF REMOVING SEX-HUNGER
BY INDULGENCE

The Mother has already told you the truth about this idea. The idea that by fully indulging the sex-hunger it will be finished and disappear for ever is a deceptive pretence held out by the vital to the mind in order to get a sanction for its desire; it has no other *raison d'être* or truth or justification. If an occasional indulgence keeps the sex-desire simmering, a full indulgence would only sink you in its mire. This hunger like other hungers does not cease by temporary satiation; it revives itself after a temporary abeyance and wants again indulgence. Neither sops nor gorgings are the right treatment for it. It can only go by a radical psychic rejection or a full spiritual opening with the increasing descent of a consciousness that does not want it and has a truer Ananda.

23-4-1937

THE MOTHER'S APPROVAL OF RIGHT EXPRESSION

Why should you think the Mother does not approve of expression, — provided it is the right expression of the right thing, — or suppose that silence and true expression are contradictory? The truest expression comes out of an absolute inner silence. The spiritual silence is not a mere emptiness; nor is it indispensable to abstain from all activity in order to find it.

THE MOTHER'S APPRECIATION OF INDIAN MUSIC

What can be stranger than this idea of yours that the Mother likes only European music and does not like or appreciate Indian music — that she only pretends to do it or that she tolerates it so as not to discourage people! Remember that it is the Mother who has always praised and supported your music and put her force behind you so that your music might develop into spiritual perfection and beauty. In your poetry it was I that supported you most, in detail; the Mother could only do it with a general force because she could not read the original (though she found them in translations very beautiful), but in music it has been just the other way round. You surely are not going to say that all that was unfelt? And the development of X? That too was Indian music, not European. And then when I write to you in praise of your music, do you think it is only my opinion that I am transmitting? Most often it is her words that I use to express our common feeling.

20-12-1932

THE MOTHER'S MUSIC

The Mother's music has often been recognised by X as Indian

of this or that *rāga*. The Mother plays whatever comes through her — she does not usually play any precisely composed music whether European or Indian — the latter in fact she has never learned.

11-9-1934

*

The Mother has played music from her childhood upwards — so it is no trouble to her to sing or play several times.

15-9-1933

*

It is not necessary to have technical knowledge in order to feel what is behind the music. Mother, of course, does not play for the sake of a technical musical effect, but to bring down something from the higher planes and that anyone can receive who is open.

15-9-1933

*

It is not by knowledge of music that the understanding [of the Mother's music] comes; nor is it by effort of the mind — it is by becoming inwardly silent, opening within and getting the spontaneous feeling of what is in the music.

1932

*

Yes. All that is very true. It is a prayer or an invocation that Mother makes in the music.

1-6-1935

*

Q: *Is it true that when the Mother plays on the organ*

she calls down the Gods of the higher planes to help us?

A: Not consciously.

9-2-1934

*

Q: Does it mean that the Gods are attracted to her music and come down?

A: They may be.

10-2-1934

*

Q: Does the Mother bring out something while playing?

A: If she did not bring something, why should she play at all?

19-4-1934

MUSIC AND MAHALAKSHMI

Q: I was so deeply moved on hearing the songs of X and Y at today's music that the question came to my mind whether it is the Mahalakshmi aspect of the Mother that is working these days.

A: On the music days it is always the Mahalakshmi aspect that is prominent.

25-12-1933

A THRILLING EXPERIENCE

Q: When I heard the Mother reading out "Prières et Méditations" my body was thrilled. How?

A: When an intense Power is put out, it will naturally give a thrill to those who receive it.

ART AND TRADITION

The Mother finds the pictures of X hideous and monstrous, she would not dignify them with the name of art. But it is not because they depart from tradition. The Mother does not believe in tradition — she considers that Art should always develop new forms — but still these must be according to a truth of Beauty which is universal and eternal — something of the Divine. As for your picture, she finds it expressive. She felt at once what it meant — so the criticism of Y does not stand.

8-12-1933

IMPORTANCE OF CONTACTING RIGHT INFLUENCES IN ART

The Mother had told you once that in your human figures you did not seem to be in contact with the right Influence and you had said that you felt the contact with an eternal Beauty in Nature but had not the same contact with regard to the human figure. It will be better then, now that you are practising Yoga and to be in contact with right Influences only is very important, to avoid dealing with the human face and figure at present. In Yoga what may seem to the mind a detail may yet open the door to things that have strong effects on the consciousness, disturb its harmony or interfere with the sources of inspiration, vision and experience.

1933

KNOWLEDGE OF FRENCH AND CLOSENESS
TO THE MOTHER

Q: Is it right to say that those who know French will be able to serve the Mother better in the years to come?

A: It is mostly that it brings a certain closeness to one side of the Mother.

3-5-1945

IDENTIFICATION WITH THE MOTHER'S CONSCIOUSNESS
THROUGH READING HER BOOKS

Q: When I read the Mother's "Prayers" and "Con-versations" I often feel as if I come in contact with her consciousness. This makes me think whether it is possible by reading her books to make one's consciousness so intense as to identify it with hers and as a result to elevate the vital and other parts also.

A: It is possible to intensely identify oneself with the Mother's consciousness through what you read — in that case the result you speak of could come. It could also have an effect on the vital up to a certain point.

21-8-1935

THE GURU, THE DIVINE AND THE AVATAR

I have only now had time to go through the three letters you sent me. X can of course have the *Conversations*. As to what your other friend asks, it is quite possible for him to receive where he is without coming here if he has the adoration of the Mother in his heart and an intense call.

About the question of the Avatar, I do not think it is useful to press in the matter. It has become very much the tendency, especially in Bengal, to regard the Guru as the Avatar. To every disciple the Guru is the Divine, but in a special sense — for the Guru is supposed to live in the divine consciousness, to have attained union and when he gives to the disciple, it is the Divine that gives and what he gives is the consciousness of the Divine who is within the Guru. But that and Avatarhood are two different things. It is mostly in East Bengal recently that those have come who were acclaimed as Avatars; those who came had each of them the idea of a work to be done for the world and the sense of a Divine Power working through them, which shows that there was a pressure for manifestation there and something came in each case, for something of the Divine Power always comes when it is called, but it does not look as if there was anywhere the complete descent. It is this that may have created the idea that the Avatar was born there. It has always been said of the Advent that is to come now that there would be many in whom it would seem that it had come, but the real Avatar would work behind a veil until the destined hour came.

I do not gather from what is quoted as said by your Guru that he claimed to be the Avatar. It seems to me that he claimed to be a Power preparing the way for the work of the Divine Mother and even to indicate that all that he meant would be manifested not only by his own followers but by other groups (*sampradāya*), consisting evidently of those who had not had him for Guru but had some other Head and Teacher. This is also confirmed by the saying that some other one than his disciples might be the means of his *prakāśa* — that is to say, would be the means of carrying on his work and aiding the manifestation of the Mother. If this meant proclaiming him as the Avatar, I do not see how it can agree with the other saying that after his leaving of the body the Avatar would come to the Ashram he had created.

I do not quite know what is meant by *ayoni-sambhava*. An incarnation is always through a human mother, though there have been one or two cases in which a virgin birth has been proclaimed (Christ, Buddha). The only other meaning — unless we suppose an unprecedented miracle — might be a descent such as sometimes happens, the Godhead manifesting in somebody who at birth was a Vibhuti, not at once the full incarnation. But in the absence of a clear statement from your Guru himself, these are only speculations.

I have written this much as an answer to your question, but I doubt whether it is necessary or advisable to write anything of it to your friends. They have their own feeling about the matter; it seems to me better not to challenge or disturb it.

25-8-1935

THE MOTHER'S SPEAKING OF PAST BIRTHS

The Mother only speaks to people about their past births when she sees definitely some scene or memory of their past in concentration, but this happens rarely nowadays.

30-6-1933

*

Mother does not usually look into past lives; only when things come of themselves from the past she looks.

24-7-1934

MEETING THE DEAD

When Mother said that it was not good to try to meet the dead, she was speaking from a spiritual standpoint which is not usually known or regarded by the spiritists.

25-8-1936

HELP TO DEPARTED SOULS

Q: Is there any indication you have received to tell you that my brother's soul really wanted at the end to come to Mother's Light and the Master's?

A: Mother cannot say particularly because so many people come to her in the night for the passage to the other side whom she has not known in the body. Your brother may very well have been one of them and in view of X's account, there is little doubt that he must have been.

DANGER OF WEAK SYMPATHY

Q: I have observed that a sensitive disposition becomes very prone to easy admission of vital forces from persons who are full of them, especially when an attitude of emotional sympathy is taken towards them out of a philanthropic desire to help them in their difficulties.

A: That is very interesting — for it agrees with the Mother's constant insistence that to feel sympathy or any emotion of the weak philanthropic kind with those possessed by vital forces is most dangerous as it may bring an attack upon oneself which may take any form. One must do what is to be done but abstain from all such weakness.

11-10-1936

EFFECTIVE CHANNELISING OF THE MOTHER'S HELP

One can be a channel for the Mother's help, but the idea of oneself helping others comes in the way and so long as it is there one cannot be a truly effective channel.

17-4-1935

AN OCCULT EXPERIMENT OF THE MOTHER

X probably referred to an experience in which the Mother being in Algiers appeared to a circle of friends sitting in Paris and took up a pencil and wrote a few words on a paper. Having satisfied herself that it was possible she did not develop it any further. That was at a time when she was practising occultism with Théon in Algiers. Materialisation is possible but it does not happen easily — it demands a very rare and difficult concentration of forces or else an occult process with vital beings behind it such as materialises objects, like the stones that were daily thrown in the Guest House, when we were there. In neither case it is a miracle. But to do as you suggest, make it a common or everyday phenomenon, would be hardly practicable and spiritually not useful, as it is not a spiritual force which gives the power but an occult mental-vital force. It would turn the Yoga into a display of occultism, rather than a process of spiritual change.

20-10-1935

*

The Mother spent many years entering the occult worlds and learning all that was to be learnt there.... She sees things always when she goes into a trance.

8-7-1936

THE MOTHER'S SEEING OF NARAD

I am afraid I don't know much about Narad. Mother once saw him standing between the Overmind and Supermind where they join as if that was his highest station. But he has his action on the lower plane also — only I don't quite know what it is. In the Puranic tales pure love and Bhakti on the one hand and, on the other hand, a pleasure in making human beings quarrel seem to be his salient characteristics.

5-5-1935

THE MOTHER'S GOING TO OTHER PLANETS

Q: I have been wondering whether the Mother has been able to establish a direct connection with Mars or any other far off planet which is probably habitable and inhabited.

A: A long time ago Mother was going everywhere in the subtle body but she found it of a very secondary interest. Our attention must be fixed on the earth because our work is here. Besides, the earth is a concentration of all the other worlds and one can touch them by touching something corresponding in the earth-atmosphere.

13-1-1934

FACULTY OF GETTING RIGHT PERCEPTIONS

X has reported Mother's observation correctly, but he does not seem to have understood it. The Mother never meant that by merely willing one could know at once what was in someone else or that all one's impressions about him would be spontaneously and infallibly correct. What she meant was that there is a faculty or power (an occult or Yogic faculty) by which one may get the right perceptions and impressions, and if one has the will to do so, one can develop it. Not at once, not by an easy method — *tra la la* and there you are: it may take years and one has to be careful and scrupulous about it. For these are intuitive perceptions and intuition is a thing that can easily be imitated by many other movements of consciousness that are much more fallible. Your impressions may be mental or vital and a mental or vital impression may have something to justify it or may not — but even in the first case there is no certainty at all that it will be correct; even if it is the same thing, it may be incorrectly caught — or caught with much mixture of error, twisted into falsehood, put in the wrong way, etc. And there may be no justification at all; it may be a mere wrong formation of your own mind or vital or of somebody else's wrong impression conveyed to you and accepted by you as your own. Your impressions may be the result of a want of affinity between you and the person, so that if he impresses you as null and neutral, it is because you cannot feel what is in him, it does not come home to you, or if you feel that he is in the wrong condition, it may be only because his vital intuitions rub yours the wrong way. There are lots of things like that which one must have the power to distinguish very carefully and exactly; until one knows one's own consciousness and its operations well, one cannot know the operations of the consciousness of others. But it is possible to develop a certain direct sight or a certain direct feeling or contact by which one can know, but only after much time and much careful, scrupulous and vigilant observation and self-training. Till then one can't go about saying that this is an advanced Sadhak or that one is not advanced and that other is no good at all. Even if one knows, it is not necessary always to air one's knowledge.

9-2-1935

TRICK OF REVERSING THE CONSCIOUSNESS

When the Mother said that it was just a trick of reversing the consciousness, she meant that: that instead of allowing always the external mind to interfere and assert its own ordinary customary point of view, it should turn itself round, admit that things may work from in outwards, and keep itself sufficiently quiet to see that developing and being done. For then an inner mind shows itself which is capable of following and being the instrument of the invisible Forces.

2-8-1932

FEELING OF SHOCK IN EXTERIORISATION

A feeling like that of the shock and the stopping of the breath for a second and as if of falling down comes to many when the consciousness for a moment or a longer time exteriorises itself (goes up out of the body); the shock comes from the going up of the consciousness or from the return into the body. The Mother used to have that hundreds of times. It is not anything physical (the Doctor, as you say, found nothing). When this movement of the consciousness is more normal, the feeling will probably disappear.

1-10-1935

NUMERICAL HARMONIES IN THE MOTHER'S ACCOUNTS

Q: X showed me his account book today in which the total was Rs. 7 As. 7 Ps.7. It is also the 7th day of the 7th month of the year and after I decided to write to you about this I saw that the house where I was working had also number 7. Elsewhere one does not come across such a play of numbers. I think it occurs here because the numbers (perhaps the occult beings of numbers) feel at ease in our atmosphere, like the sparrows in the main Ashram Building, and like to play in such harmonies.

> *In government departments and other places they feel*
> *the atmosphere mechanical, heavy and rigorous and so*
> *they do not find any joy in such play.*

A: I suppose your explanation is correct at least from the occult
point of view. The Mother is always having these numerical
harmonies in her accounts.

7-7-1936

GIVING NAMES TO CATS

The Mother gave names for cats because they understand and
answer; she has never given any for birds and does not wish to
do it. Now even for cats she is not giving names.

28-4-1932

ACTION OF MEDICINES ON THE MOTHER'S BODY

Medicines have quite a different action on the Mother's body
than they would have on yours or X's or anybody else's and the
reaction is not usually favourable. Her physical consciousness is
not the same as that of ordinary people — though even in ordinary people it is not so identical in all cases as "science" would
have us believe.

1-2-1937

THE MOTHER'S VIEWS ON MEDICAL MATTERS

What the Mother says in the matter is what she said to Dr. X
with his entire agreement — viz. reading from symptoms by the
doctors is usually mere balancing between possibilities (of course
except in clear and simple cases) and the conclusion is a guess.
It may be a right guess and then it will be all right or it may be a
wrong guess and then all will be wrong unless Nature is too
strong for the doctor and overcomes the consequences of his

error — or at the least the treatment will be ineffective. On the contrary if one develops the diagnostic flair one can see at once what is the real thing among the possibilities and see what is to be done. That is what the most successful doctors have, they have this flashlight which shows them the true point. X agreed and said that the cause of the guessing was that there were whole sets of symptoms which could belong to any one of several diseases and to decide is a most delicate and subtle business, no amount of book knowledge or reasoning will ensure a right decision. A special insight is needed that looks through the symptoms and not merely at them. This last sentence, by the way, is my own, not X's. About development of intuition afterwards — no time tonight.

6-4-1937

*

It is no use discussing these matters. The Mother's views are too far removed from the traditional nostrums to be understood by a medical mind, except those that have got out of the traditional groove or those who after long experience have seen things and can become devastatingly frank about the limitations of their own "science".

Ideas differ. Both the Mother and X were horrified at the idea of a child of four months being given a purgative. The leading Children's Doctor in France told the Mother no child under 12 months should be given a purgative, as it is likely to do great harm and may be dangerous. But here we understand it is the practice to dose children freely with purgatives from their day of birth almost. Perhaps that and over-administration of medicines is the cause of excessive infant mortality.

4-4-1937

*

All "science" does not recommend castor oil for children — I think it is a nineteenth century fad which has prolonged itself. The Mother's "children's doctor" told her it should not be done — also in her own case when a child the doctors peremptorily stopped it on the ground that it spoiled the stomach and liver. I suppose you will say doctors disagree? They do!

9-4-1937

*

Mother meant that wrong food and the poisons created by wrong assimilation were a great obstacle to the prolongation of life.

14-1-1935

*

> Q: *The Mother once said that there is hardly a disease that cannot be cured by Yoga. Can cancer be cured by it?*

A: Of course it can, but on condition of faith or openness or both. Even a mental suggestion can cure cancer — with luck of course, as is shown by the case of the woman operated on unsuccessfully for cancer, but the doctors lied and told her it had succeeded. Result, cancer symptoms all ceased and she died many years afterwards of another illness altogether.

11-10-1935

MILLENNIUM WITHOUT HOSPITALS

> Q: *I dreamt that the Mother is building a very big hospital. Dream of a millennium in advance?*

A: It would be more of a millenium if there were no need of a hospital at all and the doctors turned their injective prodding instruments into fountain pens — provided of course they did not make misuse of the pens also....

> Q: *Why furious about injective instruments, sir? They are supposed to be very effective.*

A: That does not make an increase of hospitals, illnesses and injections the ideal of a millennium....

Q: But why the deuce are those instruments to be replaced by fountain pens?

A: I was simply adopting the saying of Isaiah the prophet, "the swords will be turned into ploughshares", but the doctor's instrument is not big enough for a ploughshare, so I substituted fountain pen.

19-7-1937

XII

INTERPRETATIONS OF SOME "PRAYERS" AND
"CONVERSATIONS" OF THE MOTHER

INTERPRETATIONS OF SOME "PRAYERS"[1] AND "CONVERSATIONS"[2] OF THE MOTHER

I. "PRAYERS AND MEDITATIONS"

Q: In some of the Mother's Prayers which are addressed to "divin Maître" I find the words: "avec notre divine Mère". How can the Mother and "divin Maître" have a "divine Mère"? It is as if the Mother was not the "divine Mère" and there was some other Mother and the "divin Maître" was not the Transcendent and had also a "divine Mère"! Or is it that all these are addressed to something impersonal?

A: The Prayers are mostly written in an identification with the earth-consciousness. It is the Mother in the lower nature addressing the Mother in the higher nature, the Mother herself carrying on the Sadhana of the earth-consciousness for the transformation praying to herself above from whom the forces of transformation come. This continues till the identification of the earth-consciousness and the higher consciousness is effected. The word "notre" is general, I believe, referring to all born into the earth-consciousness — it does not mean the Mother of the "Divin Maître" and myself. It is the Divine who is always referred to as Divin Maître and Seigneur. There is the Mother who is carrying on the Sadhana and the Divine Mother, both being one but in different poises, and both turn to the Seigneur or Divine Master. This kind of prayer from the Divine to the Divine you will find also in the Ramayana and the Mahabharata.

21-8-1936

*

[1] The "Prayers" of the Mother, originally written in French, were subsequently published under the title *Prières et Méditations*. Some of them, translated by Sri Aurobindo in English, are included in Part Three of this volume.

[2] *Conversations* is a record of the Mother's talks in English with a small group of disciples in 1929.

[1]The experience you have described is Vedic in the real sense, though not one which would easily be recognised by the modern systems of Yoga which call themselves Yogic. It is the union of the "Earth" of the Veda and Purana with the divine Principle, an earth which is said to be above our earth, that is to say, the physical being and consciousness of which the world and the body are only images. But the modern Yogas hardly recognise the possibility of a material union with the Divine.

31-12-1915

*

Q: There are some Prayers of the Mother of 1914 in which she speaks of transformation and manifestation. Since at that time she was not here, does this not mean that she had these ideas long before she came here?

A: The Mother had been spiritually conscious from her youth, even from her childhood, upward and she had done Sadhana and had developed this knowledge very long before she came to India.

23-12-1933

*

Q: Nothing is more important than: "Ta splendeur veut rayonner" as the Mother says in her Prayer of the 16th June 1914. All ideas of perfection for oneself or being an instrument seem flat and insipid when considered from the standpoint of the vast universal movement of consciousness.

A: It is correct. Perfection for oneself is not the true ideal. Sadhana and instrumentation are only useful as a means for the "rayonnement".

30-4-1936

*

---

[1] This is Sri Aurobindo's answer to the Mother's letter dated 26-11-1915 containing a record of her experience. The Mother's letter has been included in Part Three. See pp. 471-72.

Q: In her Prayer of the 17th May 1914, the Mother says, "Telles furent les deux phrases que j'écrivis hier par une sorte de nécessité absolue. La première, comme si la puissance de la prière ne serait complète que si elle était tracée sur le papier."

Is it true that a prayer is not sufficiently powerful when it is kept unexpressed by speech or writing, and that its expression is necessary to make it completely powerful?

A: It was not meant as a general rule — it was only a necessity felt with regard to that particular prayer and that experience. It all depends on the person, the condition, the need of the moment or of that stage or phase of the consciousness. These things in spiritual experience are always plastic and variable. In some conditions or in one phase or at one moment expression may be needed to bring out the effectuating force of the prayer or the stability of the experience; in another condition or phase or at another moment it may be the opposite, expression would rather disperse the force or break the stability.

21-6-1936

*

Q: The Mother's Prayer of the 12th December 1914, begins with: "Il faut à chaque instant savoir tout perdre pour tout gagner..."

The Isha Upanishad also says: "tena tyaktena bhuñjithā." Do not these two statements refer to the same truth?

A: Yes, certainly. It is essentially the same truth put in different ways. It might be put in a negative form — "if we cling to things as they are in their imperfection in the Ignorance, we cannot have them in their truth and perfection in the Divine Light, Harmony and Ananda."

16-8-1935

*

Q: In one of her Prayers the Mother says: "The joy contained in activity is superseded by a greater joy in withdrawal from activity." This implies that withdrawal from activity is preferable to activity.

A: Do you think the Mother has a rigid mind like you people and was laying down a hard and fast rule, for all time and all people and all conditions? It refers to a certain stage when the consciousness is sometimes in activity and when not in activity is withdrawn in itself. Afterwards comes a stage when the Sachchidananda condition is there in work also. There is a still further stage when both are as it were one, but that is the supramental. The two states are the silent Brahman and the active Brahman and they can alternate (1st stage), coexist (2nd stage), fuse (3rd stage). If you reach even the first stage then you can think of applying Mother's dictum, but why misapply it now?

Q: Is it possible to have the highest Sachchidananda realisation in work?

A: Certainly it is realisable in work. Good Lord! How could the integral Yoga exist if it were not?

*

Q: The Mother says in her "Prayers" that experience is willed by the Divine. Am I then to suppose that dearth or abundance of experiences is in any given case willed by the Divine?

A: To say so has no value unless you realise all things as coming from the Divine. One who has realised as the Mother had realised in the midst of terrible sufferings and difficulties that even these came from the Divine and were preparing her for her work can make a spiritual use of such an attitude. For others it may lead to wrong conclusions.

10-5-1934

*

> *Q: The Mother, in her Prayer of the 4th August 1914, says: "Les hommes, poussés par le conflit des forces, accomplissent un sublime sacrifice...." Apparently she refers to the great war; but, as a result of that war has any "pure lumière" filled the hearts of men or the "Force Divine" spread on earth or something beneficial come out from that chaos as she mentions? Since the nations are once more preparing for war and are in a state of constant conflict, there seems to be no indication of any change in the inner condition of men. People all over the world including even the Indians seem to be wanting another war and hardly anyone seems to require Peace, Light or Love.*

A: There has been a change for the worse — the descent of the vital world into the human. On the other hand except in the "possessed" nations there is a greater longing for peace and feeling that such things ought not to happen. India did not get any real touch of the war. However what the Mother was thinking of was an opening to the spiritual truth. That has at least tried to come. There is a widespread dissatisfaction with the old material civilisation, a seeking for some deeper light and truth — only unfortunately it is being taken advantage of by the old religions and only a very small minority is consciously searching for the new Light.

9-6-1936

*

> *Q: You said that after the great war there has been "the descent of the vital world into the human". But did not the vital world already descend on earth — in Matter — even before the human beings came? What other vital world remained yet to descend into the human? And how is it that it decided to come down just at present — to prevent the higher Light from coming down in the human world?*

A: When there is a pressure on the vital world due to the prepar-

ing Descent from above, that world usually precipitates something of itself into the human. The vital world is very large and
far exceeds the human in extent. But usually it dominates by influence not by descent. Of course the effort of this part of the
vital world is always to maintain humanity under its sway and
prevent the higher Light.

9-6-1936

*

> *Q: If, as you say, there has been a change for the worse
> due to the descent of the vital world, would it not make
> the supramental descent in the earth-consciousness im-
> possible or postpone its coming to some distant future
> instead of "here and now"? And since the possessed na-
> tions are endowed with all the possible material power,
> there seems to be little hope of any movement of peace
> being successful.*

A: The vital descent cannot prevent the supramental — still
less can the possessed nations do it by their material power, since
the supramental descent is primarily a spiritual fact which will
bear its necessary outward consequences. What previous vital
descents have done is to falsify the Light that came down as in
the history of Christianity where it took possession of the teaching and distorted it and deprived it of any widespread fulfilment.
But the supermind is by definition a Light that cannot be distorted if it comes in its own right and by its own presence. It is
only when it holds itself back and allows inferior Powers of consciousness to use a diminished and already deflected Truth that
the knowledge can be seized by the vital Forces and made to
serve their own purpose.

12-6-1936

*

> *Q: In her Prayer of the 16th August 1914, the Mother
> refers to "chacun des grands êtres Asouriques qui ont
> résolu d'être Tes serviteurs...."*

How was it that the Asuras determined to be the ser-
vants of the Divine? Was it to exploit the Divine or
a "coup de diplomatie"?

A: It was in reference to Asuras who had taken birth in human bodies — a thing they usually avoid if they can, for they prefer to possess human beings without taking birth — with the claim that they wanted to regenerate themselves by serving the Divine and doing his work. It did not succeed very well.

15-6-1936

*

Q: Is there really an internal progress in the universe
— "marche interne d'univers", as the Mother says?
Except in a few individuals there is hardly any progress
in mankind. Internally and externally the universe seems
to be moving in the same circle always without making
any essential progress.

A: "Univers" in French usually means not the whole universe but the "world" — the earth. There must be a progress in the earth-consciousness, otherwise there could have been no evolution. The evolution of mankind may go by circles or spirals, but there is all the time an opening of more and more complete possibilities till the possibility of the evolution of a higher race becomes valid.

1-9-1936

*

Q: In a book named "Eveillez-vous" (translated from
English), there are some ideas — like those about the
Advent, the hostile beings, etc. — similar to our own.
There is also a phrase in the book, "La Paix règnera sur
terre", which also occurs in the Mother's "Prayers".
Has the author not copied this phrase from the Mother's
"Prayers" (unpublished)?

A: Not necessarily, as the phrase can easily come to one who has read the Bible and the English are very biblical. The idea of the hostile beings also is not new, in fact it is as old as the Veda. The expectation of the Advent is also pretty widespread, as according to the old prophecies it must be when the Advent is due.

16-9-1935

II. "CONVERSATIONS"

Q: The Mother asks "What do you want the Yoga for? To get power?"[1] Does "power" here mean the power to communicate one's own experience to others? What does it precisely mean?

A: Power is a general term — it is not confined to a power to communicate. The most usual form of power is control over things, persons, events, forces.

1-1-1937

*

Q: The Mother says "What is required is concentration — concentration upon the Divine with a view to an integral and absolute consecration to its Will and Purpose."[2] Is its Will different from its Purpose?

A: The two words have not the same meaning. Purpose means the intention, the object in view towards which the Divine is working. Will is a wider term than that.

1 1 1937

*

Q: "Concentrate in the heart."[3] What is concentration? What is meditation?

---

1 *Conversations* (July 1971 edition), p. 4.   2 *Ibid.*   3 *Ibid.*

A: Concentration means gathering of the consciousness into one centre and fixing it in one object or in one idea or in one condition. Meditation is a general term which can include many kinds of inner activity.

1-1-1937

*

Q: "A fire is burning there.... It is the divinity in you —
your true being. Hear its voice, follow its dictates."[1]
I have never seen this fire in me. Yet I feel I know
the divinity in me. I feel I hear its voice and I try my
utmost to follow its dictates. Should I doubt my feeling?

A: No, what you feel is probably the intimation from the psychic being through the mind. To be directly conscious of the psychic fire, one must have the subtle vision and subtle sense active or else the direct action of the psychic acting as a manifest power in the consciousness.

2-1-1937

*

Q: "We have all met in previous lives."[2]
Who precisely are "we"? Do both of you remember
me? Did I often serve you for this work in the past?

A: It is a general principle announced which covers all who are called to the work. At the time the Mother was seeing the past (or part of it) of those to whom she spoke and that is why she said this. At present we are too much occupied with the crucial work in the physical consciousness to go into these things. Moreover we find that it encouraged a sort of vital romanticism in the Sadhaks which made them attach more importance to these things than to the hard work of Sadhana, so we have stopped speaking of past lives and personalities.

2-1-1937

*

[1] *Ibid.*, p. 4.   [2] *Ibid.*, p. 6.

*Q: "There are two paths of Yoga, one of Tapasya
(discipline) and the other of surrender."[1]
     Once you interpreted my vision as Agni, the fire of
purification and Tapasya producing the Sun of Truth.
What path do I follow? What place has Tapasya in the
path of surrender? Can one do absolutely without Tapasya
in the path of surrender?*

A: There is a *tapasyā* that takes place automatically as the result of surrender and there is a discipline that one carries out by
one's own unaided effort — it is the latter that is meant in the
"two paths of Yoga". But Agni as the fire of *tapasyā* can burn
in either case.

                                                          4-1-1937

                              *

*Q: "The strength of such impulses as those of sex lies
usually in the fact that people take too much notice
of them."[2]
     What are the other impulses referred to?*

A: It refers to strong vital impulses.

                                                          4-1-1937

                              *

*Q: "The whole world is full of the poison. You take it
in with every breath."[3]
     How long is a Sadhak subject to this fear of catching
contagion? I feel I won't catch such a contagion now.
Is my feeling trustworthy?*

A: I don't know that it is. One has to go very far on the path
before one is so secure as that.

                                                          4-1-1937

                              *

[1] *Ibid.*, p. 7.   [2] *Ibid.*, p. 8.   [3] *Ibid.*, p. 10.

Q: "But to those who possess the necessary basis and foundation we say, on the contrary, 'aspire and draw.' "[1] *Does this capacity to aspire and draw indicate a great advance already made?*

A: No. It is a comparatively elementary stage.

5-1-1937

*

Q: "Spiritual experience means the contact with the Divine in oneself (or without, which comes to the same thing in that domain)."[2] *What is meant by the Divine "without"? Does it mean the cosmic Divine or the transcendental or both?*

A: It means the Divine seen outside in things, beings, events etc., etc.

9-1-1937

*

Q: Was Jeanne d'Arc's nature transformed even a little because of her relation with the two Archangels, the two beings of the Overmind[3]*?*

A: I don't see how the question of transformation comes in. Jeanne d'Arc was not practising Yoga or seeking transformation.

9-1-1937

*

Q: How can one distinguish between a dream of deeper origin and a vision[4]*?*

A: There is no criterion, but one can easily distinguish if one is in the inward condition, not sleep, in which most visions take place, by the nature of the impression made. A vision in dream is more

[1] *Ibid.*, p. 15.   [2] *Ibid.*, p. 22.   [3] See *Ibid.*   [4] See *Ibid.*, p. 18.

difficult to distinguish from a vivid dream-experience but one gets to feel the difference.

9-1-1937

*

Q: Sometimes one remembers the dreams, sometimes one does not.[1] *Why is it so?*

A: It depends on the connection between the two states of consciousness at the time of waking. Usually there is a turn over of the consciousness in which the dream-state disappears more or less abruptly, effacing the fugitive impression made by the dream events (or rather their transcription) on the physical sheath. If the waking is more composed (less abrupt) or, if the impression is very strong, then the memory remains at least of the last dream. In the last case one may remember the dream for a long time, but usually after getting up the dream memories fade away. Those who want to remember their dreams sometimes make a practice of lying quiet and tracing backwards, recovering the dreams one by one. When the dream-state is very light, one can remember more dreams than when it is heavy.

9-1-1937

*

Q: "You have no longer anything that you can call your own; you feel everything as coming from the Divine, and you have to offer it back to its source. When you can realise that, then even the smallest thing to which you do not usually pay much attention or care, ceases to be trivial and insignificant; it becomes full of meaning and it opens up a vast horizon beyond "[2]
Is this as elementary a stage as the stage of "aspire and draw"?

A: Not so elementary.

14-1-1937

*

[1] See *Ibid.*, p. 19. [2] *Ibid.*, p. 28.

Q: "But if we want the Divine to reign here we must give all we have and are and do here to the Divine."[1]
If one does this completely has he anything more to do?

A: No. But it is not easy to do it completely.

14-1-1937

*

Q: How can we recognise who gives all he has and is and does to the Divine?

A: You can't, unless you have the inner vision.

14-1-1937

*

Q: "For there is nothing in the world which has not its ultimate truth and support in the Divine."[2]
To know this perfectly by experience is to have a very great attainment, perhaps the final attainment; am I right?

A: Yes.

19-1-1937

*

Q: "Obviously, what has happened had to happen; it would not have been, if it had not been intended."[3]
Then, what is the place of repentance in man's life? Has it any place in the life of a Sadhak?

A: The place of repentance is in its effect for the future — if it induces the nature to turn from the state of things that brought about the happening. For the Sadhak however it is not repen-

[1] *Ibid.*, p. 30. [2] *Ibid.*, p. 33. [3] *Ibid.*

tance but recognition of a wrong movement and the necessity
of its not recurring that is needed.

19-1-1937

*

Q: *"You are tied to the chain of Karma, and there, in
that chain, whatever happens is rigorously the consequence of what has been done before."*[1]
    *Does "before" mean all the past lives, beginning
from the very first up to this one?*

A: That is taking things in the mass. In a metaphysical sense
whatever happens is the consequence of all that has gone before
up to the moment of the action. Practically particular consequences have particular antecedents in the past and it is these
that are said to determine it.

        (From where are these quotations? In the exact intention
of a sentence much sometimes depends on the context.[2])

19-1-1937

*

Q: *"Many people would tell you wonderful tales of how
the world was built and how it will proceed in the future,
how and where you were born in the past and what you
will be hereafter, the lives you have lived and the lives
you will still live. All this has nothing to do with spiritual life."*[3]
    *Is what such people say a complete humbug? Is there
a process other than the spiritual by which one can know
all these things?*

A: Often it is, but even if it is correct, it has nothing spiritual in

---

[1] *Ibid.*, p. 35.
    [2] It is obvious from this remark of Sri Aurobindo that while answering this series of
questions, he was not aware that the quotations cited in the questions were from the
Mother's book *Conversations*.
    [3] *Ibid.*, p. 47.

it. Many mediums, clairvoyants or people with a special faculty, tell you these things. That faculty is no more spiritual than the capacity to build a bridge or to cook a nice dish or to solve a mathematical problem. There are intellectual capacities, there are occult capacities — that is all.

20-1-1937

*

> *Q: "They [the vampires] are not human; there is only a human form or appearance.... Their method is to try first to cast their influence upon a man; then they enter slowly into his atmosphere and in the end may get complete possession of him, driving out entirely the real human soul and personality."[1]*
>
> *X has married a girl who, the Mother has said, is vampire-like to some extent. Is he then under all these risks? What precautions should he take? Shall I warn him?*

A: First of all what is meant is not that the vampire or vital being even in possession of a human body tries to possess yet another human being. All that is the description of how a dis-embodied (vampire) vital being takes possession of a human body without being born into it in the ordinary way — for that is their desire, to possess a human body but not by the way of birth. Once thus human, the danger they are for others is that they feed on the vitality of those who are in contact with them — that is all.

Secondly in this case, Mother only said vampire-like to some extent. That does not mean that she is one of these beings, but has to some extent the habit of feeding on the vitality of others. There is no need to say anything to X. It would only disturb him and not help in the least.

27-1-1937

*

[1] *Ibid.*, pp. 49-50.

> *Q: The Mother, in her "Conversations", says that the first effect of Yoga is to take away the mental control so that the ideas and desires which were so long checked become surprisingly prominent and create difficulties.*[1]

A: They were not prominent because they were getting some satisfaction or at least the vital generally was getting indulged in one way or another. When they are no longer indulged then they become obstreperous. But they are not new forces created by the Yoga — they were there all the time.

What is meant by the mental control being removed is that the mental simply kept them in check but could not remove them. So in Yoga the mental has to be replaced by the psychic or spiritual self-control which could do what the vital cannot, only many Sadhaks do not make this exchange in time and withdraw the mental control merely.

                                                                12-5-1933

*

> *Q: In "Conversations" the Mother says: "One who dances and jumps and screams has the feeling that he is somehow very unusual in his excitement; and his vital nature takes great pleasure in that."*[2] *Does she mean that one should be usual instead of unusual in one's excitement during spiritual experience?*

A: The Mother did not mean that one must be usual in one's excitement at all — she meant that the man is not only excited but also wants to be unusual (extraordinary) in his excitement. The excitement itself is bad and the desire to seem extraordinary is worse.

                                                                7-6-1933

*

> *Q: What does Mother mean by the sentence in "Conversations": "When you eat, you must feel that it is the Divine who is eating through you"*[3] *?*

[1] See *Ibid.*, p. 8.   [2] *Ibid.*, p. 15.   [3] *Ibid.*, p. 29.

A: It means an offering of the food not to the ego or desire but to the Divine, who is behind all action.

11-1-1935

*

> *Q: In "Conversations" the Mother speaks of the power of thoughts and gives the example that if "you have a keen desire for a certain person to come and that, along with this vital impulse of desire, a strong imagination accompanies the mental formation you have made....And if there is a sufficient power of will in your thought-form, if it is a well-built formation, it will arrive at its own realisation."[1]*
>
> *In the example given, suppose there is no strong desire in the vital but only thoughts or vague imaginations in the mind, would they go and induce that person to come?*

A: It might; especially if that person were himself desirous of coming, it could give the decisive push. But in most cases desire or will behind the thought-force would be necessary.

26-8-1936

*

> *Q: In "Conversations" the Mother says that depression or discouragement cut holes in the nervous envelope and make hostile attacks more easy.[2] In one sense this means that a man with goodwill should not discourage anyone's wrong ideas, impulses or movements. But would this not be against the principles in ordinary life as well as in Sadhana? There is the way of keeping silent when dealing with such people, but even that sometimes hurts them more than a point-blank discouragement.*
>
> *Would the bad effects of depression and discouragement indicated by the Mother happen in ordinary life also?*

[1] *Ibid.*, pp. 58-9. [2] See *Ibid.*, p. 102.

A: The knowledge about the bad effect of depressions is meant for the Sadhak to learn to avoid these things. He cannot expect people to flatter his failures or mistakes or indulge his foibles merely because he has the self-habit of indulging in depression and hurting his nervous envelope if that is done. To keep himself free from depression is his business, not that of others. For instance some people have the habit of getting into depression if the Mother does not comply with their desires — it does not follow that the Mother must comply with their desires in order to keep them jolly — they must learn to get rid of this habit of mind. So with people's wish of encouragement or praise for all they do. One can be silent or non-intervening, but if even that depresses them, it is their own fault and nobody else's.

Of course, it is the same in ordinary life — depression is always hurtful. But in Sadhana it is more serious because it becomes a strong obstacle to the smooth and rapid progress towards the goal.

18-7-1936

*

Q: In "Entretiens"[1] the Mother says, "Même ceux qui ont la volonté de s'enfuir, quand ils arrivent de l'autre côté, peuvent trouver que la fuite ne sert pas à grand' chose après tout."[2] What does "arrivent de l'autre côté" mean in this sentence? Does it mean "when they come into this world" or "when they go into the world of silence which they realised".

A: No — "Arrivent de l'autre côté" simply means "when they die". What Mother intended was that when they actually arrive at their Nirvana they find it is not the ultimate solution or largest realisation of the Supreme and they must eventually come back and have their share of the world action to reach that largest realisation.

2-5-1935

*

[1] The French translation of *Conversations* by the Mother.

[2] "And as for those who have the will of running away, even they when they go over to the other side, may find that the flight was not of much use after all." *Conversations*, p. 30.

Q: The Mother has said in "Entretiens": "En fait, la mort a été attachée à toute vie sur terre."[1] The words "En fait" and "attachée" tend to give the impression that after all death is inevitable. But the preceding sentence — "Si cette croyance pouvait être rejetée, d'abord de la mentalité consciente...la mort ne serait plus inévitable"[2] — brings in an ambiguity because it does not make death so inevitable; it introduces a condition — an "if" — by which it could be avoided. But the categoricality of the sentence with "En fait" rather dilutes one's expectation of a material immortality. Moreover, the "if" in the other sentence is too formidable to be satisfied.

A: There is no ambiguity that I can see. "En fait" and "attachée" do not convey any sense of inevitability. "En fait" means simply that in fact, actually, as things are at present all life (on earth) has death attached to it as its end; but it does not in the least convey the idea that it can never be otherwise or that this is the unalterable law of all existence. It is at present a fact for certain reasons which are stated, — due to certain mental and physical circumstances — if these are changed, death is not inevitable any longer. Obviously the alteration can only come "if" certain conditions are satisfied — all progress and change by evolution depends upon an "if" which gets satisfied. If the animal mind had not been pushed to develop speech and reason, mental man would never have come into existence, — but the "if", — a stupendous and formidable one, was satisfied. So with the ifs that condition a farther progress.

31-7-1936

---

[1] "Death as a fact has been attached to all life upon earth." *Conversations*, p. 43.

[2] "If this belief could be cast out first from the conscious mind...death would no longer be inevitable." *Ibid.*

PART THREE

PRAYERS AND MEDITATIONS

This collection of the Mother's *Prayers and Meditations*
— *Prières et Méditations* — is not complete. It contains
only those that were translated by Sri Aurobindo from
the original French.

Although my whole being is in theory consecrated to Thee, O Sublime Master, who art the life, the light and the love in all things, I still find it hard to carry out this consecration in detail. It has taken me several weeks to learn that the reason for this written meditation, its justification, lies in the very fact of addressing it daily to Thee. In this way I shall put into material shape each day a little of the conversation I have so often with Thee; I shall make my confession to Thee as well as it may be; not because I think I can tell Thee anything — for Thou art Thyself everything, but our artificial and exterior way of seeing and understanding is, if it may be so said, foreign to Thee, opposed to Thy nature. Still by turning towards Thee, by immersing myself in Thy light at the moment when I consider these things, little by little I shall see them more like what they really are, — until the day when, having made myself one in identity with Thee, I shall no more have anything to say to Thee, for then I shall be Thou.

This is the goal that I would reach; towards this victory all my efforts will tend more and more. I aspire for the day when I can no longer say "I", for I shall be *Thou*.

How many times a day, still, I act without my action being consecrated to Thee; I at once become aware of it by an indefinable uneasiness which is translated in the sensibility of my body by a pang in my heart. I then make my action objective to myself and it seems to me ridiculous, childish or blameworthy; I deplore it, for a moment I am sad, until I dive into Thee and, there losing myself with a child's confidence, await from Thee the inspiration and strength needed to set right the error in me and around me, — two things that are one; for I have now a constant and precise perception of the universal unity determining an absolute interdependence of all actions.

November 3, 1912

Let Thy Light be in me like a Fire that makes all alive; let Thy divine Love penetrate me. I aspire with all my being for Thy reign as sovereign and master of my mind and heart and body; let them be Thy docile instruments and Thy faithful servitors.

I said yesterday to that young Englishman who is seeking for Thee with so sincere a desire, that I had definitively found Thee, that the Union was constant. Such is indeed the state of which I am conscious. All my thoughts go towards Thee, all my acts are consecrated to Thee; Thy Presence is for me an absolute, immutable, invariable fact, and Thy Peace dwells constantly in my heart. Yet I know that this state of union is poor and precarious compared with that which it will become possible for me to realise tomorrow, and I am as yet far, no doubt very far, from that identification in which I shall totally lose the notion of the "I", of that "I", which I still use in order to express myself, but which is each time a constraint, like a term unfit to express the thought that is seeking for expression. It seems to me indispensable for human communication, but all depends on what this "I" manifests; and how many times already, when I pronounce it, it is Thou who speakest in me, for I have lost the sense of separativity.

But all this is still in embryo and will continue to grow towards perfection. What an appeasing assurance there is in this serene confidence in Thy All-Might!

Thou art all, everywhere, and in all, and this body which acts is Thy own body, just as is the visible universe in its entirety; it is Thou who breathest, thinkest and lovest in this substance which, being Thyself, desires to be Thy willing servant.

What a hymn of thanksgiving should I not be raising at each moment unto Thee! Everywhere and in everything around me Thou revealest Thyself and in me Thy Will and Consciousness express themselves always more and more clearly even to the point of my having almost entirely lost the gross illusion of "me" and "mine". If a few shadows, a few flaws can be seen in the great Light which manifests Thee, how shall they bear for long the marvellous brightness of Thy resplendent Love? This morning, the consciousness that I had of the way Thou art fashioning this being which was "I" can be roughly represented by a great diamond cut with regular geometrical facets, a diamond in its cohesion, firmness, pure limpidity, transparency, but a brilliant and radiant flame in its intense ever-progressive life. But it was something more, something better than all that, for nearly all sensation inner and outer was exceeded and that image only presented itself to my mind as I returned to conscious contact with the outer world.

It is Thou that makest the experience fertile, Thou who renderest life progressive, Thou who compellest the darkness to vanish in an instant before the Light, Thou who givest to Love all its power, Thou who everywhere raisest up matter in this ardent and wonderful aspiration, in this sublime thirst for Eternity.

Thou everywhere and always; nothing but *Thou* in the essence and in the manifestation.

O Shadow and Illusion, dissolve! O Suffering, fade and disappear! Lord Supreme, art Thou not there!

The outer life, the activity of each day and each instant, is it not the indispensable complement of our hours of meditation and contemplation? And is not the proportion of time given to each the exact image of the proportion which exists between the amount of effort to be made for the preparation and realisation? For meditation, contemplation, Union is the result obtained — the flower that blooms; the daily activity is the anvil on which all the elements must pass and repass in order to be purified, refined, made supple and ripe for the illumination which contemplation gives to them. All these elements must be thus passed one after the other through the crucible before outer activity becomes needless for the integral development. Then is this activity turned into the means to manifest Thee so as to awaken the other centres of consciousness to the same dual work of the forge and the illumination. Therefore are pride and satisfaction with oneself the worst of all obstacles. Very modestly we must take advantage of all the minute opportunities offered to knead and purify some of the innumerable elements, to make them supple, to make them impersonal, to teach them forgetfulness of self and abnegation and devotion and kindness and gentleness; and when all these modes of being have become habitual to them, then are they ready to participate in the Contemplation, and to identify themselves with Thee in the supreme Concentration. That is why it seems to me that the work must be long and slow even for the best and that striking conversions cannot be integral. They change the orientation of the being, they put it definitively on the straight path; but truly to attain the goal none can escape the need of innumerable experiences of every kind and every instant.

....O Supreme Master who shinest in my being and each thing, let Thy Light be manifest and the reign of Thy Peace come for all.

December 2, 1912

So long as one element of the being, one movement of the thought is still subjected to outside influences, not solely under Thine, it cannot be said that the true Union is realised; there is still the horrible mixture without order and light, — for that element, that movement is a world, a world of disorder and darkness, as is the entire earth in the material world, as is the material world in the entire universe.

December 3, 1912

Last night I had the experience of the effectivity of confident surrender to Thy guidance; when it is needful that something should be known, one knows it, and the more passive the mind to Thy illumination, the clearer and the more adequate is its expression.

I listened to Thee as Thou spokest in me, and I would have liked to write down what Thou saidst so that the formula in all its precision might not be lost — for now I should not be able to repeat what was said. Then I thought that this care for conservation was again an insulting lack of confidence towards Thee, for Thou canst make of me all that I need to be, and in the measure in which my attitude allows Thee to act on me and in me, Thy omnipotence has no limits. To know that at each instant what must be surely is, as perfectly as is possible, for all those who know how to see Thee in everything and everywhere! No more fear, no more uneasiness, no more anguish; nothing but a perfect Serenity, an absolute Confidence, a supreme unwavering Peace.

December 5, 1912

In Peace and Silence the Eternal manifests; allow nothing to disturb you and the Eternal will manifest; have perfect equality in face of all and the Eternal will be there.... Yes, we should not put too much intensity, too much effort into our seeking for Thee; the effort and intensity become a veil in front of Thee; we must not desire to see Thee, for that is still a mental agitation which obscures Thy Eternal Presence; it is in the most complete Peace, Serenity and Equality that all is Thou even as Thou art all, and the least vibration in this perfectly pure and calm atmosphere is an obstacle to Thy manifestation. No haste, no inquietude, no tension, Thou, nothing but Thou, without any analysis or any objectivising, and Thou art there without a possible doubt, for all becomes a Holy Peace and a Sacred Silence.

And that is better than all the meditations in the world.

December 7, 1912

Like a flame that burns in silence, like a perfume that rises straight upward without wavering, my love goes to Thee; and like the child who does not reason and has no care, I trust myself to Thee that Thy Will may be done, that Thy Light may manifest, Thy Peace radiate, Thy Love cover the world. When Thou willest I shall be in Thee, Thyself, and there shall be no more any distinction; I await that blessed hour without impatience of any kind, letting myself flow irresistibly toward it as a peaceful stream flows toward the boundless ocean.

Thy Peace is in me, and in that Peace I see Thee alone present in everything, with the calm of Eternity.

December 10, 1912

O Supreme Master, Eternal Teacher, it has been once more granted me to verify the unequalled effectivity of a full confidence in Thy leading. Thy Light was manifested through my mouth yesterday and it met no resistance in me; the instrument was willing, supple, keen of edge.

It is Thou who art the doer in each thing and each being, and he who is near enough to Thee to see Thee in all actions without exception, will know how to transform each act into a benediction.

To abide always in Thee is the one thing that matters, always and ever more and more in Thee, beyond illusions and the deceptions of the senses, not drawing back from action, refusing it, rejecting it — a struggle useless and pernicious — but living Thee alone in the act whatever it may be, ever and always Thee; then the illusion is dispelled, the falsehoods of the senses vanish, the bond of consequences is broken, all is transformed into a manifestation of the glory of Thy Eternal Presence.

So let it be. Amen.

December 11, 1912

I await, without haste, without inquietude, the tearing of another veil, the Union made more complete. I know that the veil is formed of a whole mass of small imperfections, of attachments without number.... How shall all these disappear? Slowly, as the result of countless small efforts and a vigilance not faltering even for a moment, or suddenly, through a great illumination of Thy All-Puissant Love? I know not, I do not even put to myself the question; I wait, keeping watch as best as I can, in the certitude that nothing exists save Thy Will, that Thou alone art the doer and I am the instrument; and when the instrument is ready for a completer manifestation, the manifestation will quite naturally take place.

Already there is heard from behind the veil the wordless symphony of gladness that reveals Thy sublime Presence.

February 5, 1913

Thy voice is heard as a melodious chant in the stillness of my heart, and is translated in my head by words which are inadequate and yet replete with Thee. And these words are addressed to the Earth and say to her: — Poor sorrowful Earth, remember that I am present in you and lose not hope; each effort, each grief, each joy and each pang, each call of thy heart, each aspiration of thy soul, each renewal of thy seasons, all, all without exception, what seems to thee sorrowful and what seems to thee joyous, what seems to thee ugly and what seems to thee beautiful, all infallibly lead thee towards me, who am endless Peace, shadowless Light, perfect Harmony, Certitude, Rest and Supreme Blessedness.

Hearken, O Earth, to the sublime voice that arises,
Hearken and take new courage!

February 8, 1913

O Lord, Thou art my refuge and my blessing, my strength, my health, my hope, and my courage. Thou art supreme Peace, unalloyed Joy, perfect Serenity. My whole being prostrates before Thee in a gratitude beyond measure and a ceaseless worship; and that worship goes up from my heart and my mind towards Thee like the pure smoke of incense of the perfumes of India.

Let me be Thy herald among men, so that all who are ready may taste the beatitude that Thou grantest me in Thy infinite Mercy, and let Thy Peace reign upon earth.

February 10, 1913

My being goes up to Thee in thanksgiving, not because Thou usest this weak and imperfect body to manifest Thyself, but because *Thou dost manifest Thyself*, and that is the Splendour of splendours, the Joy of joys, the Marvel of marvels. All who seek Thee with ardour should understand that Thou art there whenever there is need of Thee; and if they could have the supreme faith to give up seeking Thee, but rather to await Thee, at each moment putting themselves integrally at Thy service, Thou wouldst be there whenever there was need of Thee; and is there not always need of Thee with us, whatever may be the different, and often unexpected, forms of Thy manifestation?

Let Thy glory be proclaimed,
And sanctify life;
Let it transform men's hearts,
And Thy Peace reign on earth.

February 12, 1913

As soon as all effort disappears from a manifestation, it becomes very simple, with the simplicity of a flower opening, manifesting its beauty and spreading its fragrance without clamour or vehement gesture. And in this simplicity lies the greatest power, the power which is least mixed and least gives rise to harmful reactions. The power of the vital should be mistrusted, it is a tempter on the path of the work, and there is always a risk of falling into its trap, for it gives you the taste of immediate results; and, in our first eagerness to do the work well, we let ourselves be carried away to make use of this power. But very soon it deflects all our action from the right course and introduces a seed of illusion and death into what we do.

Simplicity, simplicity! How sweet is the purity of Thy Presence!...

March 13, 1913

.....Let the pure perfume of sanctification burn always,
rising higher and higher, and straighter and straighter, like the
ceaseless prayer of the integral being, desiring to unite with
Thee so as to manifest Thee.

May 11, 1913

As soon as I have no longer any material responsibilities, all thoughts about these things flee far away from me, and I am solely and entirely occupied with Thee and Thy service. Then, in that perfect peace and serenity, I unite my will to Thine, and in that integral silence I listen to Thy truth and hear its expression. It is by becoming conscious of Thy Will and identifying ours with Thine that there is found the secret of true liberty and all-puissance, the secret of the regeneration of forces and the transfiguration of the being.

To be constantly and integrally at one with Thee is to have the assurance that we shall overcome every obstacle and triumph over all difficulties, both within and without.

O Lord, Lord, a boundless joy fills my heart, songs of gladness surge through my head in marvellous waves, and in the full confidence of Thy certain triumph I find a sovereign Peace and an invincible Power. Thou fillest my being, Thou animatest it, Thou settest in motion its hidden springs, Thou illuminest its understanding, Thou intensifiest its life, Thou increasest tenfold its love; and I no longer know whether the universe is I or I the universe, whether Thou art in me or I in Thee; Thou alone art and all is Thou; and the streams of Thy infinite grace fill and overflow the world.

Sing O lands, sing O peoples, sing O men,

The Divine Harmony is there.

June 18, 1913

To turn towards Thee, unite with Thee, live in Thee and for Thee, is supreme happiness, unmixed joy, immutable peace; it is to breathe infinity, to soar in eternity, no longer feel one's limits, escape from time and space. Why do men flee from these boons as though they fear them? What a strange thing is ignorance, that source of all suffering! How miserable that obscurity which keeps men away from the very thing which would bring them happiness and subjects them to this painful school of ordinary existence fashioned entirely from struggle and suffering!

July 21, 1913

.... Yet what patience is needed! How imperceptible the stages of progress!...

Oh! how I call Thee from the very depths of my heart, True Light, Sublime Love, Divine Master who art the source of our light and of our living, our guide and our protector, the Soul of our soul and the Life of our life, the Reason of our being, the supreme Knowledge, the immutable Peace!

November 28, 1913

Mother Divine, grant that today may bring to us a completer consecration to Thy Will, a more integral gift of ourselves to Thy work, a more total forgetfulness of self, a greater illumination, a purer love. Grant that in a communion growing ever deeper, more constant and entire, we may be united always more and more closely to Thee and become Thy servitors worthy of Thee. Remove from us all egoism, root out all petty vanity, greed and obscurity. May we be all ablaze with Thy divine Love; make us Thy torches in the world.

January 24, 1914

O Thou who art the sole reality of our being, O sublime Master of love, Redeemer of life, let me have no longer any other consciousness than of Thee at every instant and in each being. When I do not live solely with Thy life, I agonise, I sink slowly towards extinction; for Thou art my only reason for existence, my one goal, my single support. I am like a timid bird not yet sure of its wings and hesitating to take its flight; let me soar to reach definitive identity with Thee.

February 1, 1914

I turn towards Thee who art everywhere and within all
and outside all, intimate essence of all and remote from all,
centre of condensation for all energies, creator of conscious
individualities: I turn towards Thee and salute Thee, O liberator
of the worlds, and, identified with Thy divine love, I contemplate
the earth and its creatures, this mass of substance put into forms
perpetually destroyed and renewed, this swarming mass of aggre-
gates which are dissolved as soon as constituted, of beings who
imagine that they are conscient and permanent individualities
and who are as ephemeral as a breath, always alike or almost the
same, in their diversity, repeating indefinitely the same desires,
the same tendencies, the same appetites, the same ignorant errors.

But from time to time Thy sublime light shines in a being
and radiates through him over the world, and then a little wisdom, a little knowledge, a little disinterested faith, heroism and
compassion penetrates men's hearts, transforms their minds
and sets free a few elements from that sorrowful and implacable
wheel of existence to which their blind ignorance subjects them.

But how much greater a splendour than all that have gone

before, how marvellous a glory and light would be needed to draw these beings out of the horrible aberration in which they are plunged by the life of cities and so-called civilisations! What a formidable and, at the same time, divinely sweet puissance would be needed to turn aside all these wills from the bitter struggle for their selfish, mean and foolish satisfactions, to snatch them from this vortex which hides death behind its treacherous glitter, and turn them towards Thy conquering harmony!

O Lord, eternal Master, enlighten us, guide our steps, show us the way towards the realisation of Thy law, towards the accomplishment of Thy work.

I adore Thee in silence and listen to Thee in a religious concentration.

February 14, 1914

Peace, peace upon all the earth!

May all escape from the ordinary consciousness and be delivered from the attachment for material things; may they awake to the knowledge of Thy divine presence, unite themselves with Thy supreme consciousness and taste the plenitude of peace that springs from it.

Lord, Thou art the sovereign Master of our being. Thy law is our law, and with all our strength we aspire to identify our consciousness with Thy eternal consciousness, that we may accomplish Thy sublime work in each thing and at every moment.

Lord, deliver us from all care for contingencies, deliver us from the ordinary outlook on things. Grant that we may henceforth see only with Thy eyes and act only by Thy will. Transform us into living torches of Thy divine love.

With reverence, with devotion, in a joyful consecration of

my whole being I give myself, O Lord, to the fulfilment of Thy
law.

Peace, peace upon all the earth!

February 15, 1914

O Thou, sole Reality, Light of our light and Life of our life, Love supreme, Saviour of the world, grant that more and more I may be perfectly awakened to the awareness of Thy constant presence. Let all my acts conform to Thy law; let there be no difference between my will and Thine. Extricate me from the illusory consciousness of my mind, from its world of fantasies; let me identify my consciousness with the Absolute Consciousness, for that art Thou.

Give me constancy in the will to attain the end, give me firmness and energy and the courage which shakes off all torpor and lassitude.

Give me the peace of perfect disinterestedness, the peace that makes Thy presence felt and Thy intervention effective, the peace that is ever victorious over all bad will and every obscurity.

Grant, I implore Thee, that all in my being may be identified with Thee. May I be nothing else any more than a flame of love utterly awakened to a supreme realisation of Thee.

March 7, 1914

On board the Kaga Maru

This morning my prayer rises to Thee, always with the same aspiration: to live Thy love, to radiate Thy love, with such potency and effectiveness that all may feel fortified, regenerated and illumined by our contact. To have power to heal life, to relieve suffering, to generate peace and calm confidence, to efface anguish and replace it by the sense of the one true happiness, the happiness that is founded in Thee and never fades....

O Lord, O marvellous Friend, O all-powerful Master, penetrate all our being, transfigure it till Thou alone livest in us and through us.

March 8, 1914

In front of this calm sunrise which turned all within me into silence and peace, at the moment when I grew conscious of Thee and Thou alone wast living in me, O Lord, it seemed to me that I adopted all the inhabitants of this ship, and enveloped them in an equal love, and that so in each one of them something of Thy consciousness would awake. Not often had I felt so strongly Thy divine power, and Thy invincible light, and once again total was my confidence and unmixed my joyful surrender.

O Thou who relievest all suffering and dispersest all ignorance, O Thou the supreme healer, be constantly present on this boat in the heart of those whom it shelters that once again Thy glory may be manifested!

March 9, 1914

Those who live for Thee and in Thee may change their physical surroundings, their habits, climate, "milieu", but everywhere they find the same atmosphere; they carry that atmosphere in themselves, in their thought constantly fixed on Thee. Everywhere they feel at home, for everywhere they are in Thy house. No longer do they marvel at the novelty, unexpectedness, picturesqueness of things and countries; for them, it is Thy presence that is manifest in all and Thy unchangeable splendour, which never leaves them, is apparent in the least grain of sand. The whole earth chants Thy praises; in spite of the obscurity, misery, ignorance, through it all, it is still the glory of Thy love which we perceive and with which we can commune ceaselessly everywhere.

O Lord, my sweet Master, all this I constantly experience on this boat which seems to me a marvellous abode of peace, a temple sailing in Thy honour over the waves of the subconscient passivity which we have to conquer and awaken to the consciousness of Thy divine Presence.

Blessed was the day when I came to know Thee, O Ineffable
Eternity.

Blessed among all days be that day when the earth at last
awakened shall know Thee and shall live only for Thee.

Silent and unseen as always, but all-powerful, Thy action has made itself felt and, in these souls that seemed to be so closed, a perception of Thy divine light is awake. I knew well that none could invoke Thy presence in vain and if in the sincerity of our hearts we commune with Thee through no matter what organism, body or human collectivity, this organism in spite of its ignorance finds its unconsciousness wholly transformed. But when in one or several elements there is the conscious transformation, when the flame that smoulders under the ashes leaps out suddenly illumining all the being, then with joy we salute Thy sovereign action, testify once more to Thy invincible puissance and can hope that a new possibility of true happiness has been added to the others in mankind.

O Lord, an ardent thanksgiving mounts from me towards Thee expressing the gratitude of this sorrowing humanity which Thou illuminest, transformest and glorifiest and givest to it the peace of Knowledge.

April 10, 1914

Suddenly the veil was rent, the horizon was disclosed — and before the clear vision my whole being threw itself at Thy feet in a great outburst of gratitude. Yet in spite of this deep and integral joy all was calm, all was peaceful with the peace of eternity.

I seem to have no more limits; there is no longer the perception of the body, no sensations, no feelings, no thoughts — a clear, pure, tranquil immensity penetrated with love and light, filled with an unspeakable beatitude is all that is there and that alone seems now to be myself, and this "myself" is so little the former "I", selfish and limited, that I cannot tell if it is I or Thou, O Lord, sublime Master of our destinies.

It is as though all were energy, courage, force, will, infinite sweetness, incomparable compassion....

Even more forcibly than during these last days the past is dead and as though buried under the rays of a new life. The last glance that I have just thrown backward as I read a few pages of this book definitely convinced me of this death, and lightened of a great weight I present myself before Thee, O my divine Master, with all the simplicity, all the nudity of a child.... And still the one only thing I perceive is that calm and pure immensity....

Lord, Thou hast answered my prayer, Thou hast granted me what I have asked from Thee; the "I" has disappeared, there is only a docile instrument put at Thy service, a centre of concentration and manifestation of Thy infinite and eternal rays; Thou hast taken my life and made it Thine; Thou hast taken my will and hast united it to Thine; Thou hast taken my love and identified it with Thine; Thou hast taken my thought and replaced it by Thy absolute consciousness.

The body, marvelling, bows its forehead in the dust in mute and submissive adoration.

And nothing else exists but Thou alone in the splendour of Thy immutable peace.

O Lord, O almighty Master, sole Reality, grant that no error, no obscurity, no fatal ignorance may creep into my heart and my thought.

In action, the personality is the inevitable and indispensable intermediary of Thy will and Thy forces.

The stronger, the more complex, powerful, individualised and conscious is the personality, the more powerfully and usefully can the instrument serve. But, by reason of the very character of personality, it easily tends to be drawn into the fatal illusion of its separate existence and become little by little a screen between Thee and that on which Thou willest to act. Not at the beginning, in the manifestation, but in the transmission of the return; that is to say, instead of being, as a faithful servant, an intermediary who brings back to Thee exactly what is Thy due — the forces sent forth in reply to Thy action, — there is a tendency in the personality to want to keep for itself a part of the forces, with this idea: "It is I who have done this or that, I who am thanked...." Pernicious illusion, obscure falsehood, now are you discovered and unmasked. That is the maleficent canker corroding the fruit of the action, falsifying all its results.

O Lord, O my sweet Master, sole Reality, dispel this feeling of the "I". I have now understood that so long as there will be a manifested universe, the "I" will remain necessary for Thy manifestation; to dissolve, or even to diminish or weaken the "I", is to deprive Thee of the means of manifestation, in whole or part. But what must be radically and definitively suppressed is the illusory thought, the illusory feeling, the illusory sensation of the separate "I". At no moment, in no circumstances must we forget that our "I" has no reality outside Thee.

O my sweet Master, my divine Lord, tear out from my heart this illusion so that Thy servant may become pure and faithful and faithfully and integrally bring back to Thee all that is Thy due. In silence let me contemplate and understand this supreme ignorance and dispel it for ever. Chase the shadow from my heart, and let Thy light reign in it its uncontested sovereign.

May 12, 1914

More and more it seems to me that we are in one of those periods of activity in which the fruit of past efforts becomes apparent, — a period in which we act according to Thy law in the measure in which it is the sovereign controller of our being, without having even the leisure to become conscious of the law.

This morning passing by a rapid experience from depth to depth, I was able, once again, as always, to identify my consciousness with Thine and to live no longer in aught but Thee; — indeed, it was Thou alone that was living, but immediately Thy will pulled my consciousness towards the exterior, towards the work to be done, and Thou saidst to me, "Be the instrument of which I have need." And is not this the last renunciation, to renounce identification with Thee, to renounce the sweet and pure joy of no longer distinguishing between Thee and me, the joy of knowing at each moment, not only with the intellect but by an integral experience, that Thou art the unique Reality and that all the rest is but appearance and illusion. That the exterior being should be the docile instrument which does not even need to be conscious of the will which moves it, is not doubtful; but why must I be almost entirely identified with the instrument and why should not the "I" be entirely merged in Thee and live Thy full and absolute consciousness?

I ask, but I am not anxious about it. I know that all is according to Thy will, and with a pure adoration I trust myself joyously to Thy will. I shall be what Thou wouldst have me be, O Lord, conscient or inconscient, a simple instrument as is the body or a supreme knowledge as art Thou. O the sweet and peaceful joy when one can say "All is good" and feel Thee at work in the world through all the elements which lend themselves to that transmission.

Thou art the sovereign Master of all, Thou art the Inaccessible, the Unknowable, the eternal and sublime Reality.

O marvellous Unity, I disappear in Thee.

May 21, 1914

Outside all manifestation, in the immutable silence of Eternity, I am in Thee, O Lord, an unmoving beatitude. In that which, out of Thy puissance and marvellous light, forms the centre and reality of the atoms of matter I find Thee; thus without going out of Thy Presence I can disappear in Thy supreme consciousness or see Thee in the radiant particles of my being. And for the moment that is the plenitude of Thy life and Thy illumination.

I see Thee, I am Thyself, and between these two poles my intense love aspires towards Thee.

May 22, 1914

When we have discerned successively what is real from what is unreal in all the states of being and all the worlds of life, when we have arrived at the perfect and integral certitude of the sole Reality, we must turn our gaze from the heights of this supreme consciousness towards the individual aggregate which serves as the immediate instrument for Thy manifestation upon earth, and see in it nothing but Thee, our sole real existence. Thus each atom of this aggregate will be awakened to receive Thy sublime influence; the ignorance and the darkness will disappear not only from the central consciousness of the being but also from its most external mode of expression. It is only by the fulfilment, by the perfection of this labour of transfiguration that there can be manifested the plenitude of Thy Presence, Thy Light and Thy Love.

Lord, Thou makest me understand this truth ever more clearly; lead me step by step on that path. My whole being down to its smallest atom aspires for the perfect knowledge of Thy presence and a complete union with it. Let every obstacle disappear, let Thy divine knowledge replace in every part the darkness of the ignorance. Even as Thou hast illumined the central consciousness, the will in the being, enlighten too this outermost substance. And let the whole individuality, from its first origin and essence to its last projection and most material body, be unified in a perfect realisation and a complete manifestation of Thy sole Reality.

Nothing is in the universe but Thy Life, Thy Light, Thy Love.

Let everything become resplendent and transfigured by the knowledge of Thy Truth.

Thy divine love floods my being; Thy supreme light is shining in every cell; all exults because it knows Thee and because it is one with Thee.

May 26, 1914

On the surface is the storm, the sea is in turmoil, waves clash and leap one on another and break with a mighty uproar. But all the time, under this water in fury, are vast smiling expanses, peaceful and motionless. They look upon the surface agitation as an indispensable act; for matter has to be vigorously churned if it is to become capable of manifesting entirely the divine light. Behind the troubled appearance, behind the struggle and anguish of the conflict, the consciousness remains firm at its post; observing all the movements of the outer being, it intervenes only to rectify direction and position, so as not to allow the play to become too dramatic. This intervention is now firm and a little severe, now ironical, a call to order or a mockery, full always of a strong, gentle, peaceful and smiling benevolence.

In the silence I beheld Thy infinite and eternal Beatitude.

Then softly a prayer rises towards Thee from what is still in the shadow and the struggle: O sweet Master, O supreme Giver of illumination and purity, grant that all substance and every activity may be no more anything other than a constant manifestation of Thy divine Love and Thy sovereign Serenity....

And in my heart is the song of gladness of Thy sublime magnificence.

August 27, 1914

To be the divine love, love powerful, infinite, unfathomable, in every activity, in all the worlds of being — it is for this I cry to Thee, O Lord. Let me be consumed with this love divine, love powerful, infinite, unfathomable, in every activity, in all the worlds of being! Transmute me into that burning brazier so that all the atmosphere of earth may be purified with its flame.

O, to be Thy Love infinitely....

August 31, 1914

In this formidable disorder and terrible destruction can be seen a great working, a necessary toil preparing the earth for a new sowing which will rise in marvellous spikes of grain and give to the world the shining harvest of a new race.... The vision is clear and precise, the plan of Thy divine law so plainly traced that peace has come back and installed itself in the hearts of the workers. There are no more doubts and hesitations, no longer any anguish or impatience. There is only the grand straight line of the work eternally accomplishing itself in spite of all, against all, despite all contrary appearances and illusory detours. These physical personalities, moments unseizable in the infinite Becoming, know that they will have made humanity take one farther step, infallibly and without care for the inevitable results, whatever be the apparent momentary consequences: they unite themselves with Thee, O Master eternal, they unite themselves with Thee, O Mother universal, and in this double identity with That which is beyond and That which is all the manifestation they taste the infinite joy of the perfect certitude.

Peace, peace in all the world....

War is an appearance,

Turmoil is an illusion,

Peace is there, immutable peace.

Mother, sweet Mother who I am, Thou art at once the destroyer and the builder.

The whole universe lives in Thy breast with all its life innumerable and Thou livest in Thy immensity in the least of its atoms.

And the aspiration of Thy infinitude turns towards That which is not manifested to cry to it for a manifestation ever more complete and more perfect.

All *is*, in one time, in a triple and clairvoyant total Consciousness, the Individual, the Universal, the Infinite.

O Mother Divine, with what fervour, what ardent love
I came to Thee in Thy deepest consciousness, in Thy high
status of sublime love and perfect felicity, and I nestled so close
into Thy arms and loved Thee with so intense a love that I became
altogether Thyself. Then in the silence of our mute ecstasy a
voice from yet profounder depths arose and the voice said, "Turn
towards those who have need of thy love." All the grades of
consciousness appeared, all the successive worlds. Some were
splendid and luminous, well ordered and clear; there knowledge
was resplendent, expression was harmonious and vast, will was
potent and invincible. Then the worlds darkened in a multiplicity more and more chaotic, the Energy became violent and the
material world obscure and sorrowful. And when in our infinite
love we perceived in its entirety the hideous suffering of the world
of misery and ignorance, when we saw our children locked in a
sombre struggle, flung upon each other by energies that had
deviated from their true aim, we willed ardently that the light of
Divine Love should be made manifest, a transfiguring force at
the centre of these distracted elements. Then, that the will might
be yet more powerful and effective, we turned towards Thee, O

unthinkable Supreme, and we implored Thy aid. And from the unsounded depths of the Unknown a reply came sublime and formidable and we knew that the earth *was saved*.

September 25, 1914

O Divine and adorable Mother, with Thy help what is there that is impossible? The hour of realisations is near and Thou hast assured us of Thy aid that we may perform integrally the supreme Will.

Thou hast accepted us as fit intermediaries between the unthinkable realities and the relativities of the physical world, and Thy constant presence in our midst is a token of Thy active collaboration.

The Lord has willed and Thou dost execute:
A new Light shall break upon the earth.
A new world shall be born,
And the things that were promised shall be fulfilled.

My pen is mute to chant Thy presence, O Lord; yet art Thou like a king who has taken entire possession of his kingdom. Thou art there, organising, putting all in place, developing and increasing every province. Thou awakenest those that were asleep. Thou makest active those that were sinking towards inertia; Thou art building a harmony out of the whole. A day will come when the harmony shall be achieved and all the country shall be by its very life the bearer of Thy word and Thy manifestation.

But meanwhile my pen is mute to chant Thy praise.

September 30, 1914

O Thou, Sublime Love, to whom I gave never any other name but who art so wholly the very substance of my being, Thou whom I feel vibrant and alive in the least of my atoms even as in the infinite universe and beyond, Thou who breathest in every breath, movest in the heart of all activities, art radiant through all that is of good will and hidden behind all sufferings, Thou for whom I cherish a cult without limit which grows ever more intense, permit that I may with more and more reason feel that I am Thyself wholly.

And Thou, O Lord, who art all this made one and much more, O sovereign Master, extreme limit of our thought, who standest for us at the threshold of the Unknown, make rise from that Unthinkable some new splendour, some possibility of a loftier and more integral realisation, that Thy work may be accomplished and the universe take one step farther towards the sublime Identity, the supreme Manifestation.

And now my pen falls mute and I adore Thee in silence.

October 5, 1914

In the calm silence of Thy contemplation, O Divine Master, Nature is fortified and tempered anew. All principle of individuality is overpassed, she is plunged in Thy infinity that allows oneness to be realised in all domains without confusion, without disorder. The combined harmony of that which persists, that which progresses and that which eternally is, is little by little accomplished in an always more complex, more extended and more lofty equilibrium. And this interchange of the three modes of life allows the plenitude of the manifestation.

Many seek Thee at this hour in anguish and incertitude. May I be their mediator with Thee that Thy light may illumine them, that Thy peace may appease. My being is now only a point of support for Thy action and a centre for Thy consciousness. Where now are the limits, whither have fled the obstacles? Thou art the sovereign Lord of Thy kingdom.

Oh, let Light be poured on all the earth and Peace inhabit every heart.... Almost all know only the material life heavy, inert, conservative, obscure; their vital forces are so tied to this physical form of existence that, even when left to themselves and outside the body, they are still solely occupied with these material contingencies that are yet so harassing and painful.... Those in whom the mental life is awakened are restless, tormented, agitated, arbitrary, despotic. Caught altogether in the whirl of the renewals and transformations of which they dream, they are ready to destroy everything without knowledge of any foundation on which to construct and with their light made only of blinding flashes they increase yet more the confusion rather than help it to cease.

In all there lacks the unchanging peace of Thy sovereign contemplation and the calm vision of Thy immutable eternity.

And with the infinite gratitude of the individual being to whom Thou hast accorded this surpassing grace, I implore Thee, O Lord, that under cover of the present turmoil, in the very heart of this extreme confusion the miracle may be accomplished and

Thy law of supreme serenity and pure unchanging light become visible to the perception of all and govern the earth in a humanity at last awakened to Thy divine consciousness.

O sweet Master, Thou hast heard my prayer, Thou wilt reply to my call.

October 14, 1914

Mother Divine, Thou art with us; every day Thou givest me the assurance and, closely united in an identity that grows more and more total, more and more constant, we turn to the Lord of the Universe and to That which is beyond in a great aspiration towards the new Light. All the earth is in our arms like a sick child who must be cured and for whom one has a special affection because of his very weakness. Cradled on the immensity of the eternal becomings, ourselves those becomings, we contemplate hushed and glad the eternity of the immobile Silence where all is realised in the perfect Consciousness and immutable Existence, miraculous gate of all the unknown that is beyond.

Then is the veil torn, the inexpressible Glory uncovered and, suffused with the ineffable Splendour, we turn back towards the world to bring it the glad tidings.

Lord, Thou hast given me the happiness infinite. What being, what circumstances can have the power to take it away from me?

My aspiration to Thee, O Lord, has taken the form of a beautiful rose, harmonious, full in bloom, rich in fragrance. I stretch it out to Thee with both arms in a gesture of offering and I ask of Thee: If my understanding is limited, widen it; if my knowledge is obscure, enlighten it; if my heart is empty of ardour, set it aflame; if my love is insignificant, make it intense; if my feelings are ignorant and egoistic, give them the full consciousness in the Truth. And the "I" which demands this of Thee, O Lord, is not a little personality lost amidst thousands of others. It is the whole earth that aspires to Thee in a movement full of fervour.

In the perfect silence of my contemplation all widens to infinity, and in the perfect peace of that silence Thou appearest in the resplendent glory of Thy Light.

November 8, 1914

For the plenitude of Thy Light we invoke Thee, O Lord! Awaken in us the power to express Thee.

All is mute in the being as in a desert crypt; but in the heart of the shadow, in the bosom of the silence burns the lamp that can never be extinguished, the fire of an ardent aspiration to know Thee and totally to live Thee.

The nights follow the days, new dawns unweariedly succeed to past dawns, but always there mounts the scented flame that no storm-wind can force to vacillate. Higher it climbs and higher and one day attains the vault still closed, the last obstacle opposing our union. And so pure, so erect, so proud is the flame that suddenly the obstacle is dissolved.

Then Thou appearest in all Thy splendour, in the dazzling force of Thy infinite glory; at Thy contact the flame changes into a column of light that chases the shadows away for ever.

And the Word leaps forth, a supreme revelation.

February 15, 1915

O Lord of Truth, thrice have I implored Thy manifestation invoking Thee with deep fervour.

Then, as always, the whole being made its total submission. At that moment the consciousness perceived the individual being mental, vital and physical, covered all over with dust, and this being lay prostrate before Thee, its forehead touching the earth, dust in the dust, and it cried to Thee, "O Lord, this being made of dust prostrates itself before Thee praying to be consumed with the fire of the Truth that it may henceforth manifest only Thee." Then Thou saidst to it, "Arise, thou art pure of all that is dust." And suddenly, in a stroke, all the dust sank from it like a cloak that falls on the earth, and the being appeared erect, always as substantial but resplendent with a dazzling light.

March 3, 1915

Solitude, a harsh intense solitude, and always this strong impression of having been flung headlong into a hell of darkness! Never at any moment of my life, in any circumstances have I felt myself living in surroundings so entirely opposite to all that I am conscious of as true, so contrary to all that is the essence of my life. Sometimes when the impression and the contrast grow very intense, I cannot prevent my total submission from taking on a hue of melancholy and the calm and mute converse with the Master within is transformed for a moment into an invocation that almost supplicates, "O Lord, what have I done that Thou hast thrown me thus into the sombre Night?" But immediately the aspiration rises, still more ardent, "Spare this being all weakness; suffer it to be the docile and clear-eyed instrument of Thy work, whatever that work may be."

March 7, 1915

I am exiled from every spiritual happiness, and of all ordeals this, O Lord, is surely the most painful that Thou canst impose: but most of all the withdrawal of Thy will which seems to be a sign of total disapprobation. Strong is the growing sense of rejection, and it needs all the ardour of an untiring faith to keep the external consciousness thus abandoned to itself from being invaded by an irremediable sorrow....

But it refuses to despair, it refuses to believe that the misfortune is irreparable; it waits with humility in an obscure and hidden effort and struggle for the breath of Thy perfect joy to penetrate it again. And perhaps each of its modest and secret victories is a true help brought to the earth....

If it were possible to come definitively out of this external consciousness, to take refuge in the divine consciousness! But that Thou hast forbidden and still and always Thou forbidst it. No flight out of the world! The burden of its darkness and ugliness must be borne to the end even if all divine succour seems to be withdrawn. I must remain in the bosom of the Night and walk on without compass, without beacon-light, without inner guide.

I will not even implore Thy mercy; for what Thou willst for me, I too will. All my energy is in tension solely to advance, always to advance step after step, despite the depth of the darkness, despite the obstacles of the way, and whatever comes, O Lord, it is with a fervent and unchanging love that Thy decision will be welcomed. Even if Thou findest the instrument unfit to serve Thee, the instrument belongs to itself no more, it is Thine; Thou canst destroy or magnify it, it exists not in itself, it wills nothing, it can do nothing without Thee.

For the most part the condition is one of calm and profound indifference; the being feels neither desire nor repulsion, neither enthusiasm nor depression, neither joy nor sorrow. It regards life as a spectacle in which it takes only a very small part; it perceives its actions and reactions, conflicts and forces as things that at once belong to its own existence which overflows the small personality on every side and yet to that personality are altogether foreign and remote.

But from time to time a great breath passes, a great breath of sorrow, of anguished isolation, of spiritual destitution, — one might almost say, the despairing appeal of Earth abandoned by the Divine. It is a pang as silent as it is cruel, a sorrow submissive, without revolt, without any desire to avoid or pass out of it and full of an infinite sweetness in which suffering and felicity are closely wedded, something infinitely vast, great and deep, too great, too deep perhaps to be understood by men — something that holds in it the seed of To-morrow....

November 26, 1915*

The entire consciousness immersed in divine contemplation, the whole being enjoyed a supreme and vast felicity.

Then was the physical body seized, first in its lower members and next the whole of it, by a sacred trembling which made all personal limits fall away little by little even in the most material sensation. The being grew in greatness progressively, methodically, breaking down every barrier, shattering every obstacle, that it might contain and manifest a force and a power which increased ceaselessly in immensity and intensity. It was as a progressive dilatation of the cells until there was a complete identification with the earth: the body of the awakened consciousness was the terrestrial globe moving harmoniously in ethereal space. And the consciousness knew that its global body was thus moving in the arms of the universal Being, and it gave itself, it abandoned itself to It in an ecstasy of peaceful bliss. Then it felt that its body was absorbed in the body of the universe and one with it; the consciousness became the consciousness of the universe, immobile in its totality, moving infinitely in its internal complexity.

* This is the letter which the Mother sent to Sri Aurobindo and to which he answered on 31-12-1915. See Part Two, p. 384 for Sri Aurobindo's answer.

7 31

The consciousness of the universe sprang towards the Divine in an ardent aspiration, a perfect surrender, and it saw in the splendour of the immaculate Light the radiant Being standing on a many-headed serpent whose body coiled infinitely around the universe. The Being in an eternal gesture of triumph mastered and created at one and the same time the serpent and the universe that issued from him; erect on the serpent he dominated it with all his victorious might, and the same gesture that crushed the hydra enveloping the universe gave it eternal birth. Then the consciousness became this Being and perceived that its form was changing once more; it was absorbed into something which was no longer a form and yet contained all forms, something which, immutable, sees, — the Eye, the Witness. And what It sees, is. Then this last vestige of form disappeared and the consciousness itself was absorbed into the Unutterable, the Ineffable.

The return towards the consciousness of the individual body took place very slowly in a constant and invariable splendour of Light and Power and Felicity and Adoration, by successive gradations, but directly, without passing again through the universal and terrestrial forms. And it was as if the modest corporeal form had become the direct and immediate vesture, without any intermediary, of the supreme and eternal Witness.

Always the word Thou makest me hear in the silence
is sweet and encouraging, O Lord. But I see not in what this
instrument is worthy of the grace Thou accordest to it or how it
will have the capacity to realise what Thou attendest from it. All
in it appears so small, weak and ordinary, so lacking in intensity
and force and amplitude in comparison with what it should be to
undertake this overwhelming role. But I know that what the
mind thinks is of little importance. The mind itself knows it and,
passive, it awaits the working out of Thy decree.

Thou biddest me strive without cease, and I could wish to
have the indomitable ardour that prevails over every difficulty.
But Thou hast put in my heart a peace so smiling that I fear I
no longer know even how to strive. Things develop in me, faculties and activities, as flowers bloom, spontaneously and without
effort, in a joy to be and a joy to grow, a joy to manifest Thee,
whatever the mode of Thy manifestation. If struggle there is, it
is so gentle and easy that it can hardly be given the name. But
how small is this heart to contain so great a love! and how weak
this vital and physical being to carry the power to distribute it!
Thus Thou hast placed me on the threshold of the marvellous

Way, but will my feet have the strength to advance upon it?...
But Thou repliest to me that my movement is to soar and it
would be an error to wish to walk.... O Lord, how infinite
is Thy compassion! Once more Thou hast taken me in Thy
omnipotent arms and cradled me on Thy unfathomable heart,
and Thy heart said to me, "Torment not thyself at all, be confident like a child: art thou not myself crystallised for my work?"

December 27, 1916

O my beloved Lord, my heart is bowed before Thee, my arms are stretched towards Thee imploring Thee to set all this being on fire with Thy sublime love that it may radiate from there on the world. My heart is wide open in my breast; my heart is open and turned towards Thee, it is open and empty that Thou mayest fill it with Thy divine Love; it is empty of all but Thee and Thy presence fills it through and through and yet leaves it empty, for it can contain also all the infinite variety of the manifested world....

O Lord, my arms are outstretched in supplication towards Thee, my heart is wide open before Thee, that Thou mayest make of it a reservoir of Thy infinite love.

"Love me in all things, everywhere and in all beings" was Thy reply. I prostrate myself before Thee and ask of Thee to give me that power.

December 29, 1916

O my sweet Lord, teach me to be the instrument of
Thy Love.

March 30, 1917

There is a sovereign royalty in taking no thought for oneself. To have needs is to assert a weakness; to claim something proves that we lack what we claim. To desire is to be impotent; it is to recognise our limitations and confess our incapacity to overcome them. If only from the point of view of a legitimate pride, man should be noble enough to renounce desire. How humiliating to ask something for oneself from life or from the Supreme Consciousness which animates it! How humiliating for us, how ignorant an offence against Her! For all is within our reach, only the egoistic limits of our being prevent us from enjoying the whole universe as completely and concretely as we possess our own body and its immediate surroundings.

March 31, 1917

Each time that a heart leaps at the touch of Thy divine breath, a little more beauty seems to be born upon the Earth, the air is embalmed with a sweet perfume, all becomes more friendly.

How great is Thy power, O Lord of all existences, that an atom of Thy joy is sufficient to efface so much darkness, so many sorrows and a single ray of Thy glory can light up thus the dullest pebble, illumine the blackest consciousness!

Thou hast heaped Thy favours upon me, Thou hast unveiled to me many secrets, Thou hast made me taste many unexpected and unhoped for joys, but no grace of Thine can be equal to this Thou grantest to me when a heart leaps at the touch of Thy divine breath.

At these blessed hours all earth sings a hymn of gladness, the grasses shudder with pleasure, the air is vibrant with light, the trees lift towards heaven their most ardent prayer, the chant of the birds becomes a canticle, the waves of the sea billow with love, the smile of children tells of the infinite and the souls of men appear in their eyes.

Tell me, wilt Thou grant me the marvellous power to give birth to this dawn in expectant hearts, to awaken the consciousness of men to Thy sublime presence, and in this bare and sorrowful world awaken a little of Thy true Paradise? What happiness, what riches, what terrestrial powers can equal this wonderful gift!

O Lord, never have I implored Thee in vain, for that which speaks to Thee is Thyself in me.

Drop by drop Thou allowest to fall in a fertilising rain the living and redeeming flame of Thy almighty love. When these drops of eternal light descend softly on our world of obscure ignorance, one would say a rain upon earth of golden stars one by one from a sombre firmament.

All kneels in mute devotion before this ever-renewed miracle.

A deep concentration seized on me, and I perceived that I was identifying myself with a single cherry-blossom, then through it with all cherry-blossoms, and, as I descended deeper in the consciousness, following a stream of bluish force, I became suddenly the cherry-tree itself, stretching towards the sky like so many arms its innumerable branches laden with their sacrifice of flowers. Then I heard distinctly this sentence:

"Thus hast thou made thyself one with the soul of the cherry-trees and so thou canst take note that it is the Divine who makes the offering of this flower-prayer to heaven."

When I had written it, all was effaced; but now the blood of the cherry-tree flows in my veins and with it flows an incomparable peace and force. What difference is there between the human body and the body of a tree? In truth, there is none: the consciousness which animates them is identically the same.

Then the cherry-tree whispered in my ear:

"It is in the cherry-blossom that lies the remedy for the disorders of the spring."

April 28, 1917

O my divine Master, who hast appeared to me this night in all Thy radiant splendour, Thou canst in an instant make this being perfectly pure, luminous, translucid, conscious. Thou canst liberate it from its last dark spots, free it from its last preferences. Thou canst... but hast Thou not done this tonight when it was penetrated with Thy divine effluence and Thy ineffable light? It may be... for in me is a superhuman strength made all of calm and immensity. Grant that from this summit I may not fall; grant that peace may for ever reign as the master of my being, not only in my depths of which it has long been the sovereign but in the least of my external activities, in the smallest recesses of my heart and of my action.

I salute Thee, O Lord, deliverer of beings!

"Lo! here are flowers and benedictions! here is the smile of divine Love! It is without preferences and without repulsions. It streams out towards all in a generous flow and never takes back its marvellous gifts!"

Her arms outstretched in a gesture of ecstasy, the Eternal Mother pours upon the world the unceasing dew of Her purest love!

September 24, 1917

Thou hast subjected me to a hard discipline; rung after rung, I have climbed the ladder which leads to Thee and, at the summit of the ascent, Thou hast made me taste the perfect joy of identity with Thee. Then, obedient to Thy command, rung after rung, I have descended to outer activities and external states of consciousness, re-entering into contact with these worlds that I left to discover Thee. And now that I have come back to the bottom of the ladder, all is so dull, so mediocre, so neutral, in me and around me, that I understand no more....

What is it then that Thou awaitest from me, and to what use that slow long preparation, if all is to end in a result to which the majority of human beings attain without being subjected to any discipline?

How is it possible that having seen all that I have seen, experienced all that I have experienced, after I have been led up even to the most sacred sanctuary of Thy knowledge and communion with Thee, Thou hast made of me so utterly common an instrument in such ordinary circumstances? In truth, O Lord, Thy ends are unfathomable and pass my understanding....

Why, when Thou hast placed in my heart the pure diamond of Thy perfect Felicity, sufferest Thou its surface to reflect the shadows which come from outside and so leave unsuspected and, it would seem, ineffective the treasure of Peace Thou hast granted me? Truly all this is a mystery and confounds my understanding.

Why, when Thou hast given me this great inner silence, sufferest Thou the tongue to be so active and the thought to be occupied with things so futile? Why?... I could go on questioning indefinitely and, to all likelihood, always in vain....

I have only to bow to Thy decree and accept my condition without uttering a word.

I am now only a spectator who watches the dragon of the world unrolling its coils without end.

October 15, 1917

I have cried to Thee in my despair, O Lord, and Thou hast answered my call.

I have no right to complain of the circumstances of my existence; are they not consonant with what I am?

Because Thou ledst me to the threshold of Thy splendour and gavest me the joy of Thy harmony, I thought I had reached the goal: but, in truth, Thou hast regarded Thy instrument in the perfect clarity of Thy light and plunged it back into the crucible of the world that it may be melted anew and purified.

In these hours of an extreme and anguished aspiration I see, I feel myself drawn by Thee with a dizzy rapidity along the road of transformation and my whole being vibrates to a conscious contact with the Infinite.

It is so that Thou givest me patience and the strength to surmount this new ordeal.

November 25, 1917

O Lord, because in an hour of cruel distress I said in the sincerity of my faith: "Thy Will be done", Thou camest garbed in Thy raiment of glory. At Thy feet I prostrated myself, on Thy breast I found my refuge. Thou hast filled my being with Thy divine light and flooded it with Thy bliss. Thou hast reaffirmed Thy alliance and assured me of Thy constant presence. Thou art the sure friend who never fails, the Power, the Support, the Guide. Thou art the Light which scatters darkness, the Conqueror who assures the victory. Since Thou art there, all has become clear. Agni is rekindled in my fortified heart, and his splendour shines out and sets aglow the atmosphere and purifies it....

My love for Thee, compressed so long, has leaped forth again, powerful, sovereign, irresistible — increased tenfold by the ordeal it has undergone. It has found strength in its seclusion, the strength to emerge to the surface of the being, impose itself as master on the entire consciousness, absorb everything in its overflowing stream....

Thou hast said to me: "I have returned to leave thee no more."

And, my forehead on the soil, I have received Thy promise.

Suddenly, before Thee, all my pride fell. I understood how futile it was in Thy Presence to wish to surmount oneself, and I wept, wept abundantly and without constraint the sweetest tears of my life. Tears sweet and beneficent, tears that opened my heart without constraint before Thee and melted in one miraculous moment all the remaining obstacles that could separate me from Thee!

And now, although I weep no longer, I feel so near, so near to Thee that my whole being quivers with joy.

Let me stammer out my homage:

I have cried too with the joy of a child, "O supreme and only Confidant, Thou who knowest beforehand all we can say to Thee because Thou art its source!

"O supreme and only Friend, Thou who acceptest, Thou who lovest, Thou who understandest us just as we are, because it is Thyself who hast so made us!

"O supreme and only Guide, Thou who never gainsayest our highest will because it is Thou Thyself who willest in it!

"It would be folly to seek elsewhere than in Thee for one who will listen, understand, love and guide, since always Thou art there ready to our call and never wilt Thou fail us!

"Thou hast made me know the supreme, the sublime joy of a perfect confidence, an absolute serenity, a surrender total and without reserve or colouring, free from effort and constraint.

"Joyous like a child I have smiled and wept at once before Thee, O my Well-Beloved!"

Since the man refused the meal I had prepared with so much love and care, I invoke the God to take it.

My God, Thou hast accepted my invitation, Thou hast come to sit at my table, and in exchange for my poor and humble offering Thou hast granted to me the last liberation. My heart, even this morning so heavy with anguish and care, my head surcharged with responsibility, are delivered of their burden. Now are they light and joyful as my inner being has been for a long time past. My body smiles to Thee with happiness as before my soul smiled to Thee. And surely hereafter Thou wilt withdraw no more from me this joy, O my God! for this time, I think, the lesson has been sufficient, I have mounted the calvary of successive disillusionments high enough to attain to the Resurrection. Nothing remains of the past but a potent love which gives me the pure heart of a child and the lightness and freedom of thought of a god.

June 22, 1920

After granting me the joy which surpasses all expression, Thou hast sent me, O my beloved Lord, the struggle, the ordeal and on this too I have smiled as on one of Thy precious messengers. Before, I dreaded the conflict, for it hurt in me the love of harmony and peace. But now, O my God, I welcome it with gladness: it is one among the forms of Thy action, one of the best means for bringing back to light some elements of the work which might otherwise have been forgotten, and it carries with it a sense of amplitude, of complexity, of power. And even as I have seen Thee, resplendent, exciting the conflict, so also it is Thou whom I see unravelling the entanglement of events and jarring tendencies and winning in the end the victory over all that strives to veil Thy light and Thy power: for out of the struggle it is a more perfect realisation of Thyself that must arise.

November 24, 1931

O my Lord, my sweet Master, for the accomplishment of Thy work I have sunk down into the unfathomable depths of Matter, I have touched with my finger the horror of the falsehood and the inconscience, I have reached the seat of oblivion and a supreme obscurity. But in my heart was the Remembrance, from my heart there leaped the call which could arrive to Thee: "Lord, Lord, everywhere Thy enemies appear triumphant; falsehood is the monarch of the world; life without Thee is a death, a perpetual hell; doubt has usurped the place of Hope and revolt has pushed out submission; Faith is spent, Gratitude is not born; blind passions and murderous instincts and a guilty weakness have covered and stifled Thy sweet law of love. Lord, wilt Thou permit Thy enemies to prevail, falsehood and ugliness and suffering to triumph? Lord, give the command to conquer and victory will be there. I know we are unworthy, I know the world is not yet ready. But I cry to Thee with an absolute faith in Thy Grace and I know that Thy Grace will save."

Thus, my prayer rushed up towards Thee; and, from the

depths of the abyss, I beheld Thee in Thy radiant splendour; Thou didst appear and Thou saidst to me: "Lose not courage, be firm, be confident, — I COME."

(*A prayer for those who wish to serve the Divine*)

Glory to Thee, O Lord, who triumphest over every obstacle.

Grant that nothing in us shall be an obstacle in Thy work.

Grant that nothing may retard Thy manifestation.

Grant that Thy will may be done in all things and at every moment.

We stand here before Thee that Thy will may be fulfilled in us, in every element, in every activity of our being, from our supreme heights to the smallest cells of the body.

Grant that we may be faithful to Thee utterly and for ever.

We would be completely under Thy influence to the exclusion of every other.

Grant that we may never forget to own towards Thee a deep, an intense gratitude.

Grant that we may never squander any of the marvellous things that are Thy gifts to us at every instant.

Grant that everything in us may collaborate in Thy work and all be ready for Thy realisation.

Glory to Thee, O Lord, Supreme Master of all realisation.

Give us a faith active and ardent, absolute and unshakable in Thy Victory.

BIBLIOGRAPHICAL NOTE

All the writings of Sri Aurobindo relating to the Mother have been brought together in this volume and placed in three parts.

PART ONE: *The Mother*
This book consists of six sections. The first section, written in 1927, was distributed as a "Darshan message" on 21 February of that year. The second, third, fourth and fifth sections were written separately as letters to disciples; while the sixth, which includes the descriptions of the four aspects of the Mother was, like the first, "written independently and not as a letter". All these six sections were first published together in book-form in 1928. Since then the book has gone into eleven editions up to 1980. The sixth edition was issued in three impressions, the ninth in eight impressions and the tenth in two impressions. The eleventh was a special calligraphic edition brought out to commemorate the Mother's Birth Centenary on 21 February 1978.

PART TWO: *Letters on the Mother*
A compilation of Sri Aurobindo's letters on the Mother, arranged under ten sections, was first published in 1951 under the title *Letters of Sri Aurobindo on the Mother*. These letters, with additional material rearranged under eleven sections, formed Part Three of *Sri Aurobindo on Himself and on the Mother* published in 1953 as Volume I of Sri Aurobindo International University Centre Collection. In the present volume, No. 25 of Sri Aurobindo Birth Centenary Library, this part has been further expanded by the inclusion of a large number of additional letters and the material has been rearranged under twelve sections.

PART THREE: *Prayers and Meditations*
Some portions of the Mother's *Prières et Méditations* were translated in English by Sri Aurobindo from the original in French. Only these translations are included in this part. These were first brought out in book-form in 1941. With the addition of three more translations, also done by Sri Aurobindo, four more editions of this book were brought out in 1962, 1969, 1971 and 1975. In 1948 a complete edition containing Sri Aurobindo's translations as well as translations of the remaining portions done by a sadhak was brought out. Two more editions of the complete translations were issued in 1954 and 1979. In the last edition, which forms Volume I of the Centenary Edition of the Collected Works of the Mother, all the translations excepting those by Sri Aurobindo have been newly done.

The first edition of this Volume 25 in Sri Aurobindo Birth Centenary Library was brought out in de luxe and popular impressions in 1972. It was also reproduced in a reduced format in a third impression in the same year. The present fourth impression is a facsimile reproduction of the third impression; only a few typographical errors have been corrected.